East Timor, René Girard and Neocolonial Violence

Violence, Desire, and the Sacred

Series Editors
Scott Cowdell, Chris Fleming, and Joel Hodge

Volumes in the series
Vol. 1. *Girard's Mimetic Theory Across the Disciplines*
edited by Scott Cowdell, Chris Fleming, and Joel Hodge
Vol. 2. *René Girard and Sacrifice in Life, Love, and Literature*
edited by Scott Cowdell, Chris Fleming, and Joel Hodge
Vol. 3. *Mimesis, Movies, and Media*
edited by Scott Cowdell, Chris Fleming, and Joel Hodge
Vol. 4. *René Girard and Raymund Schwager: Correspondence 1974–1991*
edited by Scott Cowdell, Chris Fleming, Joel Hodge, and Mathias Moosbrugger
Vol. 5. *Mimesis and Atonement: René Girard and the Doctrine of Salvation*
edited by Michael Kirwan and Sheelah Treflé Hidden
Vol. 6. *Möbian Nights: Literary Reading in a Time of Crisis*
by Sandor Goodhart
Vol. 7. *Does Religion Cause Violence?: Multidisciplinary Perspectives on Violence and Religion in the Modern World*
edited by Scott Cowdell, Chris Fleming, Joel Hodge, and Carly Osborn
Vol. 8. *Mimetic Theory and Film*
edited by Paolo Diego Bubbio and Chris Fleming
Vol. 9. *Mimesis and Sacrifice*
edited by Marcia Pally
Vol. 10. *Violence in the Name of God*
by Joel Hodge
Vol. 11. *Tragic Novels, the American Dream and René Girard*
by Carly Osborn
Vol. 12. *East Timor, René Girard and Neocolonial Violence*
by Susan Connelly

East Timor, René Girard and Neocolonial Violence

Scapegoating as Australian Policy

Susan Connelly

BLOOMSBURY ACADEMIC
LONDON • NEW YORK • OXFORD • NEW DELHI • SYDNEY

BLOOMSBURY ACADEMIC
Bloomsbury Publishing Plc
50 Bedford Square, London, WC1B 3DP, UK
1385 Broadway, New York, NY 10018, USA
29 Earlsfort Terrace, Dublin 2, Ireland

BLOOMSBURY, BLOOMSBURY ACADEMIC and the Diana logo are
trademarks of Bloomsbury Publishing Plc

First published in Great Britain 2022
This paperback edition published 2023

Copyright © Susan Connelly, 2022

Susan Connelly has asserted her right under the Copyright, Designs and
Patents Act, 1988, to be identified as Author of this work.

For legal purposes the Acknowledgements on pp. x–xii constitute an
extension of this copyright page.

All rights reserved. No part of this publication may be reproduced or transmitted in
any form or by any means, electronic or mechanical, including photocopying,
recording, or any information storage or retrieval system, without prior
permission in writing from the publishers.

Bloomsbury Publishing Plc does not have any control over, or responsibility for,
any third-party websites referred to or in this book. All internet addresses given
in this book were correct at the time of going to press. The author and publisher
regret any inconvenience caused if addresses have changed or sites have
ceased to exist, but can accept no responsibility for any such changes.

A catalogue record for this book is available from the British Library.

Library of Congress Cataloging-in-Publication Data
Names: Connelly, Susan, author.
Title: East Timor, René Girard and neocolonial violence: scapegoating as
Australian policy / Susan Connelly.
Description: London; New York: Bloomsbury Academic, 2022. |
Series: Violence, desire, and the sacred; vol. 12 | Revision of author's PhD thesis. |
Includes bibliographical references and index.
Identifiers: LCCN 2021038568 (print) | LCCN 2021038569 (ebook) |
ISBN 9781350161474 (hardback) | ISBN 9781350161481 (pdf) |
ISBN 9781350161498 (ebook)
Subjects: LCSH: Girard, René, 1923-2015. | Imitation. | Desire. |
Violence. | Australia–Foreign relations–Timor-Leste. |
Timor-Leste–Foreign relations–Australia. | Australia–Foreign
relations–Indonesia. | Indonesia–Foreign relations–Australia.
Classification: LCC DU113.5.T56 C66 2022 (print) |
LCC DU113.5.T56 (ebook) | DDC 327. 5987094–dc23/eng/20211027
LC record available at https://lccn.loc.gov/2021038568
LC ebook record available at https://lccn.loc.gov/2021038569

ISBN: HB: 978-1-3501-6147-4
PB: 978-1-3502-8555-2
ePDF: 978-1-3501-6148-1
eBook: 978-1-3501-6149-8

Series: Violence, Desire, and the Sacred

Typeset by Newgen KnowledgeWorks Pvt. Ltd., Chennai, India

To find out more about our authors and books visit www.bloomsbury.com
and sign up for our newsletters.

'Crucify him!'
'Why?' Pilate asked them,
'What harm has he done?'

(Mk 15.13b-14)

Contents

Map of East Timor	viii
List of illustrations	ix
Acknowledgements	x
Introduction	1
1 A new way of seeing: Mimetic theory	11
2 Australian identity and relationships	21
3 World War II	41
4 The Indonesian invasion of East Timor	65
5 The occupation of East Timor	93
6 Collapse and resurgence	125
7 Solidarity and conversion	143
Afterword	171
Appendix: René Girard at a Glance	173
Glossary of Key Girardian Terms	176
Notes	185
Bibliography	219
Index	235

Figure 1 Map of East Timor in relation to Indonesia and Australia. Wikimedia Commons.

Illustrations

1	Map of East Timor in relation to Indonesia and Australia	viii
2	Timorese people supported Australian soldiers during World War II	54
3	Australian soldiers and Timorese friends	56
4	John 'Paddy' Kenneally and Rufino Alves Correia	63
5	Starving Timorese children in Laga, East Timor	96
6	Starving Timorese children in Laga, East Timor	97
7	Laurentino Pires and Rob Wesley-Smith on 'Radio Maubere'	152
8	Timorese students at a rally in Dili	154
9	Various religious sisters at a demonstration in support of East Timor	157
10	A gathering of Australian prime ministers and foreign ministers	161
11	Alexander Downer giving advice to Timorese prime minister Mari Alkatiri	162

Acknowledgements

I wish to thank my religious congregation, the Sisters of St Joseph of the Sacred Heart, for the time, space and support needed to engage with a PhD thesis and then have it published as a book. I am indeed blessed to belong to these friends of Mary MacKillop, whose commitment to education has always inspired me and from whose spring of friendship, good example and down-to-earth championing of humanity I have drunk deep. In particular, I thank my home community for the interest, stimulation and encouragement I received. Frequent kitchen-table and prayer-space discussions on René Girard's work and East Timor have proven beneficial to all but to me in particular. I am indebted to the Australian Catholic University, its staff and librarians for providing all that was necessary during my study and for granting me the doctorate. I learned an immense amount from the examiners of my thesis, and I thank them. My family, as ever, has my enduring love and thanks for so much.

Dr Joel Hodge has been an inspiration and support, introducing me to many facets of René Girard's thought and guiding me through the doctoral research process. Joel's thorough perusal of my work led to much rewriting and much learning. His ever-courteous manner and diligence as supervisor contributed greatly to the enjoyment I swam in while researching. Without him, this book would not exist. Dr Terry Veling opened up further vistas of perception, and I appreciated his warm and insightful assistance.

The Australian Girard Seminar enabled the publication of this book, and to them I am very thankful. Dr Scott Cowdell, Dr Chris Fleming, Dr Carly Osborn and Joel have been wholly supportive and inspiring. I am grateful to Sheelah Treflé-Hidden for her insights and friendship and for sharing with me the delight of presenting some of Girard's wealth to others. The teaching of pastors James Alison and Paul Nuechterlein remain a source of Girardian delight and amazement and have enriched this book. I owe great thanks to all reviewers of my thesis, especially Pat Walsh AM, Dr Michael Kirwan SJ and Prof. Wolfgang Palaver, and to all reviewers of the resulting book. To have discovered René Girard at this time and to learn from these people is indeed a great boon.

It is an enormous honour to have had the opportunity to write about the people of Timor-Leste (East Timor). While I did not live in Timor for extended periods of time, I had the privilege of being part of the Australian support for their struggle for justice for over twenty years. My work formed the background of this book, and its conclusions – still in the process of being formed and interiorized in me – arise from the example of people who fashioned themselves as the best of humanity despite the greed and violence which sought to enslave them. During the years that I was part of the Mary MacKillop ministry in the now Timor-Leste, I worked with wonderful staff, Timorese and Australian, experiencing with them the dilemmas and effects of many of the issues described in this book. I met numerous people in Timor, young and old, religious and not-so-religious, some strong, some broken. All had their backs to the wall, all had experienced poverty and oppression and all were on fire for freedom. They remain a beacon to me, and my hope is that this book will contribute fittingly to the telling of their extraordinary story. I appreciate my present connections with the Timorese people in Australia, and I am grateful to the church community which meets at Ashcroft, so many of whom endured the situations I have tried to interpret here. Celebrating Eucharist together, the bedrock of our shared faith, goes to the inexpressible heart of the meaning of human suffering and triumph. I thank them all sincerely.

Australian support for the Timorese people is long-standing and is driven by committed people with a strong sense of justice and truth. Josephine Mitchell RSJ has given me over many years an example of dedication, insight, perseverance and empathy. Her constant love for the Timorese people makes her an outstanding exemplar of the best that civil society has to offer. The commitment of Jan Barnett RSJ to human good and justice for the poor has been a source of strength to me. Both of these sisters have lived alongside the writing of this book.

Other activists and supporters of the Timorese with whom I have worked and whose integrity shines through the historical record are too numerous to mention, as they know only too well. To them all I owe a great deal, and I am proud to be one of their number. While this book is a different way of looking at the tragedy that is the Australia-East Timor relationship, I will continue to gain from the writings of others on the subject. Of particular importance for appreciating the facts of the history and for shouldering responsibility is *Chega! The Final Report of the Timor-Leste Commission for Reception, Truth and Reconciliation*. My understanding of the situation has been deepened by the writings and experiences of those who know the debt we Australians owe the Timorese, but any deficiencies in this book are entirely my own.

I thank Bloomsbury Academic for the opportunity to have this book published in their Girard Series, with special thanks to Becky Holland and Colleen Coalter. I congratulate Bloomsbury for making available to people all over the world so many opportunities to engage with one of humanity's most remarkable recent thinkers – René Girard.

Introduction

One year after the Dili massacre, in which over two hundred young people were shot down by the Indonesian military in East Timor's capital, I attended an event that moved me to the core. I walked around the room, looking at the photographs on the walls: lines of bloated bodies, mangled bodies, dead bodies. I saw the skeletons with eyes, the living dead children. And I saw the man with the barbed wire cutting into his skin, the flay marks on his buttocks. They were dead, all dead. How many dead? I knew very little of the story, so I went to the desk and bought the book.

This event, a book launch in December 1992, had brought together about seventy people of various political and religious persuasions, all earnest, all keen to know more and read Michele Turner's *Telling East Timor: Personal Testimonies, 1942–1992*.[1] The gathering was a small band of Australians in sympathy with the Timorese people and wondering what could be done. Faces were upturned as Justice Michael Kirby spoke from the landing, the stairs to either side of him filled with the overflow of people. The venue was Callan Park, a former mental hospital at Rozelle in Sydney, full of its own history of heartache, bewilderment, schizophrenia, desperation – a deteriorating place earmarked for development.

The frenzied, arresting summons of the *babadook*, a small Timorese drum, accompanied the beautiful young man in the traditional dress of a warrior-king, dipping and weaving with his sword, his feet prancing high, his shoulders rippling in the light. There were speeches: mind-blowing, incomprehensible, their sorrow hanging heavily in the air. Applause. A question or two. Sorrow.

My dominant feelings were of shock and anger. I could hardly believe that this was happening in Timor, the former Portuguese colony so near to Australia and now under Indonesian rule. In the next few months connections with the Timorese community in Sydney gave me some understanding of their lives, their memories and their fears. I caught glimpses of the history of East Timor, including its connections with Australia. Following this, my Catholic religious congregation, the Sisters of St Joseph of the Sacred Heart, allowed me for many years to pursue this story of injustice as part of a ministry with the Timorese people in the preservation and promotion of their culture. Efforts to support the people's threatened identity brought me to the narrative of death, torture and destruction which was the Timorese story since World War II. I tried to make a difference and became involved with the Timorese people both in Australia and in Timor itself. Yet I was always confronted by the question: *Why?* What could account for the suffering of this small group of people, so closely aligned with Australia, both geographically and historically? How could one comprehend the scale of the suffering? What justification could there be for such experiences so close to my nation and within my lifetime?

As with many Australians, I am a witness: a witness from afar, not having suffered atrocity or the violent death of loved ones. Being a witness is an involvement, as one cannot see violence without decision. In a sense, it is easy to be a prosecutor, to be against the Indonesian invasion and oppression, to oppose the Australian involvement. It is easy to start as a defender of the Timorese, to draw attention to their courage, their tenacity, their victimization. But it is far more difficult to be a witness for humanity, a witness summoned to appear before a judgement on the mangled mess of human life and challenged to understand its complexity. Here the discovery of the work of René Girard (1923–2015) opened for me a means of articulating the witness, providing me with an avenue through which to understand justice, violence, mercy, deceit, sorrow and death in relation to East Timor.

Numerous analyses and commentaries exist which detail the political and economic realities of the history of the relationship between Australia and East Timor. However, as Australia's small neighbour consolidates its hard-won independence and as Australians become further distanced from the events recounted here, there is a need for an analysis which considers the deeper reasons behind Australian decisions and actions. This need has become all the more dire as facts continue to emerge concerning the Timor Sea intrigues that are affecting the fledgling Timorese nation and further implicating Australians.[2]

Application of the 'mimetic theory' of René Girard provides a comprehensive anthropological lens to understand the dynamics of the Australian-Timorese relationship, particularly those involving violence. It is a new approach that opens up a variety of fresh insights into individual and social motivations. These insights prove to be a valuable force for interpreting complex political situations, reflecting on responses and modifying behavior.

Aim and method

In this book, I analyse the relationship between Australia and East Timor (now Timor-Leste),[3] attempting to understand the background and implications of Australian forces affecting the Timor tragedy. Such a reflection entails assessment of historical actions arising from Australian policies and practice that affected the relationship. The study covers three major historical periods: the Australian presence in Timor in 1942; the Indonesian invasion of 1975; and the twenty-four-year Indonesian occupation, culminating in the definitive changes that occurred in 1999. This is an attempt to understand and see through the violence that has characterized the relationship and brought so much suffering to many. The anthropology of René Girard's mimetic theory provides the structure for this understanding of the events and the suffering which occurred.

Three aspects of mimetic theory are applied to the Australia-Timor relationship in these time periods: the scapegoat, texts of persecution and conversion. Girard's understanding of scapegoating was built on his perception of the origins of violence. Human beings imitate each other in many ways, including at the fundamental level of desire, termed 'mimetic desire'. Humans desire what others desire, generating situations of rivalry which often resolve through violence. Girard detected through studies in ancient mythology, cultural anthropology and psychology that destructive social violence was quelled through the scapegoating of one individual or a group. A focus on one deflected the violence away from the dominant group, thus saving it from itself. The success of this method of retaining group cohesion required the community's belief in the actual guilt of the scapegoat or victim. Cultural and religious practices were built on scapegoating, providing communities with a method of dealing with disharmony that was, however, only partially successful, as recurring strife required repeated scapegoating, producing countless victims over generations. Myths are narratives of such scapegoating events, woven by communities to allow them to strengthen their sense of identity and to conceal or justify the violent sacrifice of scapegoated victims. 'Texts of persecution' is the term used to describe modern-day narratives that blame scapegoats and exonerate their persecutors. By 'conversion', Girard refers to the possibilities of transformation from scapegoating and acquisitive violence in human society to positive mimesis grounded in mutual recognition.

The concept of 'relationship' especially between nations is difficult to define, as the people of any nation are unable to describe their shared identity adequately. Rather than thinking of a 'nation' as a concrete reality, Charles Taylor envisages it as being an 'imagined' entity, where widely held memories, stories and practices validate the claiming of common attributes and a sense of 'self'.[4] In regard to each of the separate communities of Australia and East Timor, application of Taylor's concept of the 'social imaginary' reveals the remarkable differences of colonial history, culture, opportunities and size that exist in each, alongside the human commonalities that they share. It signifies the shared assumptions of each society as to how its members 'fit together'. There is a recognizable – if mostly inexpressible – coherence within each society, enabling the people to identify themselves as belonging to that society regardless of the fact that most individuals forever remain unknown to each other.

Ironically, in grappling with questions concerning 'who we are' and 'how we relate to others', it is possible that the image citizens have of their own nation may be inaccurate or biased – in Taylor's words, a 'false imaginary'. In regard to the history of Australian involvement with the Timorese people this proves to be poignant and even distressing. This book reflects on how the group which identifies as 'Australian' related to that identifying itself as 'Timorese' and how historical events generated, influenced and changed that relationship. In that reflection, aspects of the Australian imaginary, such as fairness and loyalty, have too often been found wanting.

Personal and national identities depend on relationships. This book describes and interprets major Australian decisions and actions that formed the Australian part of the relationship, drawing conclusions about 'Australia' (as a shared social imaginary) rather than 'East Timor'. Reflection back to the self by the 'other' in the course of a relationship is a unique means of evaluation of the self. Thus the effects of Australian actions on the Timorese people are an indispensable part of Australian self-reflection. How a person, or indeed a nation, treats another is a gauge of its professed values and principles. It is undeniable that the treatment of the weaker and more vulnerable other demonstrates conclusively the character of the self. Numerous claims as to their national identity are proposed by Australians, but it is through Australian actions, in this case in relation to East Timor, that the veracity of those claims is demonstrated.

This book's considerations of fear, suffering, non-violence, forgiveness and conversion form a comprehensive analysis of the relationship. The study embarks on new territory: to dissect a relationship between two nations – characterized by the presence of oppression, violence and scapegoating – using mimetic theory.

East Timor as scapegoat

Within the broad range of insights that Girard termed 'mimetic theory', scapegoating is an expression of the victim mechanism by which human societies have traditionally functioned.[5] Girard identifies certain defining elements of scapegoating which he describes as 'stereotypes of persecution'.[6] These elements include crisis, crime, criteria for the selection of victims and the consequent violence done to them, all of which are used in this study to interpret the historical events and discern their effects and ramifications.

Crisis

Girard explained that the catalyst for scapegoating is a social crisis. Australians have experienced significant crises mostly concerned with political and military threats from foreign powers and ideologies, especially from Asia. The first crisis relevant to this study occurred when the ferment of World War II and regional threat threw Australia's vulnerable isolation into relief. Japan's expansionism and Australia's defensive determination made them rivals. Australian troops were inserted into what was then known as 'Portuguese Timor' against the wishes of the Portuguese administration, an incursion that breached Portuguese neutrality. Two months later Japanese troops also arrived, their numbers increasing greatly over the next fourteen months because of the success of the Australians and their Timorese supporters. While the Australians withdrew early in 1943, the Japanese stayed until the end of the war.

Further crises arose in the decades after the war that were countered by Australian alignments with larger powers for security. The threat of communism intensified Australian ties with the vehemently anti-communist Indonesia, and the alliance with the United States was strengthened and formalized. As ways of ensuring national security and wealth, agreements bound Indonesia and Australia together more firmly, allowing for the sharing of resources and mutual protection. As a result, Australia did not oppose Indonesia's invasion of East Timor upon the withdrawal of the Portuguese in 1975. With contradictory policies, wariness of Indonesia's growing strength and the prospects of gain, Australia proved supportive of the attack. East Timor was occupied for the next twenty-four years, presenting Australian governments with an ongoing crisis that burgeoned as a result of dependence on Indonesia's favour and the effects of divisive and immoral policy regarding East Timor.[7]

Crime

The second element identified by Girard as a feature of scapegoating is that of the crime, believed by those under threat to be the cause of the crisis and the threatened harm to the community. In the case of East Timor there was no crime committed by the Timorese for which they could be blamed, either in World War II or under the Indonesian regime. In both cases, however, the perception of the antagonists was pivotal to the events. In each case Timor was seen to occupy the role of obstacle to the attainment of the shared desires of greater forces. It was also seen to be a weak territory that required the intervention of larger powers to prevent it from becoming a threat, either from Japanese or communist use and influence.

The crime of Timor during World War II was its very existence, occupying a geographical position which was seen as either opportunity or threat, depending on the views of the wartime rivals. Timor was the object over which they fought, but its status as the colony of a neutral power rendered it an obstacle to the realization of each rival's dream. The crime of East Timor in relation to Australia and Indonesia during the 1975 invasion and subsequent occupation was based on its geography and colonization and as the locus of a possible threat. As the outpost of an unstable Portugal on the Indonesian archipelago it invited the designs of Indonesian expansionism, with which Australia concurred. Furthermore, the spread of communism into Southeast Asia placed the fledgling political aspirations of the Timorese into question, thus providing useful excuses for the Indonesian invasion. The crime attributed to the Timorese was not something which had happened, but something which its neighbours calculated might happen: the possibility of either independence or communist control. As the Indonesian occupation took hold (with Australian approval), the Timorese desire for their own identity and for freedom was treated as a further crime.

Criteria for the selection of the victim

The third stereotype is the criteria for the choosing of the victim. Girard identifies victims as needing to be both marginal to the persecuting society and credible suspects. As a small half-island whose population was generally tribal,

East Timor provided the insignificance required of scapegoats. Appearing to lack the capacity to be either politically or economically self-sufficient marked it as unviable in the eyes of its neighbours and as weak and exploitable in the brutal politics of nation states. Moreover, it was accused of having communist leanings, thus providing its scapegoating with a veneer of validity. Of greatest consequence was its position of being friendless among suspicious and fearful neighbours who thus avoided, and have continued to avoid, any accountability for their scapegoating acts. There was no one to take up the Timorese cause; there was no one to counter the lies; there was no one to champion the people.[8] As a negligible and undefended entity, East Timor was a feasible candidate for sacrifice and victimization.

Violence

Regarding the fourth aspect of Girard's persecution stereotypes – the violence done to the scapegoat – the Timorese people are notable among the world's victims as their history from 1942 to 1999 is catastrophic. The World War II death toll in this colony of neutral Portugal estimated to be at least 40,000, and all civilians, is comparable to that of major nations in that same war. During the Indonesian occupation, between 102,000 and 183,000 Timorese people out of a population of 650,000 died (according to one estimate) due to unnatural causes, such as extrajudicial killings, torture and politically induced starvation.[9] This period of the history saw deliberate, wholesale violence by an invading state for its political and expansionist objectives.[10] The Australian journalists known as the 'Balibó Five' and another, Roger East, were murdered at the time of the invasion. Despite numerous inquiries, their deaths remain the subject of conjecture, denial and official inaction.[11]

There are levels of Australian complicity in both of these violent tragedies. Throughout the occupation, Australian governments supported Indonesian sovereignty in East Timor. Australia argued that the matter of East Timor be taken off the agenda of the United Nations.[12] It provided weapons and military training to the Indonesians as the Timorese people were being subjugated, leading to well-substantiated claims of complicity.[13] Publication of the facts of the oppressive situation and the opposition of the Timorese to Indonesian rule resulted in increasing unease internationally and in Australia.[14] Thus, a variety of policies and practices of support for Indonesia rendered Australia a partner in the victimization of East Timor. While this book deals with the shared history of Timor and Australia up to 1999, at the time of writing, events subsequent to that time frame demonstrate that the Australian sacrifice of Timor for its own gain has continued in matters associated with the resources of the Timor Sea for more than twenty years after 1999.

Myths and lies

Girard connected scapegoating with the production of ancient myths. As communities killed or expelled their scapegoats over millennia they constructed narratives that disguised the violence in order to conceal their guilt. These cultural stories exonerate communal violence and ensure that any blame remains on the head of the victim or else is disguised to the extent that the violence is justified or written out of the narrative.[15]

In modern times, such myths are not written, but records of scapegoating events are ubiquitous and are termed by Girard as 'texts of persecution'. This book discusses official Australian texts of persecution concerning the scapegoating of East Timor since 1942. I argue that the revelation of the scapegoat mechanism is a means of historical interpretation, opening up essential insights into human culture and politics. I do this by showing how the complicity of Australian governments in Timor's victimization is revealed in official documents. An abundance of that material is accurately described as 'texts of persecution' because of the omissions, embellishments and lies which, as modern-day myths, continue the scapegoating. There is reference to the paucity of material available to the Australian public that gives adequate recognition to the Timorese people's wartime loyalty to Australian soldiers and consequent suffering. The absence of such material is interpreted here as an overarching 'text of persecution' in its own right.

Furthermore, I apply to existing official documents concerning the Indonesian invasion and occupation Girard's designation of 'romantic lie'. Most of the documents released for public perusal regarding this period of the Australia-East Timor relationship display an ignorance of one of the basic premises of mimetic desire, that of unawareness of mimetic dependence on others. The Australian and Indonesian mutual dependence is apparent in cables, inquiries and reports which demonstrate contradictory and self-serving policies. Moreover, Girard's incisive textual interpretations distinguish between scapegoats *in* the text and scapegoats *of* the text. I show this classification to be particularly relevant to material issued by the Australian government as a current and generally accessible history of the time. A case study concerning ex-prime minister Whitlam and Monsignor da

Costa Lopes, a leader of the Catholic Church, also demonstrates the power of textual scapegoating.

Turning towards the victim

Significant popular opposition to government policies and monumental political changes in Indonesia in the late 1990s influenced the Australian government to modify its stance on East Timor. Internal Australian dissent and solidarity were inspired by the Timorese people and accompanied increasing international abhorrence of the situation, all of which led to policy change and comprehensive national support for the Timorese people. The United Nations administered a referendum in 1999 in which the Timorese decisively separated themselves from Indonesian control. An Australian-led military force InterFET (International Force for East Timor) was formed and supported the transition to local rule, while the UN administered the country in preparation for the Democratic Republic of Timor-Leste's Declaration of Independence in 2002. Many ordinary Australians actively supported the Timorese struggle to form an independent nation. I endeavour to capture some of this momentum using Girard's concept of 'conversion' to identify the profound changes that occurred in the late 1990s when the suffering of the victim, East Timor, became increasingly apparent and movements of solidarity strengthened. Flowing from the inspiration of non-violence, non-retaliation and a tendency towards forgiveness displayed by the Timorese people and coupled with changes in Indonesia itself and in Australian policy, this development eventuated in freedom and independence for the new nation of Timor-Leste.

Essential to this study is the revelation of the scapegoat's innocence, which Girard sees in the Gospel accounts of the passion of Christ. The gradual but inexorable decline in the power of scapegoating to achieve the desired effect of communal peace has continued since that time. However, this revelation does not automatically give human beings the capacity to live without the scapegoat mechanism and its attendant violence as is clear from the state of the world today. It is impossible for us who are bound by violence to release ourselves from the bind. I agree with Girard that it is Christ who reveals the truth about violence, because as God, he is the one capable of rising above the violence that had previously 'absolutely transcended' humanity.[16]

Integrally woven in with that faith, it is the Timorese non-violence and forgiveness which interrogates those who were complicit in persecution and calls them to conversion. Influenced by the Timorese non-violent response to suffering and committed resistance to oppression, all levels of Australian society ultimately contributed positively to the resolution of what was an appalling moral crisis. While deep questions remain concerning the application of justice, redress for the suffering and ongoing violence (both in Australian policy and in Timor-Leste), I believe that the application of mimetic theory to global situations is both possible and profitable, and I suggest that in the face of the upheavals and violence that mark the present age, such analyses are indispensable.

This study begins with an overview of mimetic theory in Chapter 1, followed in the next chapter by a discussion of certain claimed Australian values or characteristics and of Australian relationships with other nations. These reflections are necessary because they demonstrate the contradictory nature of much of the self-perception of Australians and the sweeping desire for security that was a driving force across decades that affected the relationship with the Timorese people so decidedly. Chapters 3, 4 and 5 deal with the Australia-East Timor connection during World War II, the invasion and the occupation, respectively. Chapter 6 begins with a discussion of the political changes in the late 1990s and reflects on the force of the inspiration of the Timorese people as their plight became more vivid. Their willingness to display aspects of the 'forgiving victim' demonstrates Girard's insights into the essential nature of forgiveness in the light of the inability of the scapegoat mechanism to produce peace as in times past. The final chapter gives a brief overview of the role of the Australian solidarity movement which grew in strength in the final years of the Indonesian regime in East Timor. It ends with comments on future possibilities: either to regress into blindness towards the victim and accept increasing violence or to undertake a course of action that Girard identified within mimetic theory – positive mimesis – imitating the good and abstaining from violence.

1

A new way of seeing: Mimetic theory

The major historical events in the Australia-East Timor relationship that saw so much violence and suffering are interpreted in this book through key concepts within René Girard's 'mimetic theory': 'the scapegoat', 'texts of persecution' and 'conversion'.

A fundamental premise of Girard's theory concerns desire and the often violent rivalry that can follow in its wake. Not only do humans imitate each other in diverse, intense and sophisticated ways but we also imitate other people's desires. Girard states that we desire according to the desire of others.[1] This imitative desire is not readily recognized, however, as we misperceive ourselves as the autonomous originators of our desires. Mimetic desire is neither autonomous nor spontaneous; rather it is the attraction to an object because of another's possession of it or desire for it.

Girard maintains that the desiring person imitates the desire of another – the model or mediator – who possesses or desires an object. Paradoxically, the desire of a person for another's object signals to the other that the object is indeed desirable, thus enhancing its desirability in the eyes of that other. With both subject and model desiring the same thing, each becomes a 'model' for the other. An appreciation of this contagious nature of human desire throws light on conflict and violence, although Girard acknowledged that positive mimesis also exists, where people embrace their better selves through imitation of worthy models. However, shared desire – such as for possessions, position, a love match or power – is prone to result in rivalry. Not only does each party model desire to the other but each can become an obstacle to the other's attainment of the object of that desire. They are harnessed together in mimetic rivalry. Hence, unless there is some form of peaceful resolution, capitulation or withdrawal by one or both parties, violence is inevitable. Imitation, desire, rivalry and violence are observable on personal and public levels.

Girard developed mimetic theory over the course of an academic career that ranged across a number of disciplines, beginning with history and literary criticism and moving into anthropology, psychology and biblical studies. Criticisms levelled against his theses include that they are too ambitious, attempting to explain all aspects of human nature, culminating in a far-too-elaborate theoretical system. It is said his theses are not verifiable by scientific controls and thus lack scientific rigour.[2] As there are no means of testing or refuting them, they become meaningless theories. Girard is said to discard larger methodological frameworks in favour of historical particularities and references to a relatively limited range of literature to construct his proposals.[3] Such a concentration, some claim, leads him to ignore other plausible explanations of the matters he considers. Others criticize Girard's theories as being too religious, lessening the possibility of scientific explanation. He is accused of being indulgent towards the Bible, especially the New Testament, and of proposing an unmerited uniqueness to Christianity.

It is to be expected that a theory so new and so comprehensive would attract criticism and argument. However, it is evident that recognition of the value of mimetic theory in a variety of fields is increasing, for example, in psychology, literature, theology, business and neuroscience.[4] This book demonstrates that mimetic theory is a valuable means of developing an intriguing and satisfying interpretation of political and moral choices that formed the relationship between Australia and East Timor. Thus it would be a worthy tool for analysing Australian relationships with first peoples, cultural history and regional neighbours and to illuminate a broad range of global affairs.

Major questions arise before a discussion of these aspects can begin. How can a theory that deals with essentially personal human categories such as 'desire' be applied to relations between nations, or in the case of Australia and East Timor, between an established nation and one in the process of becoming? Girard himself applies the theory to political situations only rarely and in relatively few articles and interviews, although he is reported to have said that the 2001 attack on the United States was 'mimetic rivalry on a planetary scale'.[5] However, the growing interest in mimetic theory has seen the establishment of bodies through which scholars engage internationally to discuss its richness, development and applications. Journal articles, conferences, websites and books applying Girard's theses to the wider world are multiplying.[6] While he may not have commented extensively on mimetic theory in relation to concrete political matters, others are successfully mining its depths.

As will be discussed, mimetic theory proposes that innocent people are often victimized – scapegoated – to maintain order and security in the face of violent social collapse. Wolfgang Palaver refers to Girard's belief that the origins of political institutions can be found in the practice of scapegoating, the genesis of all types of violence, including that practised in political circles.[7] Mimetic theory has the capacity to identify the scapegoating process in both personal and wider relationships, such as those dictated by a nation's foreign policy.[8] In his last book (in which he warns about the dire necessity to refrain from violence) Girard states: 'Politics is part of violence, not violence part of politics.'[9]

Fundamental political questions about authority, law and the nature and origin of the state are continually asked in societies. They generate an incessant ebb and flow of ideas, challenges and often violence. In the application of mimetic theory to such political situations, it becomes political theory. Paul Dumouchel states that Girardian theory does not have to explain everything in the domain of politics, but it does have claim to relevance within that domain.[10] Application of mimetic theory to the relationship between Australia and East Timor entails discussion of historical, social and political realities. The particular aspects of the scapegoat, texts of persecution and conversion that are used in this book to throw light on the relationship – an arena which spawned so much violence – are now discussed.

The scapegoat

Girard wrote extensively that the violence resulting from mimetic rivalry in ancient societies was quelled by means of the scapegoating of one individual or a group.[11] The scapegoated victim was killed or expelled, providing a focus upon which violent resolution of social conflict could be heaped. Aiming such responses onto one entity relieved the members of the wider group from attacking each other, thus saving the community from itself. However, scapegoating acts to achieve group harmony had to be repeatedly employed as rivalrous violence or inexplicable natural disaster frequently threw communities into disarray. Girard concluded that the sacrifice of a scapegoated victim was a successful way of dealing with rivalry, internal strife and violence and thus became the basis for religious and cultural measures which enabled communities to cohere. While violent, it also prevented further violence for a time. It 'contained' violence, in both senses of the verb. The wholesale violence of 'all against all' was replaced with an 'all against one' method of bringing peace and calm, however short-lived.[12]

The word 'victim' is used in this book in the technical sense in which Girard defined it and which is central to his work. In this context 'victim' means the 'scapegoat' – the one sacrificed by killing or expulsion by a crowd for social protection or order. While the scapegoat may well be guilty of a crime or transgression, in Girard's usage the victim is structurally innocent as it cannot be responsible for all the rivalries and tensions that split a community and lead to mob violence. This structural innocence removes the victim, in Girard's view, from ordinary notions of guilt or innocence. Osama bin Laden was not innocent in the usual meaning of the word, yet his execution, complete with footage of the US president and important administrators in virtual attendance, functions as an act of scapegoating when seen in the context of the ambiguous and highly questionable response of the United States to the attacks on 11 September 2001. Furthermore, while the word 'victim' does not have the pejorative or colloquial connotations of helplessness or passivity usually ascribed to it, Girard does identify how victims are powerless before a mob. However, given the facts of the history yet to be related, it is clear that the more common understanding of 'innocence' may also be applied to the scapegoated Timorese people, alongside a strictly Girardian use of the term.

Throughout this book an application of the concept of scapegoating to East Timor as a vulnerable and inconvenient entity within global politics provides a different perspective to judgements based solely on political or economic considerations. Girard's theories provide material for an analysis that is a more comprehensive way of understanding the reasons behind Australian attitudes, policies and actions in the relationship. In particular, the focus on major events in the light of Girard's insights reveals key aspects neglected in the general literature. The literary and anthropological resources in Girard's theory allow for an acutely insightful identification of the status of East Timor in its shared history with Australia and the depths of Australian complicity in its victimization. It illuminates the situation by applying the concept of scapegoating to the reversal of fortunes of a vulnerable people in relation to a rich and dominant neighbour.

There are certain consistent features of ancient scapegoaters and their victims. The scapegoaters needed to be oblivious to the innocence of their victim if the scapegoating process was to provide a satisfactory solution to social problems. In their view, the victim was truly responsible for the social crisis, and they were unable to see how they were uniting to transfer their own guilt, rivalries and tensions onto the substitutionary victim.[13] The status of the scapegoat itself depended on its marginality to the dominant group. The scapegoat had to be familiar, but somewhere on the edge and easily made an outsider – similar enough to the group to be an adequate substitution but different enough to uphold a suspicion of guilt. Girard describes the essential vulnerability of the victim as one who can be expunged from society 'since he lacks a champion'.[14] These aspects of scapegoating – levels of unanimity and unconsciousness (or misapprehension) in the scapegoaters and the marginality and vulnerability of scapegoats – are apparent in the shared Australian-East Timorese history, as will be demonstrated in further chapters.

The process of scapegoating as described by Girard included elements that will be employed in this study: a crisis, a corresponding crime, the criteria for the choice of the scapegoat and the violence committed to resolve the problem. Girard also detected in ancient scapegoating a fifth aspect which he termed 'double transference'.[15] The act of killing or expelling the scapegoat brought unity to the group and a sense of peace and relief that the cause of the crisis had been despatched. Order was reinstated, and prosperity could be sought once again. The community then believed that the death of the victim was responsible for the return of social harmony, and thus the victim was seen in an ambiguous light. In the first place, it was worthy of blame and had to be sacrificed, but then because of its death it was credited with reintroducing peace. In Girard's view, this 'double transference' – the status of being simultaneously blameworthy and therapeutic – was recorded in ancient myths in ways that raised victims to the level of gods.

Here can be seen a crucial difference between modern and archaic scapegoating that has bearing on this study. In modern times a scapegoat is not ultimately seen as a god, because the collapse of the power of scapegoating is well underway (although it is still often successfully attempted). In Girard's view, and as will be discussed, this collapse is a result of the Gospel's depiction of the passion of Christ in which the basic lie of scapegoating was revealed. A scapegoat is innocent of the guilt for which it is executed. The influence of this unveiling of the innocent victim over millennia means that people are now more likely to *see through* efforts to load single entities with responsibility for social difficulties, and hence victims are not divinized, and any weaving of myths no longer compels. The lack of divinization indicates the ongoing crumbling of the scapegoat mechanism as a dependable way of restoring harmony as in ancient times. The thoroughly beneficial realization of the innocence of the victim means that humanity is released from the lie of scapegoating and can see the truth of victimization more clearly. However, the revelation of the innocence of the scapegoat and the consequent collapse of the mechanism has had other outcomes. Girard maintains that the absence of the age-old means of restoring concord is leading to escalating global violence.[16] Another consequence is that the mantle of 'innocent victim' can now be donned by those who are not victims.[17] For example, convinced of attack by Japan via Portuguese Timor in World War II, and fearful of repercussions from any deviation from supporting the clear desires of Indonesia during its invasion and occupation of the area in 1975, Australian governments saw their nation as victim for decades. The Australian appropriation of the role of victim in its relationship with East Timor is clear from the historical record and will be discussed in detail later.

'Texts of persecution' and myth

Girard demonstrated the integral connection of scapegoating to ancient myth and to the modern expressions of myth, which he termed 'texts of persecution'. The violent dispatch of scapegoated victims, committed by ancient communities in order to prevent or limit greater violence, was accompanied by oral, enacted and later written accounts of those killings or expulsions. These accounts evolved over millennia as fanciful mythic stories, but stories that disguised the violence in order to conceal the guilt of those responsible for the sacrifice of the victims. Myths are thus supernatural and fantastical tales of violent events told from the point of view of the powerful but unconscious majority who met natural disaster or community unrest by blaming a scapegoat. They are cultural narratives that distort communal violence, displace it onto the victim and conceal the guilt of the community.[18]

Girard's insights into mimesis in literature and anthropology reached their zenith in his investigations into the Jewish and Christian scriptures which he saw as the groundbreaking means of recognizing the innocence of the victim and thus the reversal of myth. While the scriptures contain some mythic elements, the Gospel accounts of the passion and death of Christ invert myth. The texts comprehensively place the blame for the violent death onto the guilty ones – the political rulers, religious leaders and the crowd – and they display the complicity and cowardice of the disciples. Contrary to myth, the innocence of the victim is clearly and unambiguously displayed. For Girard, the Christian scriptures definitively unveil the scapegoat mechanism as the violent foundation of religion and culture that unconsciously dominates societies.[19] Girard looks on the Gospel revelation of the innocent victim not solely in spiritual terms but as an intellectual feat, the accomplishment of which forms a major step forward in human consciousness.[20]

This progress in humanity's ability to appreciate the innocence of the victim is developing, although at a glacial pace. As a result, scapegoating too has persisted albeit in diluted forms. Unsurprisingly, the production of distorted accounts of scapegoating accompanies this current tortuous advancement. While myths are no longer generated, attempts to exonerate persecutors in present-day scapegoating efforts continue through narratives that conceal guilt and deflect blame. These 'modern-day myths' have the same structure and serve the same purpose as ancient myths, presenting the situation entirely from the rationalizing point of view of the persecutor, with the victims seen as guilty. Girard interprets such modern efforts to exonerate violent perpetrators as 'texts of persecution'.[21]

The concept of persecutory texts is a valuable tool with which to investigate official written accounts of the relationship between Australia and East Timor. It will be demonstrated that official Australian documentary records attempt to soften the circumstances of the scapegoating of East Timor, distort the facts and exonerate those responsible. The documents are thus fairly described as texts of persecution. The evident bias, while designed to camouflage the truth, can have the opposite result. This book presents only readily available Australian government resources, but nevertheless, those resources clearly demonstrate that official actions regarding East Timor were characterized by fear, deceit and the willingness to sacrifice a weaker entity. Other researchers and commentators have experienced extreme difficulty in trying to access a more extensive range of relevant government documents.[22] One wonders what further revelations about the Australia-Timor relationship would flow from the documents that remain concealed by government.

Conversion

The responses of the Australian people to the suffering of the Timorese people are considered in this book in the light of another major Girardian insight forming part of mimetic theory, that of human 'conversion' towards the vulnerable other. Girard's insight into this 'conversion' is integral to his overall theory and, as an interpretative category, is an appropriate and significant way to understand aspects of the Australian role in the relationship with East Timor.

Girard's profound and extensive work on mimetic theory involved investigating the writings of certain modern novelists in whom he perceived a growth towards an understanding of human beings as mimetically dependent on the desires of others. He detected in this literature the movement in various characters from self-centred notions of desire and identity to recognition of the other-centred nature of desire, a development essential to human maturation. Girard maintained that the novelists had experienced this insight in their own lives and then projected it onto characters in their novels. He labelled this change of perspective as a 'conversion'[23] and described this growth in the careers of the novelists as a movement away from the 'romantic lie' of narratives that depict humans as autonomous and independent of the influence of others, towards a recognition of the motivating power of shared desire and its attendant rivalry and then a turning towards the other. A person comes to realize his or her dependence on the other, including the rival or the victim, for identity. This change, or conversion, generates relationship and solidarity in a new way so that one's desire and identity can be formed explicitly with the other rather than unconsciously over against the other. This movement in literature away from mistaken notions of the self and towards a recognition of the influence of the other on one's identity mirrors the passage from myth to Gospel. The distorted mythic view of the scapegoat as deserving of punishment by dominant, self-righteous groups is unveiled by the Gospel texts which reveal the fears, rivalries and violence of such groups.

The written record of the scapegoating process found in Australian government, media and other documents can be described as examples of the 'romantic lie'. Alongside this, the concept of 'conversion' away from the self-promoting immaturity of false independence is considered in relation to the unparalleled success of the movement supporting East Timor that climaxed in 1999, a movement away from, and against, the 'romantic lie'. Important in this regard are the various solidarity movements, which demonstrated the growing gap between the responses of government and those of civil society groups and individuals. Ordinary Australians took the lead by challenging official Australian complicity in the victimization of Timor. In the process of their personal advocacy, and in concert with others at home and abroad, Australians strengthened the existence of levels of openness towards the victim. A wholesale 'conversion' or turning towards the victim occurred on the part of general civil society and those in power, contributing to the gradual erosion of dominant narratives based on lies and deception. It was integral to the change in official policies that occurred. While the conversion did not need to involve an explicitly religious character, it did follow the pattern of conversion that Girard outlines: a movement from self-centred desire to interdependence with others, and accepting responsibility for the other, particularly the victimized. Assessing the success of the movement supporting East Timor, especially against significant political forces, is an important factor for understanding the solidarity that grew between the Australians and the Timorese.[24]

Significantly, the call to Australians to practise the values proclaimed as traditional was provoked by the example of the Timorese people's forgiving responses to violence and suffering. As the events of Timor's oppression became known, the actions and attitudes of the Timorese in facing overwhelming persecution showed that it was they, the victimized other, who embodied the values and characteristics traditionally claimed by the dominant Australian culture, such as independence, courage and the capacity to battle on against the odds. Thus the Timorese people became a 'model', in Girardian terms, to which Australians could aspire. The Timorese response to violence in large part imitated the non-retaliation and forgiveness of the victimized Christ, making reflection on insights into the power of the victim to restore the humanity of both oppressor and oppressed compelling.[25]

Conclusion

A series of major historical events, including wars and invasions, formed the Australia-East Timor relationship. These realities are interpreted in this book using pivotal aspects of the theories of René Girard to provide a structure for a different understanding of the events themselves and the wholesale suffering that occurred throughout. This new interpretation of the relationship is grounded in Girard's mimetic theory, specifically the aspects of 'the scapegoat', 'texts of persecution' and 'conversion'. East Timor was the scapegoat sacrificed for the benefit of Australia, the official records weaving myth-like narratives which concealed the suffering of the victim. Growing solidarity with the victim demonstrated the gradual collapse of the scapegoat mechanism as a valid means of attaining harmony and led to a turning towards the victim, a type of conversion away from a national self-focus to a more realistic and genuine appreciation of the victimized other.

2

Australian identity and relationships

This chapter analyses certain characteristics which Australians generally apply to their nation, and discusses in broad terms Australian relationships with other significant and regional powers. Consideration of the dominant discourse around 'Australian' values and heroic archetypes, particularly as they operated within the Australia-East Timor relationship and affected it, is important for later assessment of this relationship. Outlining some of the dominant Australian cultural values and self-perceptions and considering how they have operated within significant Australian national relationships provide a context for reflection on ways in which they were challenged by the relationship with East Timor.

The two parties to the relationship being studied in this book, Australia and East Timor, can be described as 'imagined communities'. Benedict Anderson's phrase points to the limited yet sovereign status of nations, where no one member could ever know all the others, yet from its cultural roots the nation generates communities willing both to kill and to die for it.[1] Charles Taylor expands this idea, writing of the 'social imaginary' which allows the society to make sense of itself, its history and its practices, thus enabling it to cohere and develop.[2] Far from fictitious, the social imaginary is present in large groups, if not the whole society, covering expectations between people, how they 'fit together with others'.[3]

Despite major differences of size, ethnicity, colonial history, culture and status as recognized nations, the social imaginaries of both Australia and East Timor have the common purposes of nurturing their respective communities, protecting and ennobling shared existence, and finding and expressing the meaning of human life. Bound together psychologically, socially and sometimes physically, and also with the past and the dead, the separate, unique and recognizable entities of each society are constructed.[4]

Nevertheless, while Taylor's 'social imaginary' embraces essential if indefinable aspects of nations, it also allows for reflection on the possibility of a false imaginary.[5] Taylor states, for example, that belief in the principle of democracy could lead people to imagine that it is already realized in their society, whereas they may ignore or deny the evidence of some people's exclusion.[6] The claiming of certain characteristics within a social imaginary, therefore, does not guarantee their actual existence. Thus, Australian projections of national ideals such as fairness or loyalty did not assure their practice in relation to the Timorese people any more than lack of political experience undermined the Timorese capacity for independence. The official tendency of Australian self-congratulation in the wake of Timorese independence lacks strong foundations and thus skews appraisal of the situation towards falsehood. Additionally, the existence of some oppositional forces within the Timorese people was incapable of negating the desire for independence which came to form the overarching Timorese imaginary, just as the false Australian social imaginary of white superiority was not universal. It is in this sense that this book assesses how the group which identifies as 'Australian' related to that identifying as 'Timorese', how that relationship was influenced and changed, and the effects that are observable in the history of that relationship.

Identity is created through relationships with others upon whom we rely for constant re-evaluation of self. What is done in those relationships, especially concerning the vulnerable other, expresses who we are. It is therefore essential to an understanding of Australian identity to consider whether values generally claimed as 'Australian' can be demonstrated in the events which affect close neighbours in situations of poverty and oppression, such as the Timorese people.

Whilst the focus here is not to add to the various inconclusive efforts to define an Australian identity, documentary record shows that in its relationship with East Timor, Australia in many ways did not live up to the values it claims as its identifying features. I suggest that official Australian actions throughout Timor's history contributed to an overall Australian identity which contains traits opposite to those claimed, that is, one where loyalty, the 'fair go', independence and support for the underdog were neglected or betrayed. In this regard, the impact of a realpolitik foreign policy markedly influenced Australian identity. Certain significant official Australian responses to the East Timorese situation illustrate underlying contradictions between what governments and agencies say and what they do.

Unpalatable aspects of history and the tendency to ignore or deny them illustrate the need for a continuing reflection on established facts and on discourse about identity.[7] A willingness to accept the darker side of the history and culture of one's nation involves being able to discern the ethical value of attitudes and actions. This is particularly so in relation to the vulnerable and through principled choice to determine possibilities for the future.[8] An honest appraisal of Australian values and their practice in both formal and informal history is required 'to determine who we might be as much as who we think we were'.[9] In particular, analysis of the Australia-Timor relationship reveals how a victimized people can pose a challenge to and provoke change in a politically stable and economically affluent neighbour. Because of the level of Timorese suffering and the substantial factors which currently remain unresolved, such scrutiny is essential.

Values, self-perceptions and contradictions

Popular descriptions of Australian characteristics which are generally accepted as constituting the 'social imaginary' include values such as egalitarianism, loyalty, courage, self-confidence, independence, a certain disrespect for authority, freedom and perseverance in adversity.[10] At the same time, the complexities of Australia's past and present relationships present an array of contradictions alongside these qualities. These considerations are integral to any scrutiny of the Australia-East Timor relationship.

Australia is a nation comprising a mix of people from different ethnic origins within a highly structured state. It is a society extolling freedom which emerged from a penal colony but a nation where the presence of its ancient Indigenous cultures was not legally recognized until 1992. The first immigrants from the British Isles established European settlements, while programmes of immigration, especially after World War II, contributed to its strongly multicultural character. Australia is a nation state which had a foundational Christian influence but which developed to be both secular and multireligious, one with a strong military tradition yet without the experience of a modern foreign war on its soil.

Similar contradictions are found in characteristics seen by many as 'Australian'. Certain values of 'the bush' are often proclaimed as important in popular discourse despite the fact that most people live in urban settings. In the same way, irreverence and anti-authoritarianism have been championed as 'Australian', while there is also a long history of paternalism and legalism. Freedom is prized but is compromised by highly restricted ownership of media and business and by these vested interests having marked influence on government. Australia is successful and rich but displays high levels of fear and insecurity in policymaking and social interaction. A long-standing sense of inferiority, a 'cultural cringe', is amply matched by an abundance of celebrated heroes. Australians are descended from many racial and cultural groups making the country one of the most multicultural nations on earth, yet it usually projects images of cultural homogeneity, particularly in popular media. Moreover, the relatively tolerant relationships in this rich diversity are held together successfully, in the main, by formal structures inherited from the British. But perhaps most paradoxically of all, a past military defeat – at Gallipoli during World War I – is presented as an iconic and central source of the nation's pride.

Independence and egalitarianism are values particularly important to Australian self-perception and therefore are relevant to any investigation of the history of Australia's relationship with East Timor. These values are often popularly expressed through the image of 'the bush'. In this imagery, grit, hard work and an independent streak are the hallmarks of 'battlers' who eke out an existence from an unforgiving land, considering others as equals and treating them fairly without the compromises brought by class or status. Efforts to define 'Australianness' in terms of 'the bush' were fed by the growing nationalism which characterized Europe and its colonies in the nineteenth and twentieth centuries. The focus on the bush served a sense of independence because it distinguished colonial society from the British in a positive way.[11] The uniqueness of the Australian bush made it 'distinctive, not representative', but because of its accessibility through art and literature it permeated the Australian psyche and grew to be a significant 'social imaginary' – the Australian legend.[12] Nevertheless, despite their questionable status as true reflections of some innate quality of 'Australianness', images of the dominant culture are promoted by authorities and opinion-makers in ways which reinforce stereotypes. The bush, along with Anzacs and mateship, continues to be used to promote the particular views of advertisers and governments for their various political, cultural and financial interests.

Blanket application of certain values as images of the 'real' Australia, however, omits the balance of other views which also have resonances of fact without themselves necessarily being the complete truth. Australian racism has been described as more fundamental than egalitarianism.[13] Additionally, when referring to apparent contradictions and inadequacies displayed by Australia as a member of the international community, Alan Renouf, a former head of the Department of Foreign Affairs, stated that 'Australians have been a frightened and intimidated people'.[14]

Significantly, the attitudes of cultural or political 'elites' – establishment figures and opinion-makers – have the capacity not only to reflect the views of a multifaceted people but also to shape them. The image of the rugged independence of battlers in the bush, whilst seizing on aspects of reality, may have been rather a mental morality-play addressing the hardships and disappointments of industrialized cities and towns in the grip of drought and depression. Art and literature may have made a lasting contribution to the development of an Australian ethos or myth, yet contrary realities, such as settlement at the rim of Australia rather than in the outback, and acceptance of prevailing notions of inferior races rather than egalitarianism indicate some distance between the theories of the privileged and talented and the experience of ordinary people. The phenomenon of an appreciable difference between the views and priorities of elites (including the intelligentsia) and those of ordinary Australians arises again in considering Australian international relationships and is pertinent to the relationship with East Timor. Of particular relevance is the contradiction between projections of calm confidence and the demonstrated Australian fear which substantially influenced decisions concerning East Timor from World War II onwards. The contradictions that can be identified when considering Australia and its people indicate the strong probability of the reign of false imaginaries.

Civic and ethnic nationalism

Efforts to understand these contradictions are assisted by Winton Higgins's reflections on the effects of ethnicity in the development of nationalism in Europe and his comparison between civic and ethnic nationalism.[15] Higgins describes the emergence of nation states over centuries as being associated with national identities dependent on the cohesiveness contributed by race, religion and cultural similarities, which provided the evolving political entities with a dependable core. This ethnic nationalism guarded itself carefully, tending to conceal or assimilate all groups other than the dominant one.[16] Identity relied on the exclusion of others. Civic nationalism, however, is based on popular sovereignty, the rule of law and citizens' rights. Higgins maintains that Australian national development was a hybrid but one that tended more towards the ethnic side.[17] The early dominance of the British and the Irish which entailed the exclusion of the Indigenous peoples entrenched the Australian self-projection as a white society.

However, the massive influx of immigrants after World War II changed the ethnic make-up of Australian society irrevocably, with hundreds of thousands of Europeans impelled to find security away from their homelands. Having signed the 1951 United Nations Refugee Convention, Australia presented many displaced people with the means to escape the war and its aftermath. Between 1945 and 1965 assisted migration programmes brought two million migrants, who enjoyed the chance of employment and better living conditions and boosted Australia's population and its agricultural and industrial progress. Although non-Europeans were excluded from migration programmes until the 1970s when the White Australia policy was finally rescinded, the Colombo Plan established in 1950 was an advance towards countering adverse international opinions about Australian policy and a means of providing regional neighbours with higher education opportunities. Greater Asian migration occurred in the 1970s and 1980s with the final demise of anti-Asian policies.

Despite strong European dominance, Australia's multicultural reality is increasingly diverse, but it is generally harmonious and stable because of the strength of the 'civic nationalism' components of the inherited British Westminster parliamentary system and the strong tradition of the rule of law. The balancing of civic and ethnic nationalism is not a task that can be claimed to be complete, however, particularly in a nation such as Australia. Here the European, and especially Anglo-Celtic, ethnicity remains the underlying standard by which social and political realities are judged with varying degrees of consciousness. Belief in white racial supremacy and its attendant denigration or paternalism towards difference exists within the Australian population. Official multiculturalism veils a fundamental suspicion and distrust of difference.[18]

Ghassan Hage makes an insightful comment about the unconscious supposition inhabiting prevailing cultural thought that suggests the existence of a 'real' Australia which now includes other cultures as a set of appendages:

> The 'we appreciate' diversity, 'we value' ethnic contributions, etc., attitudes which abound in the dominant political discourse in Australia create a gulf between the 'we' and that which is appreciated and valued. In so doing, they work to mystify the real possibility, grounded in the very composition of Australian society, of a national 'we' which is itself diverse. It is this 'we' that is at the core of the multicultural Real: we are diversity.[19]

Thus in any assumption of an ethnic Australian core which sees others as apart or lesser, there lies an expression of the ethnic nationalism which, Higgins is at pains to explain, must give way in every instance to the hard-won civic nationalism.

These reflections are integrally tied to the idea of the 'nation' which requires some definition to advance the discussion in this book. A focus on the actions of a nation risks reification, where an abstract reality is treated as a concrete thing: in this context to consider states, for example, as acting on their own behalf. Thus, reference to 'Australia' in this book concerns particularly the government acting with the general compliance of the population at a particular time and in a particular set of circumstances and not as a completely definable totality. Yet, as Higgins points out, the ways in which populations conceive of and identify themselves vary dramatically. As the most basic political entities in the modern world are nation states, these variations influence and express the responses of each national community to 'morally significant issues'.[20] The historical response of the Australian national community to the situation in East Timor remains one such moral issue.

The effort to understand a nation's past actions is intimately linked with the general population's perception of the nation, which in turn is influenced by the people's approach to history, that is, how a population remembers and celebrates its history dramatically influences its self-concept.[21] Higgins emphasizes the importance of facing history, however inconvenient or disgraceful, but more especially with the willingness to grapple with 'the moral significance of the facts'.[22] This book claims that certain facts significant to Australia's official historical relationship with East Timor attest to denial, deceit, indifference and ignorance, challenging the self-images of fairness, equality and independence that many Australians accept as reality.

'We Australians have trouble in identifying ourselves, in saying what we are, and what we are coming to be.'[23] This insight reflects the number of published attempts undertaken since the 1950s to describe the 'Australian identity', many concluding that if such an identity exists, it is impossible to define. It is possible, however, to demonstrate whether claimed national values are applied in concrete situations through which Australians establish and build relationships with other nations and peoples.

A multiplicity of distinctive cultural traits operates within Australia and has done so as long as people have inhabited this land, as demonstrated by the Indigenous cultures. The dominant cultural traditions have attempted to mediate different and sometimes competing cultures and groups, and have generally done it successfully, whilst recognizing unresolved aspects of the relationship with the Indigenous peoples. However, claims to the independence which arises from freedom and courage, essential to the images of battlers and the bush, are challenged by the history of Australia's international relations and dependencies. Too often, fear, insecurity and consequent dependency have characterized Australia in the modern world. The veracity of Australia's claims to independence and belief in equality for all can be tested by considering their practice in relating to others. The foremost consideration is how the expanding Australian nation 'fits together' with its Indigenous peoples, a reflection on whose history raises matters of relevance to East Timor.

Relationships

Indigenous peoples

A strong aspect of the Australian social imaginary that existed in colonial Australia was equality, but the ideal was not applied to Indigenous peoples. The concept of 'mateship' was part of the egalitarian ethos, but it had little, if any, connection to Aborigines or to other races, such as the Chinese on the goldfields or Pacific Islanders in the cane fields.[24] Race was integral to the concept of nationality prevalent at the time. This ethnic nationalism held the belief that threat and conflict could be avoided through the exclusion of coloured races; hence Indigenous people were excluded by being dispossessed, ignored or assimilated.[25] The inability of the dominant groups to incorporate these peoples as contributors to society contradicts claims of egalitarianism and demonstrates that the Australian interpretation of equality was limited and insular from the beginning of white settlement.

This exclusion of Indigenous people is connected to questions concerning the use of the historical record and is a matter of importance to this book. The absence of a unifying narrative of the historical relationship between Indigenous and non-Indigenous Australia arises partly from the absence of comprehensive records but also from interpretations of the available record based on commentators' differing world views.

During the twentieth century, awareness of the prejudice towards and mistreatment of Indigenous people grew. It culminated in the overwhelming support for the 1967 referendum, which recognized the Aboriginal peoples' right to vote and charged the Commonwealth government with legislating for Indigenous affairs, giving impetus to positive action and organization at a national level. W. E. H. Stanner in his Boyer Lectures of 1968 voiced a growing recognition within the dominant Australian society of the time that Aboriginal people had suffered 'the great Australian silence'.[26] He maintained that Aboriginal people had not been treated as integral players in Australian history but rather had been reduced to subjects to be studied. Bain Attwood states that they were valued by anthropologists as 'artefacts of the human past'.[27] In colonial art, Aborigines did not appear as social actors but were seen as part of nature whilst being deleted from the unfolding history.[28]

Poignant descriptions of the initial attempts of the first governor of New South Wales, Arthur Phillip, to obey the orders given him to engage with the natives and 'to live in amity and kindness with them' can, unfortunately, now be viewed in the light of the threat of near extinction subsequently experienced by Aboriginal Australians.[29] The inability to establish a relationship of 'amity and kindness' was a tragedy arising from numerous causes, not the least of which were the inability of colonial leaders (including Phillip) to comprehend the situation, the taking of the land by convicts and settlers and the status of Indigenous peoples in the minds of eighteenth- and nineteenth-century Westerners as a 'stone-age' people.

Alongside Stanner's insights, serious research into Aboriginal history accompanied growing international recognition of the rights of Indigenous peoples and greater understanding of the effects of colonialism in the ensuing half-century. Aboriginal strength in political and cultural arenas led to greater knowledge of their status and history in mainstream society. On the journey towards recognition and equality the nation formally expressed sorrow particularly for the removal of Indigenous children from their families – the stolen generation – in 2008.

Despite such positive changes, there still remain many challenges to reconciliation and to improving the material position of many Indigenous communities. Conflicting and ongoing argument about the place of Aboriginal people in Australian society accompanies polarization concerning the historical record of race relationships in modern Australian history.

Stanner refers to the exclusion of Aboriginal people's experience from that record as arising not only from indifference towards them but also from deliberate forgetfulness and denial.[30] The silence cannot be seen as the unfortunate effect of simple misunderstandings but as a structural reality arising from colonial acquisition and particular views of racial and social superiority which gained strength in the nineteenth century. Attempts to redress the exclusion of Aborigines from the record of Australian history since Stanner's time were many and varied, but divisions among some historians, politicians and commentators remain.

These divisions coalesced around what has been called 'the history wars', which involved prominent historians such as Henry Reynolds and Keith Windschuttle. Opposing views of the record of Indigenous history include the disputes concerning the 2002 publication of Windschuttle's work, *The Fabrication of Aboriginal History*. The introduction to this work states clearly that it is a study of 'the nature of the written history' of the relationship between the early settlers and the Aboriginal people.[31] Windschuttle maintains that there is a consensus among historians and intellectuals that Australia was guilty of deliberate genocide of the Indigenous peoples. He claims that such assertions disparage the character not only of the Australian nation but of British civilization.[32] He aimed to refute these opinions by examining the credibility of this interpretation of Aboriginal history.[33] His trilogy was received with acclaim in some politically conservative circles.[34]

In response in 2003, Robert Manne edited *Whitewash*, a book of essays by fifteen historians, archaeologists, curators or lawyers who criticize Windschuttle's work as being rushed, superficial and inaccurate. In the collection, James Boyce sees *The Fabrication of Aboriginal History* as seriously flawed because of the limited sources consulted.[35] Attwood refers to Windschuttle's omission of available information and questions the premises on which he bases his conclusions.[36] Prominent historian Geoffrey Blainey however, writing elsewhere, supports Windschuttle's accusation that selective use of evidence underpins currently accepted versions of Aboriginal history.[37]

The Windschuttle debate is an element in the 'history wars' in which government, media, historians and members of the public continue to be engaged, particularly since Stanner's unsettling phrase began to inhabit the Australian psyche. That highly educated historians, opinion-makers, politicians and commentators continue to exchange accusations about selective use of sources and manipulation of evidence on Indigenous questions indicates fundamental unease and frustration at an academic level, thus weakening the ability of that stratum of knowledge to influence this fundamental relationship more popularly. Pertinent to the matter in this book, the fact that Australia is still grappling with the written record of its relationship with its Indigenous peoples contrasts markedly with celebrated versions of its self-projection, demonstrating the embedding of a false imaginary. The inability of the dominant culture over the years to understand, accept and then describe this fundamental historical relationship suggests that Australia's relationships in the region with other Indigenous peoples, including the Timorese, would have similar challenges.

It must be asked what political, social and racial currents affect that later relationship, to what extent government, media and church silence contributed to East Timor's situation and whether there are forces at work which continue to ignore, falsify or misinterpret the record of dealings with the Timorese people, as is still being claimed and counterclaimed regarding Australia's Indigenous peoples.

Britain

Self-images of Australian independence are challenged in some ways by Australia's relationship with Britain, a connection of singular importance to self-understanding and the development of its later relationships.[38] A kind of 'love-hate' relationship exists between the British-influenced Australian culture and that of Britain in which feelings of loyalty and affection as well as of competitiveness and disdain arise. The closeness of the relationship since the beginning of colonization in 1788 developed on the basis of the white population being predominantly made up of convicts and settlers from the British Isles, with administration by appointed British governors, and all institutions being modelled on that of Britain. There was a tendency in the colonies to judge everything by British standards which in some quarters remained well into the twentieth century. Even the values which Australians claimed as distinctive to them were recognized by others as British: courage, independence, self-reliance and loyalty.[39] Whilst the class system did not have the hold in Australia that it did in Britain, the use of the colony for the excess of convicts, the presence of the lower classes and a significant minority of Irish among both the convicts and the free settlers contributed to an opinion of the low status and lack of quality of the new venture. When Australian was compared with British, it was always in the context of British superiority.[40]

Despite such comparisons, Australia remained culturally, politically and emotionally tied to Britain.[41] Strong ties held sway in diplomatic and trade matters, both forming and illustrating Australia's dependence on the colonizer. In 1901, when the Australian colonies became a Federation of States, the Commonwealth of Australia became a Dominion of the British Empire. Britain's declaration of war in 1914 automatically included Australia, with Australian troops being counted as British. In fact, all Australians were seen as British subjects until 1949.[42] It was not until 1984 that Australian citizens ceased to be British subjects altogether.[43] Sports traditionally enjoyed by Australians (and subsequently seized upon as evidence of a nation devoted to sport) for the most part were based on British models: cricket, versions of rugby and boxing.

The threats posed by distance, difficulty of communication and the status of being a small population inhabiting a large land mass so close to Asia encouraged continued dependence on Britain, so much so that Australian foreign policy was dictated by London throughout the 1920s and 1930s, with Australia only gradually moving towards the exercise of greater international diplomacy. Trade, security and diplomatic support from Britain was a matter of course until World War II when, with the fall of Singapore and the war in the Pacific, the reality of Britain's inability to provide expected levels of support forced Australia to look elsewhere for security. With Britain's decision to join the European Economic Community in 1973, economic relations declined, further weakening the traditional British-Australian relationship.[44] Nevertheless, while strong levels of migration, trade and investment continued, and military and intelligence sharing alliances were retained, Australia chose to retain the Union Jack in its flag and the British monarch as head of state.

Such a strong history of dependence on the founding culture for institutions, symbols and protection indicates an insecurity requiring multiple levels of support. Ann Curthoys alludes to the experience of the early settlers, soldiers and convicts as being uprooted from Europe and believes that a sense of dispossession applied to them.[45] Gregory Melleuish discusses Simone Weil's belief that those uprooted from their environments can manifest their suffering by dispossessing others without in any way healing their own anguish.[46] This can describe the experience of Europeans in Australia who, having dispossessed the Indigenous peoples, found themselves in a vacuum, where insecurity expressed their shallow hold on the country.[47] This insecurity required dependence on greater powers, a phenomenon which characterizes Australian modern history, providing constant challenge to aspects of the social imaginary, such as rugged individualism.

The Australian relationship with Britain, with all its dependency and inferiority, raises questions. Given the tendency in Australia in the nineteenth and twentieth centuries to measure itself in relation to Britain, what echoes arise in the relationship with East Timor? To what extent could it be claimed that the apparent backwardness, weakness and impoverishment of East Timor reflected Australia back to itself? Could the later demonstration that East Timor was of little account in many Australian eyes flow from the Australian sense of self in relation to Britain? Did Australians subsume into their social imaginary elements of Girard's designation of the victim?

United States of America

Australian recourse to American protection in 1942 was a realistic response to Japan's expansionism and Britain's inability to provide essential support. The ANZUS Treaty, which came into effect in 1952, cemented the Australian-New

Zealand-American security alliance and became the bedrock of Australian foreign policy, influencing its other relationships.[48] Alan Renouf states that it was Australia's need for security, fear of communism and inferiority complex which required the treaty, a formality which was not the preference of the United States, given Australia's already demonstrated strategic importance to the United States in its dealings in Asia.[49] The treaty is actually ambiguous as to the practical requirements of the parties in response to threats. In both its advantages and disadvantages the relationship can be seen as a continuation and then replacement of the strategic dependence which the former prime minister Malcolm Fraser states described Australia's relationship with Britain.[50] Long after his years in leadership, Fraser actually advocated terminating the alliance, citing the diminishment of the Australian capacity to act independently as a sovereign nation through too great adherence to America.[51] Claiming protection and security through dependence on a greater power exposes Australia to the threats faced by that power, thereby heightening the very insecurity it seeks to avoid.

The implications of Australia's efforts to engage with its regional neighbours whilst retaining a favoured position with the Americans were seen in regard to East Timor. The United States' thrust towards regional dominance accounted substantially for its decades-long support of Indonesia's anti-communist regime. The effects of that balance of power were felt in Australia which also had its own fears of communism and worked closely with the United States to counter that threat, all of which contributed to the compromised Australian response to Indonesia regarding East Timor for many years.

Asia

Australian relationships with Asia have historically involved a degree of ambivalence, insecurity and fear, heightened by Japan's role in World War II, the Cold War and communism. As time passed, Australia's desire to receive support from Britain and the United States was concurrent with efforts to strengthen defence and trade ties with Asia. The interplay of these forces had direct bearings on East Timor in its place as part of the Indonesian archipelago.

As a predominantly European culture with its geographical place in the Asian region far from Europe, the Australian social imaginary harboured currents of negativity towards Asia. Gary Smith alludes to a sense of isolation arising from the state of being a small number of people in a vast continent which produced fears of being 'vulnerable, indefensible, and desirable'.[52] Lack of interaction and familiarity between Australians and Asians brought misunderstanding of mutual needs and perceptions, with suspicion and fear accompanying racial and cultural differences. Political attempts to engage with Asia were not necessarily shared by large sections of the Australia population, forming a challenge to government and indicating that underlying fear and suspicion dominated the Australian psyche. It can be seen that enthusiasm for engagement with Asia was a project of the political and intellectual elites far more than that of the general public. This hiatus between the positions of ordinary people and the establishment regarding Asia will be demonstrated as significant in relation to both Indonesia and East Timor.

An expression of the deep-seated Australian mistrust of Asian peoples, and a significant contributor to that position, was contained initially in the *Bulletin*, the widely popular weekly newspaper founded in 1880. Nationalistic, anti-Semitic and racist in its early issues, the *Bulletin* lampooned leaders in every field, supported Australian independence and took a hard line in favour of the White Australia policy. Through this magazine, images of exclusion and violent opposition to people and ideas considered alien were presented to a wide Australian reading public for many years. The motto 'Australia for the White Man' was part of its masthead until the 1960s, testimony to Australian fear, insecurity and sense of racial superiority.[53]

The maintenance of difference and division in the population had been strengthened by the White Australia policy, introduced for a mix of economic and racial reasons. It passed into Federal law in 1901, described as a way of protecting white citizens' employment opportunities from Asian and Islander workers and ensuring a homogenous population similar to that of Britain. Post-war immigration remained solely for Europeans, with restricted opportunities for non-Europeans. While the policy expressed ideas concerning race and nationalism current at the time of its promulgation, it lasted in Australia into the 1970s. Its isolationism not only affected the composition of the population and a protectionist economy but also nurtured the defensiveness and sense of superiority which existed among many Australians of Anglo-Celtic or European descent. These realities influenced decisions regarding East Timor over decades – not only the political considerations thought necessary at the time of the events but in succeeding decades concerning official government presentation of the history.

Engagement with Asia

Threats to Australia, whether perceived or real, ensured that the nation's security within Asia remained a matter of major concern. In particular, Japan's expansionism increased Australian belief in its vulnerability to aggression from the north, underlining fears of Asian nations generally. Interestingly, the experience of World War II and reliance on the United States rather than on Britain were accompanied by Australia's realization of the importance of active engagement for its national interest in the Southeast Asian region. At that time, Australian governments endeavoured to ensure that all other considerations, including traditional fears, loyalties and images of independence, were subordinated to the main national interest: security.

The interactions of dominant world powers in the subsequent Cold War affected their interests in the region. With Australia in alliance with the United States, its approach to Asia was governed by the demands of anti-Soviet politics.[54] Furthermore, the communist ascendancies in some newly independent Asian states heightened the sense of threat, linking Australia to the Cold War which was gripping Europe. The rise of Mao Zedong's communist China brought the impasse between the USSR and the West into the Asian region, presenting Australia with further reason to fear Asia through the 1950s and 1960s, with the 'domino' theory posing broad perceptions of serious menace. Thus Indonesian accusations of Timorese communist sympathies in the 1970s made Timor's position in Australia's regard an invidious one, given the breadth and intensity of Australia's wariness of communism within its own borders as well as in the region.

Following World War II, Australia sought to engage with Asia as a way of protection of its interests. This was represented at an early stage by Australia's membership of the South East Asian Treaty Organization (SEATO) in 1954, where alliances were formed with Asian nations under the overarching relationships with the United Kingdom and the United States. While pursuing better relations in Asia, Australia also firmly retained its position of alliance with the United States, often cooperating on foreign policy in Asia, but showing willingness to demonstrate such dependency regardless of its effects on relationships in the region. According to Renouf, this resulted in major disadvantages for Australia, which was seen widely as retaining its traditional dependence on colonial powers. He states that as SEATO enjoyed strong British influence, Australia's membership weakened the ANZUS alliance, while conversely the continuing Australian dependence on the United States alienated Asian opinion.[55] With its security dependent on amicable relations between the United States and an increasingly powerful Asia, Australia viewed East Timor as relatively unimportant, determining not to allow it to interfere with those other relationships, especially that with Indonesia.

Particularly from the 1970s onwards, governments on both sides of Australian politics were avid in pursuit of Asian trade, engaging with the region through treaties, foreign aid, military cooperation, education, regular multilevel visits, conferences and immigration. With the trade focus shifting from declining European markets to closer Asian ones, and with the restrictions on immigration lifted from the 1970s onwards, greater cultural interaction was possible between Australia and Asia. Immigration and tourism brought a degree of greater tolerance and mutual understanding. However, while economic prosperity increased in both Australia and Asia, the increasing wealth of the growing economies in the region ensured that they could buy more and better weapons, thus increasing their potential threat. [56] Greater ties with Asia brought questions about the extent to which Australian economic and strategic gains in the region could, and should, influence its approach to human rights, given fundamental differences of approach between Western and Asian nations to this matter.[57] This dilemma surfaced with full force as Australia juggled its relationships with Indonesia, Britain, the United States and the United Nations in the matter of East Timor.

Indonesia

The Asian nation closest to Australia, just a few hundred kilometres to the north, is the Republic of Indonesia. The most populous Muslim nation in the world, Indonesia boasts a mix of languages and cultures. Its relatively stable democracy (following more than thirty years of dictatorship under the former military general Suharto) and swiftly developing economy mark it as a success story of the post-war era. Its proximity makes its relationship with Australia significant among Asian nations, even more so in its integral connection with events affecting East Timor.

Historically, Australia has shown consistent support for Indonesia. The struggle of the previous Dutch East Indies for independence after World War II saw military efforts by the Netherlands to regain control, a move which led the Australian government to register complaints with the United Nations. Australian trade union blockades against Dutch vessels involved in the offensives continued until the recognition of Indonesian sovereignty in 1949. Australia was among the first nations to recognize Indonesia's new status. When the first president, Sukarno, promoted policies viewed as verging on communism, the concern of the United States was echoed by Australia. His overthrow by General Suharto and Indonesia's subsequent rejection of communism allied it to the

United States and contributed to its status as a bulwark against China in the region. Although authoritarian and controversial, Suharto's long presidency, from 1967 to 1998, developed the economy and consolidated Indonesia as a significant Asian power.

Along with closer political and security ties, Australian governments secured trade and investment opportunities with Indonesia, and partnerships of the 1980s and 1990s recognized more fully the capacity for mutual economic benefits. These included opportunities for the exploitation of oil and gas reserves in the Timor Sea. Greater benefits for Indonesia through these links accompanied the likelihood of Australia's greater acceptance in the Southeast Asian region. Prime Minister Paul Keating asserted in 1994 that Indonesia was more important to Australia than any other country.[58]

While diplomatic and political interaction with Indonesia has remained a high priority of successive Australian governments, deeper cultural and social connections between the peoples of the two nations took far longer to be made.[59] Despite its highly significant democratic advances and economic progress, just over 20 per cent of the Indonesian population is vulnerable to poverty.[60] The economic disparities between Australia and Indonesia place the former ahead in terms of current opportunities, but the relative youth and size of Indonesia's population provide conditions for strong growth. While Indonesia's development benefits Australian prosperity, it has also caused insecurity and ambivalence, pointing to the ever-present Australian sense of fear of the other. Indonesia was seen from the 1980s through the 1990s as the country most likely to threaten Australia's national security.[61]

At government levels Australia and Indonesia have entered into a range of agreements and treaties since 1964 to build the relationship, including trade, seabed boundaries, investment and development, science and technology. Among the most significant is the 2006 Treaty on Security Cooperation – the Lombok Treaty – designed to maintain close cooperation for peace, prosperity and mutual security by the practical means of combatting terrorism and transnational crime.[62] Decades of combined military exercises and Indonesian officer training in Australia were designed to enhance the relationship but have had unfortunate results. Indonesia's human rights record in East Timor (and in other parts of the archipelago) contributed to credible accusations of Australian compromise and complicity. Much controversy has centred on the Indonesian elite force Kopassus, which continued to receive training from Australia during the 1980s and 1990s, throughout the struggle for Timorese independence and beyond.[63]

The relatively weak relationship between Indonesia and Australia at the levels of individuals and communities is in contrast to strong and positive aspects of the relationship concerning mutuality between leaders, and government-to-government initiatives, especially in defence, security and trade. However, in the case of East Timor, the reverse of this situation developed. As this book details, the strengthening of relationships between ordinary Australians and Timorese, with the associated analysis and public presentation of a more complete version of the narrative of East Timor's history, led to a major change in the Australian population. Alongside significant global shifts, this turning towards the Timorese in recognition of their reality as an oppressed people, a true victim in the Girardian sense, eventually influenced the change in the position of the Australian government from support of Indonesia's integration of East Timor to support for Timorese self-determination.

East Timor

The Australian relationship with East Timor is characterized by extreme geographical and historical differences. The vast continent of modern Australia is a Europe-based middle power with strong multicultural elements, still grappling with the effects on the Indigenous peoples of the arrival of white settlers at the end of the eighteenth century. Conversely, indigenous Timorese comprise the greater part of East Timor's society, although with Portuguese and Chinese influence for five centuries. Australian sovereignty evolved from its status as a colony of Britain, whereas Timor-Leste, after a European colonization twice as long as Australia's, has had recent experience of armed invasions and occupations by foreign powers, with its final independence gained as recently as 2002.

Situated in the Indonesian archipelago, the mountainous island of Timor was populated over millennia by a series of migrations which included both Melanesian and Malaysian people who developed strong and successful tribal societies. European influence came through Dutch colonization of the western half of the island, while the Portuguese arrived on the eastern side in 1515 and established trading posts in the 1560s. Throughout the sixteenth to the nineteenth centuries, resistance to the Portuguese was quelled both by military force and by manipulating tribal kingdom rivalries. Despite being recipients of over 450 years of Portuguese colonization, the Timorese remained largely poor and uneducated until the 1970s. Some conversions to Christianity occurred during earlier times, especially among Timorese elites, increasing exponentially among the general population in the latter part of the twentieth century. Internationally recognized boundaries were established in 1913 between Dutch West Timor and Portuguese East Timor. The importance of oil to the rapid industrialization of the world had a direct effect on the fortunes of the Timorese people in their dealings with Australia and became an underlying element in Australia's actions regarding East Timor throughout the shared history.[64]

The majority of people in both nations identify as Christian. Despite this, animism and superstition remain strong in Timor while in Australia meaning is increasingly sought in material success. Strong political, judicial and legal frameworks based largely on the British system and Judeo-Christian principles provide Australians with stable regulatory processes to support social life. In contrast, Timorese people's systems are evolving from Portuguese and Indonesian influences, with ancient customs and beliefs retaining strong underlying cultural significance. As a developing nation, one which suffers the effects of recent military devastation, Timor-Leste experiences major hurdles alongside recent significant improvement in education, health and political stability. Australian social systems are far stronger: on the 2020 UN Human Development Index (an international measure to rank social and economic development) Australia is at no.8 whereas Timor-Leste is at no.141.[65]

Alongside the disparities of wealth and stability, there exist certain Australian cultural attitudes which tend towards attitudes of superiority towards Timor-Leste and its people. Western ethnocentrism has tended to appropriate civilization to itself, harbouring the view that non-European civilization lacks what is required of a modern state.[66] And yet a nation is a people that existed long before and quite independently of becoming a body politic.[67] Taylor refers to the unique development of non-Western cultures which elude analysis by theories designed by and for the Western mind.[68] Thus the 'social imaginary' which conceived that a small, oppressed and linguistically diverse group could become a sovereign nation such as Timor-Leste contrasts with the 'social imaginary' in Australia which thought such an outcome impossible for the Timorese people and actively opposed it.

Conclusion

Australian society often projects images of itself which are at variance with the historical record of its attitudes, decisions and actions. Elements of both civic and ethnic nationalism are apparent in Australian history, making the task of accurately describing the 'social imaginary', or how Australians 'fit together', an important but elusive one. Contradictions abound in Australian relationships. There are long-standing attitudes of superiority and suspicion towards people of different ethnicities or cultures, including both the Indigenous and Asian peoples, forming a constant challenge to claims of egalitarianism. Dependence on Britain, on the United States and increasingly on Asian neighbours has served modern Australia's need for security but questions notions of its independence.

The relationship with East Timor demonstrates to what extent ideals such as fairness, independence, supporting the underdog, equality and courage operated in historical events in which Australia had a major role and during which the Timorese people suffered greatly. As a result, the relationship is a primary witness as to how we stand in relation to power and to others, especially the victim or scapegoat: how we imagine our society. The following chapters recount, in the light of René Girard's mimetic theory, major events which formed and affected that relationship.

3

World War II

The first situation that calls for focused attention is the Australian relationship with East Timor (Portuguese Timor) in World War II. Attempts to protect Australian security in the face of Japanese aggression included an Australian invasion of Portuguese Timor in December 1941 which was the catalyst for the subsequent Japanese invasion and occupation of the half-island. This episode was the first wide-ranging incident in the modern relationship between the Australian and Timorese people. It was highly significant in the formation of that relationship, influencing subsequent historical periods.

This chapter demonstrates that East Timor had the hallmarks of the scapegoat, a vulnerable party suffering the effects of being expendable. However, it was Australia that predominantly perceived itself as the victim under threat and was willing to sacrifice another for its security. The chapter shows that readily available documents on the subject remain fairly described as 'texts of persecution', that is, modern-day myths. Completing this Girardian interpretation, it is apparent that at the time of writing this book, only limited sections of the Australian population understand the Timor campaign. Clearly, there is need for the prevailing 'social imaginary' of heroic Australia to acknowledge the debt owed to the heroic Timorese.

War in the region

In brief, the Australian intervention in Portuguese Timor was in response to fears that the proximity of Timor may pose a threat should the Japanese incorporate it into its expansionary plans during World War II. As a result, Australia sent a few hundred commandos of the 2/2nd Independent Company, part of 'Sparrow Force', to Dili, the capital of Portuguese Timor, in December 1941, followed later by part of the 2/4th Independent Company.[1] This incursion took place against the express wishes of the Portuguese administration.[2] Two months later the Japanese also invaded East Timor. The Australians, assisted by many Timorese, conducted a guerrilla campaign over the next fourteen months against Japanese troops. The highly successful Australian commandos and the intrepid Timorese harassed the Japanese even though they were far outnumbered for the whole operation. Towards the end of 1942 thousands more Japanese troops were inserted in response to the Australians' success and the general unwillingness of the Timorese to capitulate. The success of the Australian commandos in resisting a much larger Japanese force was extraordinary. The operation, in relation to the whole war, has been referred to as 'one of the few success stories in a rather bleak year'.[3] When all other Allied resistance in Asia collapsed, this small group of Australians continued to fight the Japanese for many months with the essential help of the Timorese people.[4] Once returned to Australia, the soldiers showed how deeply affected they were by their Timor experience, some producing material to recount their experiences and their appreciation of their Timorese allies. Relatives also acknowledged the effect on their fathers of the loyalty of the Timorese.[5]

The withdrawal of the Australians early in 1943 left the Timorese in the invidious position of having supported Japan's enemy. It allowed the Japanese complete control, contributing to further death and destruction, as many thousands of troops remained on the island until the end of the war. A conservative estimate of consequent Timorese deaths at that time is at least forty thousand (all civilians) as a result of starvation, Japanese reprisals and Allied bombing.[6] This wartime experience of support of Australians by the Timorese people forms a backdrop to events in subsequent decades.

Australian fear of invasion

Discussion of the Australian presence in East Timor using a Girardian analysis begins with the perceived threat of invasion of Australia in World War II. It underlines the bitter poignancy of the Timorese experience as victim of the mimetic rivalry between larger powers. At the beginning of his comprehensive treatise on Australian foreign policy entitled *The Frightened Country*, Alan Renouf (a former head of the Australian Department of Foreign Affairs) stated that the aims of national foreign policy were to safeguard the independence of the sovereign state and to preserve it from attack and from the threat of attack.[7] It is undeniably true that every nation shares these common objectives. But as

World War II approached, major obstacles to the maintenance of Australian security were apparent, including the size of the population relative to that of the continent.[8] Isolation was a double-edged factor, supplying both the protection and the risks of distance. Consequent fear and insecurity contributed to the Australian dependency on larger powers, particularly the United States.[9] Australian fear centred on the possibility of invasion, and thus the seemingly impossible task of protecting the Australian continent constituted one of the crises facing Australians at that time, a crisis which was a catalyst for the Australian incursion into Portuguese Timor. Two factors which initially contributed to the concern in both the population and government were the existence of a genre of popular literature called 'invasion fiction' and Japan's interest in commercial possibilities in the half-island of Portuguese Timor, geographically close to Australia's north.

Fear of invasion had inhabited the Australian psyche for many years. Professor Peter Stanley, previous principal historian at the Australian War Memorial and author of many books on the military history of both world wars, describes how Australians 'frightened themselves repeatedly' with novels and stories centred on imaginary invasions.[10] From popularity as novels in the late nineteenth century, a steady stream of similar writings on invasion has continued to be produced as articles, books and websites. Urgent and didactic, novels of the Australian invasion fiction genre emphasize the imminence of disaster and seek to shock readers into an acceptance of the perceived danger.[11] The basic plot is reshaped to fit the times, but the fundamental story remains the same and is constantly repeated. As the threat, the 'other', is traditionally Asian, this collection of fiction is the textual expression of the long-held and deep-seated belief that Australia is at risk of invasion by Asians.[12] Fear of Japan featured in this literary style in the early twentieth century, mirroring political wariness of the time. Japan's growing industrial power and military strength, its successful wars against China, Korea and Russia and its 1902 alliance with Britain formed an integrated backdrop both for fiction and for political responses to Japanese expansionism. From 1901 to 1939 the main concern of Australian diplomacy was the perceived threat from Japan.[13]

The geographical position of Portuguese Timor and its proximity to Australia made it strategically important to security; hence, it became a focus of Australian wartime deliberations. By the mid-1930s there had been signs of Japanese interest in Portuguese Timor. A 1939 government submission noted that Japan had interests in two major companies in the territory, was gaining concessions in Portuguese Timor for oil and crops, was cornering that island's coffee trade and was making efforts to control the pearling trade and strengthen its shipping services.[14] These moves bolstered the belief that Japan's real objective in its interest in Portuguese Timor was its inclusion in a planned expansion southwards. There were fears of the 'possibility of Japanese penetration and infiltration into the Netherlands East Indies and Timor'.[15] With Australian foreign policy still being dictated by London, and keen to establish British interests in the face of Japanese penetration into the area, in 1937 the British government had suggested the establishment of an air service to Dili, advising the Commonwealth Government of Australia to develop closer contacts with Portuguese Timor 'for strategic reasons'.[16]

Australia's traditional reliance on Britain eroded swiftly in the face of the political and military disaster that was the fall of Singapore in 1942.[17] With Japan's southward advance, the Australian chiefs-of-staff were convinced of invasion and advised the government that such was likely by April 1942, with a landing in the east coast in May.[18] Political and military leaders realized that the Australian defence services were too ill-equipped and inexperienced to counter any threat of invasion.[19] Therefore the government deployed significant sections of the Australian forces previously in the Middle East to shore up the defence of Australia. In doing this, Australian prime minister John Curtin resisted Winston Churchill's attempt to divert Australian divisions to Burma.[20] Military strength and war effort were thus increased in Australia in view of the perceived threat by Japan.

Undoubtedly, only those who experienced the deep-seated fear and the expectation of a Japanese invasion could properly appreciate the situation in Australia in 1942. Australians were embroiled in a world war, and their traditional support by Britain was weakened. They inhabited a vast and undefended landmass and believed it would be engulfed by Japan's southward march. Australians feared for their nation and their lives. Wartime Australian citizens and government, seeing a formidable Japanese force moving south – and lacking information to the contrary – understandably believed that an invasion was imminent. The nation was in the crisis of war, in which all the fears of the past congealed and intensified.

Japanese intentions

However, Japan did not intend to invade Australia. The primary reason for its expansionist push southwards was to establish the 'Great Southeast Asia

Co-prosperity Sphere'.[21] This scheme was proposed as a Japanese economic, industrial and political empire stretching from Manchuria to the Dutch East Indies and through to New Guinea and the Pacific. Retaining this 4,000 mile sphere of influence was believed by the Japanese to guarantee a flow of oil from the Dutch East Indies and be a bulwark against invasion of Japan herself.

While Japan's designs on Australia and the region have been matters of some dispute, there is now consensus among reputable historians that the Japanese did not intend to invade Australia.[22] Stanley shows that an invasion of Australia by Japan was not planned by the Japanese High Command.[23] His evidence has been supported by English military historian Sir Antony Beevor.[24] Australian David Horner, who was professor of Australian defence history at the Australian National University and has authored many books on defence matters, also concurs.[25] A government paper from 1992 explains the reasons for the realization that Japan was not intending to invade.[26] Significantly, such historians built on the evidence of the lack of invasion plans which the Australian Official War History had detailed as far back as 1957.[27]

Suggestions of including an invasion of Australia in the push southwards did surface however, but only in Japanese naval ranks. The organization of the Japanese armed forces is relevant to this point. While the Japanese Imperial General Headquarters had operational command of the armed forces, the army and navy had administrative control, each operating their own extensive departments and generating plans and strategies. Bullard comments on the long-standing rivalries between the army and navy that could even result in contradictory policies being presented to General Headquarters and to the final authority, the emperor.[28] It appears that the general staff of the navy considered that an invasion of Australia was warranted and that three armed divisions would suffice.[29] The army staff disagreed, however, maintaining that such an invasion would require ten divisions or more.[30] They argued that the size of the continent precluded the transportation and supply of an invading force of that size and was impossible given that their forces were already stretched by offensives on a number of fronts, including Burma and China.[31] Stanley states that the Japanese army and navy commands constantly argued among themselves, unhampered by any clear direction from an authoritative body.[32] Even in the navy, states Horner, unanimity was absent concerning suggestions to invade Australia.[33] Stanley quotes the Army Imperial Headquarters war diary which laments the efforts made to restrain the navy's naïve designs on Australia.[34] As quoted in Australia's official war history, Japan's wartime prime minister Tojo Hideki said that Japan had no plans to invade:

We never had enough troops to do so. We had already far out-stretched our lines of communication. We did not have the armed strength or the supply facilities to mount such a terrific extension of our already over-strained and too thinly spread forces. We expected to occupy all New Guinea, to maintain Rabaul as a holding base, and to raid Northern Australia by air. But actual physical invasion – no, at no time.[35]

Nevertheless, while an invasion was not planned, there were attacks against the Australian mainland. These were designed to isolate the nation from its allies and to prevent the use of Darwin's strategic position by the United States. The first bombing of Darwin on 19 February 1942 killed over 240 people and wounded up to 400, with most civil and military facilities destroyed.[36] Sixty-four more attacks on Darwin happened in the following weeks, besides air attacks on inland towns in the Northern Territory through to November 1943.[37] The destruction of Darwin was a preliminary strike 'to disable its potential as a threat' to the invasion of the Dutch half of Timor, which the Japanese already controlled.[38] Occupation of the islands to Australia's north-east would cut links to US, Commonwealth and Dutch interests, thus neutralizing threats to the Japanese expansionist designs.[39] The Japanese generals were confident that Australia could be bullied into submission through such isolation and by associated psychological pressure.[40]

Contributing to heightened fears of a Japanese invasion of Australia was the New Guinea campaign, particularly the Battle of Kokoda fought between Japanese and Australian forces from July to November 1942. The Kokoda Track and the exploits of the Australian soldiers subsequently filled Australian imaginations as proof of imminent peril to the mainland.[41] In the years following, stories have abounded that the invasion plan was thwarted by the Australians at Kokoda.[42] Nonetheless, the moral triumph of the Australians at Kokoda was neither the sole reason for victory in the south-west Pacific nor can it be seen in isolation as the American victories in the Solomon Islands were crucial and costlier than the New Guinea campaign.[43] The Australians who bravely and skilfully fought against the Japanese in New Guinea did so against an enemy who was attempting to cripple Australia, not invade it.[44]

Thus the threat posed by Japan was real and had fatal consequences for parts of Australia, but it was a threat of isolation rather than invasion. The Australian population, however, did not know that at the time. Australian authorities had received information by May 1942 that there were no Japanese plans to invade. Allied intelligence reports and code-breaking had clarified the matter beyond question.[45] These reports were confirmed by diplomats who relayed to their superiors that the Indian Ocean, and not Australia, was the Japanese focus.[46] The Australian government did not make Japan's lack of intention to invade Australia known to the population, preferring instead to encourage the people to continue to 'work, fight and save' as their war effort.[47] It was a decision compounded in its intricacy by Curtin's realization that Australia's security lay with the United States and not with Britain, and his insistence on the use of Australian troops to bolster the security of the homeland.[48]

The consensus among prominent historians remains that there was not, at any time, a threat of Japanese invasion of Australia, though there was a real threat of aerial attack and isolation. Nevertheless, the situation was perceived as desperate and threatening by the small and fearful Australian population. The subsequent tragedy, however, was not primarily felt by Australians in their own country but by the Timorese in theirs.

The invasions of Portuguese Timor

The status of Portuguese Timor as 'victim' in the global conflict is demonstrated by the fact that the territory was invaded twice at that time – by both Australia and Japan. The drama of World War II in this region saw the foreign powers of Australia, Britain, the Netherlands and Portugal operating in competition with Japan for the possession and control of territory and in pursuit of national stability. This mimetic rivalry resulted in the arrival in Portuguese Timor of both Australia and Japan. Both nations breached Portugal's neutrality by entering its colonial territory against the wishes of the Portuguese authorities. Such illegality placed both incursions in the category of invasion.

The Dutch East Indies, which included the western half of the island of Timor, was included in Japan's expansionary focus.[49] Conversely, the eastern half of Timor was a possession of Portugal, whose neutrality throughout the war was a significant element affecting Japanese plans, as is discussed later in this chapter. On 12 December 1941, the Australian 'Sparrow' Force consisting of about 1,400 men joined Dutch defence troops in the area of the capital of Dutch West Timor, Kupang. The decision was then taken to land 155 men of the Australian 2/2nd Independent Company, along with 260 Dutch troops, in Portuguese Timor on 17 December 1941. Within days, many of the Dutch were replaced by the remainder of the 2/2nd who had stayed in Kupang, as a compromise to assuage the fears of the Portuguese concerning the Dutch presence on the eastern half of the island.[50] Just over two months later, on

19 February 1942, the Japanese military invaded Kupang on the Dutch-administered western end of Timor with two battalions of the 228th Infantry Regiment of the 38th Division. On the same day, one battalion from that regiment landed at Dili, the administrative centre of the eastern Portuguese region.[51] The date is significant for Australians, being the date of the bombing of the city of Darwin.

While it is true that the Australian invasion of Portuguese Timor was not of the same type as that of Japan – in that the Australians did not deliberately kill Timorese people as Japanese soldiers did – the Australian action placed the Timorese at risk and made them vulnerable. Though there may have been reasons to protect the Australian mainland from aerial or infantry attacks, the Australian decision to go into Timor set in train massive loss of life in which an expendable entity – Timor – was sacrificed for the good of the stronger, Australia. Certain features of Girard's designation of the scapegoat are apparent in Portuguese Timor's predicament. It was not the focus of blame for any part of the escalating conflict in the region, but it occupied a geographical position which became the focus of warring rivals. Its structural insignificance made it marginal and therefore superfluous, to the extent that the death and damage inflicted on it continues to receive little, if any, official Australian consideration. The victimization of Portuguese Timor thus took the form of collateral damage in the interests of Japanese expansionism and in notions of Australian protection.

Protection of Australia

The Australian incursion into Portuguese Timor in December 1941 was seen as necessary to protect Australia. In reality, it became the catalyst for the Japanese invasion of the half-island. Some background to the decision is necessary. Australian dependence on Britain for military decisions dictated actions regarding Portuguese Timor, as the cables to and from Lord Cranborne (the UK secretary of state for dominion affairs) and John Curtin (the Australian prime minister) show. These cables detail the official stated strategy of the Australian incursion: to assist the Portuguese in the defence of their territory, and by safeguarding the colony in the event of a Japanese attack, protecting it against Japanese aggression.[52]

However, the cables also reveal that the real consideration was the protection of Australia. Wray comments on the extreme anxiety of the Australian War Cabinet at the swift advance of the Japanese and the undefended airfield and flying-boat base in Dili.⁵³ Curtin wrote to Cranbourne that the defence of Timor as a whole was closely bound up with the defence of both Darwin and the Netherlands East Indies.⁵⁴ He stated that any occupation of Timor by Japan would seriously prejudice the defence of Darwin.⁵⁵ Portuguese Timor was seen to be 'the entrance door to Australia'.⁵⁶ Cranbourne had earlier stated that the object of sending Australian and Dutch troops was to safeguard vital interests by denying Portuguese Timor to the enemy.⁵⁷ As early as September 1941 the Australian War Cabinet had positively discussed the preventive occupation of Portuguese Timor by the Australian and Dutch forces.⁵⁸ Thus official communications of the time saw incursion into Portuguese Timor as crucial to the protection of Australia.⁵⁹ How the small Australian force of a few hundred men was meant to accomplish that feat was not made clear.⁶⁰

Australian breach of neutrality

Australian troops entered the territory administered by Portugal without invitation, thus breaching Portuguese neutrality. The incursion was met with vehement written and verbal opposition by Portugal and by the local authority, Senōr Manuel Ferreira de Carvalho, the governor of Portuguese Timor.⁶¹ He rejected the suggestion that Portuguese Timor required the protection which the allies said they were offering.⁶² Britain and Australia had just days earlier complied with the proposals of the governor general of the Netherlands East Indies that a combined force of Dutch and Australians was necessary to enter Portuguese Timor as Japanese aggression was imminent. This assessment was entirely false, as the Japanese decision to invade was weeks away. Honorary Consul David Ross, acting for Britain and Australia, was told to deliver a message to Governor de Carvalho on the day after the landing. The message expressed the Commonwealth of Australia's regret: 'We assure you Portuguese sovereignty will not be impaired and in fact it is to defend that sovereignty as well as to prevent Japanese aggression that our forces have co-operated with Netherlands Government in taking this action.'⁶³ It included the statement that 'in order defend against Japanese aggression it has been found necessary to prevent Japanese breach neutrality in Timor [sic]'.⁶⁴ Thus the Commonwealth of Australia claimed to uphold Portuguese neutrality by itself violating that status, blaming a possible future breach by Japan. The Australian logic thus follows the mimetic reciprocity identified by Girard: that people cling to the notion that the opponent is the attacker and that they are the victims – never the ones who initiate confrontation.⁶⁵

The Allied troops landed despite the governor's strongly worded protest: 'Under these circumstances, every disembarkation of forces will be considered as a breach of the neutrality of our territory.'[66] Further reports in the cables describe the reaction of the government in Portugal to the entry of allied forces as a violation.[67] It was denounced as most serious and violently unfavourable, thus presenting Australia and Britain with a major crisis in their relations with Portugal.[68] The governor remained steadfastly against the Australian arrival: his obstructive attitude even suggesting to the allies that he may possibly assist the Japanese.[69]

Japanese breach of neutrality

Neutral Portugal played an important political role in the international community during the war. Its capital Lisbon was a base for operatives on all sides to collect information.[70] The mimetic rivalry of the European powers is demonstrated in their fears concerning any threat to the advantages they gained from Portugal's neutral status. One of Portugal's concerns was their suspicion that the Dutch might have used any invasion of the eastern half of Timor as a means (through a separate peace with the Japanese) of later extending their reach across the whole of the island.[71] Britain, on the other hand, was fearful that the Portuguese, offended by any incursion into their territory, might allow the Germans into the Iberian Peninsula.[72] Similarly, but for different reasons, the Japanese administration opposed breaching Portugal's position in case of repercussions in Europe, choosing therefore not to target the Portuguese colonies of Macau and Timor.[73] Dunn concludes that the Germans also may have been wary that Japanese aggression towards Portuguese territories could induce Lisbon to allow the allies to use its facilities in the Azores. Such a move would have caused serious threat to the success of U-boat attacks on Allied ships.[74]

Reciprocal rivalry reigned. The allies worried that an Australian advance into Portuguese Timor may cause the Portuguese to retaliate by allowing the Germans to use their territory. The Japanese were concerned that any foray of theirs into Portuguese possessions may cause Portugal to favour the allies. However, at the time that the British and the Australians used a possible assault by Japan as a reason for their plans for invading Timor, there had been no indication that Japan would infringe the status of Portugal and its possessions. Concerning the Japanese quandary regarding violation of neutrality, Frei presents the 'agonizing debates' undertaken by the Japanese from the beginning of December 1941 which involved the army, the navy, legal experts, the foreign ministry, the prime minister and the emperor.[75] But finally the decision was made by the Japanese to enter Portuguese Timor, two months after the Australians. Since Australian and Dutch troops had already taken up positions in Portuguese Timor, Japan now felt free to attack.[76] Thus the Australian move into Portuguese Timor breached Portuguese neutrality but was claimed to be necessary to offset a Japanese incursion. Similarly, the subsequent violation by Japan was claimed to be in response to the Australian breach of neutrality.[77]

Regardless of Japanese anguish over whether to invade Portuguese Timor, the protection of their proposed Sphere of Co-Prosperity finally overrode their reluctance to risk repercussions in Europe. Their desire for expansion coupled with Australian fear produced an unforeseen and violent tragedy. Both nations demonstrated a fundamental mimetic concept, expressed by Girard as: 'the aggressor has always already been attacked'.[78] Each blamed the other for neglect of international law, each depicted the other as the aggressor and thus each appropriated the role of victim. In doing this, they each imitated their perception of the desire and threat of the other.

Control of Portuguese Timor appeared to the antagonists as a way of providing an advantage over the other, and therefore each desired to possess it. Possession was the underlying reason for the mutual invasions of Timor. The fighting that ensued was a by-product of the ultimate object of the attacks: possession.[79] Possession appeared as the salve for the concerns of each, the expansionism of Japan and the Australian anguish to protect itself. The mimetic rivalry in this situation exemplified the 'romantic lie', each party grasping for possession in the mutual imitation of desire.[80] Neither wished to shoulder the responsibility of breaching Portugal's neutrality (thus risking possible repercussions elsewhere), so each blamed the other for the situation. Each nation insisted on taking the moral high ground: Australia claiming national protection, and Japan claiming that breaking neutrality was forced onto it by the prior incursion by Australia. Each then blamed the other for the ensuing violence, while imitating the other.

It was a situation of intense competition, in which each power became an obstacle to the other, a stumbling block.[81] Australia and Japan showed that they were rivals in thoroughgoing imitation with each other in their invasions but at the same time competing with each other.[82] In their mimetic competition they were faced with Portuguese Timor, into which each felt they must intrude to gain their purposes. However, its nature as a colony of a neutral power meant that each needed to mount an illegal invasion in pursuit of their desires. Australia and Japan found Portuguese Timor an obstacle which ensnared them both.

The Timorese people, however, were not passive in this process and were the subjects of activity both as friends and rivals. Timor frustrated the desires of both Japan and Australia and became a mimetic obstacle to each, though in different ways. In Japan's regard, the East Timorese proved most unhelpful, their lack of cooperation requiring in the vicinity of a whole Japanese division to occupy the territory until the end of the war when those troops could well have been effectively used in Papua New Guinea. In regard to the Australians, most Timorese were true friends and allies, supporting, guiding and nursing them, and, in the end, losing tens of thousands of lives. The Australians withdrew in early 1943, but the devastating effects on the Timorese people continued until 1945, as the Japanese remained until the end of the war. However, subsequent events show the lasting influence of the Timor campaign in later Australian history. Australian forgetfulness of the friendship of the Timorese has remained an obstacle, a stumbling block of conscience against which the proclamation of Australian values constantly trips.

Scale of Timorese suffering

Australians in Timor

There was, of course, an actual 'victim' in all this turmoil. The element missing from the deliberations of Japanese and Australians as well as the Portuguese, the British, the Dutch and the Germans was the welfare of the local people in Portuguese Timor. There is no evidence of questions as to what 480,000 Timorese people may have thought or desired. There are no considerations expressed in the documents about their fears and anxieties and no reflection on the possible effects of armed foreigners coming into their ancient tribal society. The Japanese advance southwards ignored the welfare of all peoples it encountered, including the Timorese. Similarly, the Australian government's insecurity and fear in the face of an expected invasion by Japan rendered it insensible to the probable effects on Timorese society of its invasion of their territory. Had the allies not transformed Portuguese Timor into a war zone, the Timorese may have escaped the almost unbelievable outcome they endured.[83] In order to comprehend the enormity of the effects on the victim, the events of the following fourteen months when the Australians were present are summarized here.

The few hundred Australians who had moved into Portuguese Timor in December 1941 initially had no contact with the outside world. They lacked their own radio equipment until they constructed a wireless and made contact with Australia on 19 April 1942.[84] They were then supplied by air drops which augmented their living off the land and their dependence on the Timorese people. The commandos continued to conduct a rearguard action against the Japanese, employing with success the guerrilla tactics in which they had been trained. Apart from direct hit-and-run attacks, establishment of communication with Australia meant provision of valuable intelligence on ship and troop movements and identification of targets which were then attacked by the Royal Australian Air Force (RAAF).[85]

In May 1942 the Australians were ordered to keep harassing the Japanese forces since there was no possibility for them to be evacuated. In June, the Australian government argued for US involvement to assist with the guerrilla campaign in Timor, but it was rebuffed because of General MacArthur's conviction that the greatest danger would come from the Atlantic.[86] The Japanese increased their numbers substantially in August with specially trained troops, as a direct result of the Australians' success in killing or eluding them. The 2/2nd Company was reinforced by the 2/4th Independent Company in September 1942 although the number of Australian men in Portuguese Timor was never more than seven hundred at any one time. That month, the original Japanese garrison was withdrawn from Portuguese Timor and replaced by units of the 48th Division, one of the elite Japanese formations. Thus the few Australians were engaging, evading and frustrating thousands of Japanese along with their tank, engineer and artillery supports.[87] In November 1942, seven further battalions from the 48th division were inserted.[88] Cleary cites Japanese documents which put final Japanese troop numbers at almost twenty thousand, nearing the standard strength of a Japanese infantry division.[89]

Support by the Timorese

The Australian troops who conducted the Timor campaign credited the general support of the East Timorese people as the main reason for their success. That testimony illustrates the quality and depth of the relationship which the Australians and Timorese developed. Cleary alludes to the attitudes of the Australians which was essential to good relationships. Without the benefit of shared language or knowledge of their customs, a remarkable relationship was formed, a motley but highly successful band, unique in Australian history.[90]

Further, the Australians were friendly and, unlike the Portuguese, treated the people, particularly the women, with respect.[91] The 'criados' (in the twenty-first century more correctly referred to as 'veterans') were young Timorese men who, with the active cooperation of their families, provided the Australians with shelter, shared their food, nursed them during their bouts of malaria and tropical diseases, relayed information on Japanese troop movements, pointed out the best observation and ambush positions and protected and carried the commandos' equipment while they were engaging the Japanese.

Such assistance was essential to the success of the Australian mission in fighting the increasing numbers of Japanese and those West Timorese whom the Japanese brought in and used as militia. Up to forty men of the Independent Companies died in Portuguese Timor, but only ten of these in combat.[92] The deaths of Japanese are calculated as many hundreds.[93] The sustained and ferocious Japanese retaliation against the Timorese because of their support of the Australians caused a grievous toll. But shockingly, many Timorese deaths were also the result of Australian success, as bombing of Japanese positions wiped out villages and crops, causing death, injury and starvation.

Figure 2 Timorese youth and their families were crucial to the success of Australian soldiers during World War II, supplying food, carrying equipment, caring for the wounded and sick, giving directions and providing information about Japanese troops. Their loyalty cost them dearly when the Australians left in early 1943. Japanese reprisals, US and Australian bombing raids and famine left tens of thousands of Timorese dead. Photographer: Damien Parer © Australian War Memorial 013793.

After the war, the Australian men related the levels of loyalty they found among the Portuguese Timorese. For example, describing a youth who undertook to pretend to sell produce to a Japanese troop section as a way of spying on them for the Australians, Archie Campbell of the 2/2nd Independent Company wrote:

> It is almost incredible that he is willing to risk torture and death for the Australians who are indirectly responsible for all the misery the Japs have heaped upon the Timorese: the burning villages, the killings, the terrified women carried into slavery and defilement. Yet there he goes – no fanfare, no drama – just a casual wave and a smile, and he is gone.[94]

Lance Bomford of the 2/40th Battalion which joined up with 2/2nd in September 1942 wrote:

> Each of us had his native, called a criado. They carried our packs so we were free with our guns, and without them we just couldn't have fought like we did. The natives would spot when the Japs were making a move and relay the message to us so we could set up ambushes. Even at the end when it was tough we were dependent on them to keep one jump ahead of the Japs. It wasn't just the criados, there were lots who helped us. Early in December we got orders to move to the coast. It was a great feeling to be going home but it was a sad parting from the Timorese boys who'd done so much for us. Quite a few of us had tears in our eyes. I'd have loved to have taken my little fella back with me. He cried when the time came to leave. I gave him a note [praising him], what a good lad he was, gave him a few odds and ends. What happened to him Lord knows.[95]

Lt Col. Sir Bernard Callinan became the leader of the 2/2nd in May 1942. Interviewed by Michele Turner, he said:

> It was upsetting what the Japs did towards the end. They'd move into an area where the natives were loyal and say, 'Look, if you help Australians we'll come and burn your villages and destroy your crops.' And they did it. Then the Japs would go to another area and say, 'Over there they're helping Australians, wouldn't you like to go down and take all their pigs and goats?' – playing on greed and old antagonisms, not just releasing them from the restrictions of the Portuguese, but really encouraging them to do it.
>
> So after a while our natives thought, 'Well, we have to look after ourselves.' That's only realistic. But many would stand up to beatings by the Japanese, still saying they didn't know where we were or where we'd gone or anything, and they would get badly beaten. When the natives were getting more restless towards the end none of the *creados* [sic] was affected; they stuck right to us.[96]

Figure 3 L–R: Australian soldiers of the 2/2 Independent Company Sgt Ronald Sprigg, Lt Sydney Carton Speight, W/O John O'Brien, Sgt William Tomasetti, Signaller Donald Murray and an unidentified soldier with Timorese friends. Gordon Hart, also of the 2/2, often said, 'The only people I can't look in the eye are the Timorese.' © Australian War Memorial P11123.017.

Exhausted, the 2/2nd was evacuated to Australia in December 1942 with some Portuguese civilians, while the 2/4th was withdrawn in early 1943, which meant that their Timorese companions were left to return to their homes. They found that their support of the Australians was to be brutally repaid by the Japanese who remained in their thousands in Portuguese Timor until the end of the war.

Effects of the campaign on the Timorese people

Wartime society in Australia experienced fundamental disruptions caused by the military mobilization of many in the population, the rationing of food and clothes, the uncertainty of the world situation, the focus of the government on protecting security, the absence and deaths of loved ones and the fear which centred on the possibility of invasion from the north. Like so many societies through the ages, threat to life and well-being resulted in disruption of civil and family life and a sense of liminality not experienced in times of peace.

In contrast, even though calculations of the Timorese death toll are still being researched and remain contentious, the effects of World War II on the Timorese people is extraordinary in comparison to the Australian and worldwide death count. A comparison between the census of 1947 and that of 1930 suggests that the population of the territory had declined from 472,221 to 433,412. James Dunn calculates that the real number of wartime deaths must have been higher than the 40,000 indicated if even a minimum natural growth rate is considered.[97]

On this basis, it is concluded that between 40,000 and 60,000 Timorese died during the war, all civilians. That is, between 8 per cent and 14 per cent of Portuguese Timor's 1939 population died between 1941 and 1945, despite its status as the colony of a neutral power. This figure is startling when compared with the numbers of deaths in the populations of those nations officially at war. The enormous losses of Russia, Poland, Germany, Yugoslavia and Greece – all combatant nations – match those of Portuguese Timor in percentage terms. The number of British military and civilians who died is calculated at 0.8 per cent of the pre-war population, and that of United States deaths at 0.3 per cent of their population.[98] Australian deaths are calculated at 0.4 per cent of its 1939 population.[99]

The enormity of the effects of the war on East Timor is further seen when comparing its fortunes with those of Papua New Guinea (PNG). The support of the local New Guinean people for Australian soldiers is well known, and it is estimated that 15,000 civilians died during the conflict.[100] Australian responsibilities towards its Papua and New Guinea territories required the payment of compensation for the destruction which the local people endured. Therefore, between 1942 and 1948, the Australian government's War Damages Commission paid £6,710,799 (Australian pounds) to Papuan villagers to cover death, injury and destruction.[101] Conversely, minimal payment was made by the Australian government to local Timorese helpers, and that was by way of silver coins distributed during the time the Australians were there, and small amounts repaid for material assistance. There was no reparation for injuries, even when requested by Portuguese authorities after the war.[102] No other compensation has been paid to the Timorese people for their extraordinarily large World War II losses.

The mimetic aggression of Japan and Australia is clear when seen in the context of Girard's explanation of the measures which societies take to protect themselves. He states: 'Everywhere in the world, even today, any natural or man-made disaster intensifies the appetite for victims and causes accusation to proliferate.'[103] In World War II, the threatening disorder required the apportioning of blame which was accomplished relatively easily by identifying the aggressors – the Japanese. Thus Japan was the focus of Australian anger and fear. However, the proximity and vulnerability of Portuguese Timor involved that territory in matters of Australian security, drawing it in as a real but unwitting participant. Its use by Japan to attack Australia was seen as a possibility, and hence Timor's very existence rendered it a probable threat to the interests of Australia. Girard notes that present-day victims need not necessarily be seen as a culpable cause of social ills and disruption. The Timorese people were not blamed by the Australians for the crisis, but as their territory was seen as desirable to the enemy, they became embroiled in the aggression by potentially becoming a base of operations for the Japanese. In this way, it needed to be neutralized as a threat and so became a victim of Australia's security interests. Australia, seeing itself as victim of the Japanese, prepared to strike at the aggressor, and in the process sacrificed the Timorese to its perceived national security. The Timorese were not scapegoats in the sense of being seen as the cause of the crisis, but by virtue of their geography and vulnerability they became the real victims of the Japanese and Australians as the voiceless 'other' sacrificed by both for their own ends.

World War II texts of persecution

The effects of the Timor campaign do not end with the close of World War II or with the passing away of returned Australian soldiers and their Timorese friends. The scapegoating of East Timor has been enshrined in the written record of the campaign which further suppresses the interests of the Timorese and justifies Australian action.

As discussed earlier, Girard's mimetic theory sees ancient myths as disguised accounts of scapegoating incidents. Victims in the ancient world, sacrificed for defence or social harmony, were not honoured or even remembered. Myths buried their victimization, the stories weaving gilded fantasies of persecutors and the communities they protected, ignoring or justifying the violence. In a similar way, the victimization of Portuguese Timor by Australia in World War II has received textual treatment with myth-like resemblances and is rightly described as belonging to the 'texts of persecution' genre. This chapter now details significant examples of the textual evidence which has successfully minimized the importance of the Timor campaign.

Texts concerning the fear of invasion of Australia

First to be considered are texts generally available to the public in libraries and on the internet concerning the supposed Japanese intention to invade

Australia. The history of this episode has a direct bearing on the perception of Australia as victim and, as will be seen, on the presence of a type of unconsciousness among Australians as to the actual victims in the saga. Despite evidence to the contrary, belief in an impending Japanese invasion in World War II remains in some influential circles in Australia. Many available texts continue to suggest, and even at times specifically to declare, that Australia was in danger of invasion. The opinion of eminent historians that any Japanese naval suggestions of invasion were never countenanced as official strategy have often been ignored or challenged. For example, some of Paul Keating's speeches as prime minister used the phrase 'invasion of Australia' repeatedly.[104] A current website devoted to the theory of invasion by Japan attacks opinions which question Japanese invasion plans.[105] Recent novels make clear the fear of invasion in 1942 but do little to present information that it was a misplaced fear.[106] Admittedly, in a growing number of cases there is recognition that Japan was not intending to invade, for example, the website of the Department of Veterans Affairs correctly states that the Japanese had no such plans but that they intended to disrupt Australian-American supply lines in the south-west Pacific.[107]

Popular belief in an impending Japanese invasion was strengthened in 2008, however, when the 'Battle for Australia Day' became a commemoration to be celebrated on the first Wednesday of September annually. Astonishingly, it ranks third in importance after Anzac Day and Remembrance Day.[108] Thus the erroneous notion that Australia was the object of Japanese invasion plans has been recently officially cemented in the Australian psyche. The idea of Australia being 'victim' is unavoidably connected to this perception of events. It undoubtedly is linked to past fears, but also indicates continuing suspicions concerning possible invasion from the north. This notion is intrinsic to the precarious nature of a small population occupying a large continent. It is used as a justification for actions during World War II, but also for the subsequent Australian use of smaller territories, such as Nauru and PNG, to detain asylum seekers arriving by boat to serve its perceived security interests.[109]

There appears to be difficulty in some quarters in distinguishing between opinions understandably held in the past and historically accurate statements based on recent evidence. To be able to acknowledge that Australia was not going to be invaded does not diminish the people of the time who genuinely thought that invasion was imminent. The task of those with the present benefit of historical evidence is to concentrate on what in fact did happen. Australia was not invaded by the Japanese military, and as has been shown, there was not a credible plan to undertake such an invasion. It was Timor that became the victim – invaded and decimated – not Australia.

Texts concerning the Australian campaign in Timor

The Official Australian War History, documents in the National Archives and the War Memorial, as well as books, commentaries, articles, education curricula and websites comprise the record available to the Australian public concerning the events of World War II in which Australia and Portuguese Timor were linked.[110] However, most current Australian general history books have little on Timor and even less on the Timorese-Australian connection during World War II. Far too many ignore Australian errors and extol Australian virtues while being oblivious to the Timorese. Recent Australian histories which deal with World War II ignore the Timor campaign, mention it only minimally or are focused only on the Australians.[111] These omissions and emphases make the record incomplete and, all too often, misleading: true texts of persecution.

In light of the prevailing erroneous view that Australia was to be invaded by Japan, it is not surprising that the facts and significance of the Timor campaign itself are generally ignored. Internalization of fear in large sections of society alongside relatively simplistic notions of an ideal Australian 'character' mean that Timor's role in the war is minimized. Many Australians remain oblivious of this unique wartime narrative. Such unconsciousness relieves the population of acknowledging that notions of exceptional diggers, battlers and heroes would need to be applied as much to the Timorese as to Australians.

This suggests the unconsciousness or misperception required in the victimage mechanism. However, tempered and challenged somewhat by the testimony of some returned Australian soldiers and by a constant, if muted, *ostinato* narrative of the debt owed to the Timorese since the war, it is clear that the unconsciousness is not total. Nevertheless, the readily available popular record both reflects and feeds the general ignorance, thus distorting the facts, maintaining romantic illusions of autonomous Australian heroism and forgetting the Timorese. They are well described as 'texts of persecution' which justify military action that took no account of the Timorese people. They fail to make the connections required to influence Australian people's understanding of the place of Timor in the war. They become a means of continuing to victimize the Timorese.

In contrast, in those cases where the Timorese story is told with due recognition of the Timorese people, light is thrown on the victimization process, requiring a deeper Australian reflection on the experience. Some grassroots

Australian efforts have seen photograph exhibitions mounted and Australian sightseeing in Timor to promote the Timorese war involvement.[112] These accounts of the remarkable campaign combine to present the narrative of a feat which has few parallels in that the resourcefulness, courage and resilience of the Australians, with the sustained support of the local people, ensured that they were the only Allied fighting force which remained viable in Southeast Asia at that time. Informative as they are, these works are specialized and have not yet affected popular general knowledge about Timor's wartime role. The relative ignorance of this narrative suggests that the Australian population as a whole has not achieved an acceptance of the dependency that Girard argues is integral to conversion. It indicates that Australians generally, particularly in relation to our war history, have not yet realized that we are neither autonomous individuals nor an autonomous nation but relational beings dependent on others.

The general lack of written material about East Timor and the often skewed emphases in favour of Australia in material about the relationship in World War II are echoed in school curricula which have only very slight mention of East Timor in connection to World War II.[113] While teachers and schools with an interest in Timorese history are known to use resources to help students understand some of the current and historical realities affecting the two nations, the scant treatment of the regional neighbour Timor is extraordinary, given the loss of Timorese life as a result of Australian presence on their land. The absence of this topic from the curriculum echoes the exclusion of any realistic treatment of Indigenous peoples in Australian schools until recently. Along with the paucity of material available to the general public on Timor in World War II, such dearth of information to the next generation can be said to constitute a 'text of persecution' in its own right.

There is one printed document from World War II, however, which has come to symbolize the complex and ambiguous nature of the relationship between Australia and East Timor and its textual record. As was the practice worldwide at the time, the Australian government produced and distributed a large number of propaganda leaflets designed to lower enemy morale or to encourage civilian populations in theatres of war. One such leaflet was dropped over Timor, which declared '*Your friends do not forget you*'.[114] The leaflet invites the trust of the Timorese people, promising that Australians would remember their assistance, the small print going so far as to state that Australians would return to oust the Japanese. Unfortunately, the participle of the Portuguese verb in the heading ('do not forget') was misspelled as 'nõa' instead of não and rendered the sentence meaningless at best, thereby negating its original intention.[115] On another level the badly presented document symbolizes the Australian hubris and forgetfulness that has characterized the subsequent history and represents much of the current written record of the wartime relationship: inaccurate, self-serving and oblivious of the meaning of the war experience for the Timorese people.

The leaflet remains a challenge to Australians and expresses underlying unease in many of them concerning subsequent treatment of East Timor. The nagging sense of betrayal and victimization both in World War II and during the Indonesian occupation is evoked by the leaflet's wording, with all its mistakes. The mention of 'friends' places the relationship above simple regional connections. Denis Kevans's poem 'Never Forget You' picks up something of the betrayal, not only of Timor by Australia but (with some poetic license) of government betrayal of something dear to the ordinary Australian:

> For a promise made by the soldiers
>
> that their leaders never kept.[116]

The promise has not been kept by the Australian nation as a whole, and yet the keeping of it is daunting. How does one nation remember another when it was that other which lost tens of thousands of people as a result of its friendship? How can any such remembering take place in the face of further betrayal, as in Australia's role during the Indonesian occupation from 1975? How, indeed, could such a war memory be honoured alongside the Australian espionage committed against the post-independence Timorese government for Australian financial benefit?[117] The Australian involvement in Timor's World War II history affects the relationship significantly. When it has been remembered at key moments it has provoked consciences.

Standing as witnesses to the diplomatic anxieties, claims and counterclaims, breaches of neutrality, accusations, justifications, invasions, reinforcements and bombing were 480,000 Timorese people. The omission of their suffering from the bulk of the Australian written record in preference to the relentless promotion of a threat to Australia and the courage of Australians contrasts with the poignancy of the official history's recording of the reception which the Australian soldiers received on the afternoon of the day they arrived in Timor, 17 December 1941. It relates that the men 'were agreeably surprised to find the inhabitants apparently friendly towards them'.[118] One can imagine the brash, open-faced Australians somewhat buoyed by the attitude of the locals. One can also imagine the curious relief of the Timorese at meeting people who appeared to lack the superior disdain of many Portuguese. The friendliness of the Timorese was not solely a

Figure 4 John 'Paddy' Kenneally of the 2/2nd Independent Company, and Timorese friend Rufino Alves Correia in 2001. Rufino had been the loyal guide and supporter of Lt Tom Nisbet. Paddy visited Timor often and argued for the the Timorese cause on many fronts in Australia. 'All we brought to the Timorese was misery', he used to say. Photographer: © Jon Lewis.

result of their character but a response to the easygoing camaraderie with which the Australians treated them. The mimetic relationality was initially positive, which could be remembered to challenge later negative actions. That friendliness was to be tested by the later dire choices which awaited them.

Given that so much material continues to downplay or to challenge the evidence that Australia itself was not to be invaded, is it sadly unsurprising that so much material similarly continues to ignore the invasions endured by the Timorese. The absence of adequate reference to the Timor campaign in history books belittles the relationship, and in so doing, is testimony to the victimization of the Timorese people for Australian protection.

Conclusion

In the 'all against all' turmoil of World War II, where nations fought for supremacy, possession and self-protection, the defenceless entity of Portuguese Timor was sacrificed as a victim of Australian fear. The welfare of the Timorese people was ignored in the Australian effort to prevent conflict – whether real or imagined – from reaching Australian shores. The paradoxes are vast. Australia, the larger, richer nation which feared invasion, remained secure, while Portuguese Timor, the smaller, weaker territory, became the victim, suffering an invasion and a four-year occupation by the Japanese.

The popularly available records are well described as 'texts of persecution'. It maintains the distortions which accompany a narrative told from the perspective of a victor or a persecutor: in this case, a foreign power mounting an invasion in order to protect itself. The reiteration of the fears of the past concerning an 'invasion of Australia' ignores current historical research. Accompanied by little acknowledgement of the actual locus of invasion, Portuguese Timor, it indicates a displacement of the status of 'victim' onto Australians instead of those who endured the invasions, the Timorese people.

While documents written at the time of the invasions would naturally reflect the political and military constraints on the dissemination of factual material of those times, the passage of decades now demands more clarity and a wider perspective. Currently available material stocked by libraries, accessible on the internet and mandated for use in schools, however, continues to present a narrative almost entirely from the Australian viewpoint. Traditional images abound of courageous Australians victorious in the face of defeat: the victim under threat and the hero battling to the end. This Australian self-focus distorts the facts, belittling the enormity of the suffering of the Timorese people and ignoring their courage and service in Australia's regard. It cries out for 'conversion'.

4

The Indonesian invasion of East Timor

In the previous chapter, the extremity of Timorese suffering in World War II was described using mimetic theory as a particular type of scapegoating. The official Australian documentary record was shown as a collection of 'texts of persecution', that is, modern-day myths which recount the episode entirely from the point of view of successive Australian governments, as the dominant and victorious players, exonerating their actions and excluding appropriate recognition of the Timorese people and their suffering. Mimetic theory can be profitably applied when considering the invasion of East Timor by Indonesia in 1975 and the involvement of Australia. In this infamous event, Australian governments participated in the scapegoating of East Timor consistent with the actions and attitudes present in World War II. The outworking of the World War II attitude shown by Australia – of willingness to sacrifice East Timor for its own security – was reinforced and put on public display before, during and after the Indonesian invasion. In this scenario, communists were perceived as the external threat that needed to be opposed. The great powers of the region – Indonesia, Australia and the United States – agreed that Timor had to be sacrificed in order to prevent this enemy from threatening any of these allies.

This chapter considers the record of the Australian involvement in the Indonesian invasion that is contained in the Australian government's publication *Australia and the Indonesian Incorporation of Portuguese Timor 1974–1976*.[1] The documents therein almost completely exemplify Girard's 'romantic lie', by which he described the writings of those novelists who were oblivious to the force of mimetic dependency. The Australian documents similarly portray the imagined autonomy of policy and action, which is consistent with Girard's notion of the false sense of autonomy in that lie. In this case, the 'romantic lie' of an official document reveals Australian inability to recognize its mimetic dependence on Indonesia (and other world powers) and the resultant sacrifice of East Timor to ensure security with Indonesia.

Australia and Indonesia mimetically depended on each other to achieve security. A singular threat perceived by both nations was increasing communism in Asia. The actions of Indonesia in quelling its internal communists brought it a favoured position in the eyes of the United States, with consequent economic and military support.[2] Perceptions of East Timor as courting communism made its position in relation to Australia and Indonesia precarious.[3] Indonesian tactics capitalized on political divisions in Portugal, broadcasting suggestions of Timorese communism in a process of subversion.[4] Australian compliance with Indonesia was to thwart communism through the incorporation of Portuguese Timor into Indonesia, that is, through the sharing of a common scapegoat. The threat of social destabilization, seen by Indonesia and Australia to be promised by communism, was met by their combined channelling of national fear onto a common enemy.[5] In this way a type of unanimity between the two nations was produced, within which the violence inflicted on the perceived enemy, Portuguese Timor, was justified. Furthermore, Australia also sought to maintain and develop mutual regional protection, trade and financial gain from the resources of the Timor Sea resulting from Indonesian control of the whole archipelago. Australia thus became willingly compliant with Indonesia as the Timorese people became the sacrifice required to repudiate communism and achieve the benefits of Indonesian expansion.

The entanglement of Australia at this time flowed from a type of unconsciousness concerning Australian dependence on Indonesian desires, which presented itself as a set of politically astute decisions, but which sacrificed the weaker neighbour, Portuguese Timor. A particularly vivid example of the depths to which Australian governments descended in pursuit of Indonesian favour is discussed, that is, the matter of the deaths of the journalists the 'Balibó Five' and Roger East.[6] The invasion demonstrates how Indonesian desires became the model for Australian desires, engendering mimetic dependence, the record of which in official Australian documents remains a 'romantic lie' that shrouds this reality.

The invasion

The mimetic dependency of Australia on Indonesia is apparent in the circumstances surrounding the invasion in 1975. The Indonesian annexation of Portuguese Timor was a result of its long-held expansionist desires, evident in its acquisition of West New Guinea in 1962 and its opposition to the creation of

Malaysia up to 1966.[7] Australia was increasingly aware of Indonesian hankerings, and therefore the 1963 US advice to Canberra of the Indonesian desire to subsume the region was not news.[8] This ambition was seen as caused by dissatisfaction with the amount of territory that Indonesia had gained at independence.[9] It also suggests the Indonesian claim that Timor required rescue from the European colonizer Portugal.[10] The withdrawal of Portugal and the threat of communism provided a proximate context for the realization of those desires. The importance of Indonesia to Australia's political and economic prospects was demonstrated when, faced with Indonesia's intention to incorporate East Timor upon the withdrawal of the Portuguese, Australia was careful not to oppose it. The desire of the 'model' to possess led to Australian mimetic dependency.

The establishment of the Democratic Republic of Indonesia in 1948 had drawn together peoples from a range of neighbouring disparate cultures under one political umbrella, all of whom had experienced Dutch colonization. The historical anomaly of the Portuguese colonization of the eastern half of the island of Timor, however, prevented complete Indonesian control of the archipelago. In 1974 the Armed Forces Movement in Portugal overthrew the Salazar-Caetano regime, and Portugal began the process of decolonization of its overseas possessions – including the underdeveloped East Timor which it had administered for nearly five hundred years. A number of political parties emerged in East Timor. The UDT (*União Democrática Timorense* or Timorese Democratic Union) proposed that Portugal remain in control during preparation for independence, while FRETILIN (*Frente Revolucionária de Timor-Leste Independente* or Revolutionary Front for an Independent East Timor) advocated immediate independence as a republic.[11]

Worldwide movements against colonialism after World War II resulted in the establishment of many new independent nations in a short period of time. Portuguese Timor was not among them. In the face of the threat of the growth of communism in Southeast Asia, accusations were directed at the unfolding political consciousness in Timor, particularly against FRETILIN, although actual communist influence in Portuguese Timor was negligible.[12] Superficial verdicts based on some Timorese use of leftist terminology ignored that fact that FRETILIN's main thrust was towards nationalism, including its swift introduction of literacy programmes and other social benefits.[13] Further weakening the bid for freedom, unfavourable judgements concerning the ability of the Timorese to govern themselves were voiced by both Indonesia and Australia.[14] Division of opinion was apparent in Australia between government geopolitical interests and a certain level of popular concern for the welfare of the Timorese people, resulting in the Australian government vacillating between upholding Timorese political rights and siding with Indonesia. Significantly, Australian authorities expressed the view that it would be easier to negotiate the resources of the Timor Sea with Indonesia, rather than with Portugal or an independent East Timor.[15] Here, the Australian desire for possessions, in the form of the resources of the Timor Sea, mirrored Indonesia's desire for the benefits of territorial expansion. The mutual mimetic dependency of Indonesia and Australia ensured the victimization of Portuguese Timor. Consequently, Australian prime minister Whitlam signalled to Indonesia that integration of East Timor into Indonesia was inevitable.

Covert Indonesian operations destabilized East Timor using accusations of communism as an excuse for infiltration and border attacks as Indonesia prepared to annex the territory by force.[16] The two main Timorese political parties united in a pro-independence coalition early in 1975; however, the alliance was fragile as internal differences as to how independence was to be achieved were not resolved. The union proved susceptible to Indonesian subversion based on accusations of FRETILIN's supposed communist leanings.[17] The parties split and a two-week war (August–September 1975) resulted in the deaths of at least 1,500 people. The victorious FRETILIN party declared East Timor an independent republic on 28 November 1975.

President Gerald Ford and Secretary of State Henry Kissinger were in Jakarta for meetings with President Suharto on 6 December 1975 and discussed the impending invasion which began the following day. Successive Australian governments validated the invasion over the ensuing years as they worked to strengthen Australia's relationship with Indonesia, and with Asia generally. The policy of supporting Indonesian government policy continued with increasing determination at diplomatic levels, and the provision of arms and training to the military further underscored Australia's position. Despite years of repeated calls by the United Nations for the withdrawal of Indonesian troops, the record shows that Australia repeatedly voted against such withdrawal.[18] Australian dependence on its model Indonesia was complete.

Certain Australian residents were also victims of the invasion, although subsequent Australian governments have neglected to find out the truth of the matter or to make any formal protest to Indonesia. On 16 October 1975 five Australia-based journalists in the East Timorese border town of Balibó were killed by Indonesian troops to prevent them from reporting on Indonesian military operations preparing for the invasion.[19] Roger East, another Australian journalist reporting on the situation, was murdered in the capital Dili on the day after the invasion, 8 December 1975. The deaths received wide coverage in Australia and were the subject of much public disquiet and conjecture. Denial and inaction characterized the official response to the killings during the Indonesian occupation and despite numerous inquiries over the subsequent thirty years.[20] In 2007 a New South Wales Coroner's Inquiry found that the five in Balibó were murdered by the Indonesian military.[21] The Australian Federal Police was given the task of pursuing those named as responsible but have since determined that there is not enough evidence to take the matter any further.[22] Consequently, dissatisfaction and suspicion remain.

Australian documents a 'romantic lie'

The Australian government's 2000 publication *Australia and the Indonesian Incorporation of Portuguese Timor 1974–1976* contains many of the relevant documents concerning the events at the time of the invasion and presents the government's rationale for its decisions and actions. As will be shown, with few exceptions the record neglects or obscures negative Australian actions towards East Timor regarding the invasion of East Timor and the prior deaths of the 'Balibó Five'. In so doing, it conceals Australian complicity in Timor's persecution and betrays the influence of mimesis in the relationship between Australia and Indonesia. It demonstrates Girard's designation of narratives that display ignorance of the influence of that rival.

This fraught period was one of enormous complexity for the Australian government because of foreign policy difficulties faced at that time, especially concerning the Vietnam War. Difficult choices had to be made between conflicting interests, and the Australian response to these world problems was compounded by the internal political upheaval of the removal of the Labor prime minister Gough Whitlam towards the end of 1975 and the installation of a caretaker coalition government, followed closely by a general election. Nevertheless, the written record of Australian involvement in the events concerning Portuguese Timor must be subject to scrutiny, as Australian decisions resulted in complicity with the forces which brought to the neighbouring Timorese people suffering and death on a horrific scale.

The importance of *Australia and the Indonesian Incorporation of Portuguese Timor 1974–1976* consists in its status as a collection of major government documents with a foreword by Alexander Downer, the foreign minister at the time. Its stated purpose is to provide readers with a clearer understanding of the development of Australian foreign policy during this critical period and to go some way towards answering the many questions of those who have been concerned with obtaining the truth about Australian official thinking and action in relation to the Indonesian incorporation of East Timor and the deaths of the Australia-based journalists there.[23] The book is composed of nearly five hundred government documents which were released in 2000, before the usual thirty years had expired for the publication of Commonwealth files. Its introduction is a concise summary of the events of 1974–76, but it also offers reasons for the selection of the cables and other primary source material within it and explains their early release. The book also contains a section titled *Australia, Indonesia and Portuguese Timor 1945–1974*, with unnumbered notes, reports and memoranda from those times, prefaced by an overview.

The reasons given for the early release of the documents are stated as the desire to counter possible leaks from the Department of Foreign Affairs which the introduction to the collection claims could have given an inaccurate picture of events.[24] The writers explain the criteria for their selection of documents as their 'significance to policy formation or key issues' and to demonstrate historical complexities.[25] In this regard, there is emphasis on the great volume of material, the layers of debate and the limitations of documents to convey clearly the intricate nature of the events. Mention is made of intelligence material not released, missing files and promises of the availability of further files through the National Australian Archives. The human emotions of government officials at the time are described, such as frustration and fatigue. There are mentions of accusations and demands by Indonesian officials, the pressures of changes in staff of embassies and outbursts of angry relatives of the Balibó Five.[26] The irony of including these items of information when dealing with a situation which cost tens of thousands of Timorese lives and unimaginable long-term suffering seems to be lost on the writers. Similarly, indications appear of the dilemma of attempting to balance human rights, such as self-determination, with the 'desire to maintain close relations with an Indonesia willing to subvert those principles in Portuguese Timor'.[27] There is no acknowledgement that some contradictions are simply irreconcilable.

Nevertheless, the abundance of careful and comprehensive explanations of the Australian position suggests that justification for decisions was seen to be required for reasons other than explaining the early release of the documents. Clearly, the book serves as an effort to vindicate the Australian government's position on the Indonesian invasion and the events concerning the Balibó Five. Indeed, the introduction states:

The purpose of this action is not to challenge strongly held views, nor to blunt criticism. Rather the hope is that publication of this volume, together with early public access to all the relevant material, will permit a more measured appreciation of the bases on which recommendations on policy and decisions were made, provide a fuller context for material which has hitherto been made public, and in general replace speculation with greater knowledge.[28]

Thus the publication seeks to explain the Australian position and policies surrounding the Indonesian invasion. It hopes that, as a result, readers would understand the complexities more completely. Interpreting this material from a Girardian perspective, however, provides a way of 'seeing through the violence' but not in a form intended by the publication itself. Instead, the documents can be understood as an expression of what Girard terms the 'romantic lie': material which presents the events in a way that reflects, but does not reveal, the presence of a mediator.[29] As discussed in the introduction, the 'romantic lie' describes texts oblivious of their own mimetic dependence and rivalry. Relationships, decisions and actions are presented as though from autonomous self-sufficiency. The writers of the Australian documents demonstrate their ignorance of the influence which the mediator, in this case Indonesia, wields. 'The mediator remains hidden precisely where his revelation is of the utmost significance, in the existence of the author himself.'[30] This record of decisions and policies is clearly a 'romantic lie'. This contention is now demonstrated with reference to this government text in an overview of significant events which involved Australia at the time of the invasion.

Australian knowledge of Indonesian desires

The Indonesian expansionist mentality and desire to control the whole archipelago was apparent for decades and was known by Australian governments. It took no great leap of imagination for Australia to reflect on the attractiveness of Portuguese Timor to Indonesia in the light of that nation's acquisition of West New Guinea in 1962, its hostility towards Singapore and its opposition to the creation of Malaysia between 1962 and 1966.[31] Consequent Australian dilemmas regarding Portuguese Timor were summarized in the introduction to *Australia and the Indonesian Incorporation of Portuguese Timor 1974–1976*:

> From 1962 to 1965 the Australian Government faced the difficulty of resisting Indonesian aggression against Portuguese Timor without being seen to support Portuguese colonialism, or alternatively, trying to encourage an end

to Portuguese rule in Timor without encouraging any precipitate action by Indonesia.[32]

In 1962 an internal submission entitled *Australian Attitude in Event of Indonesian Aggression* determined that Australia could not help Portugal should a situation of Indonesian incursion arise and proposed United Nations intervention.[33] In 1963 the United States advised Canberra that Indonesian activities were already in train.[34] It was clear that there was no doubt that President Sukarno wanted control of Portuguese Timor.[35] Canberra stated that there was 'no practicable alternative to Indonesian sovereignty' but that the use of arms would be unacceptable.[36] Thus in the early 1960s there was a high level of Australian realization of Indonesian aspirations.

Diplomatic interactions at the time were testimony to the intricacies of rivalry and deceit. In March 1963 the Portuguese prime minister António Salazar wrote to Prime Minister Robert Menzies that the Indonesian government had on more than one occasion indicated that they had no desire or interest in possessing Portuguese Timor.[37] Menzies answered in October 1963 that such a denial of claims on the territory should no doubt be seen alongside Indonesia's declaration of support for all anti-colonial movements, including any which may occur in Timor.[38] He commented that he had 'no illusions about Indonesian tactics'.[39] Suspicions concerning Indonesian intentions were not allayed by Indonesian assurances, but Australian officials observed that involvement of the United Nations would make it more difficult for Indonesia to take 'unilateral, violent action'.[40]

Adding to the intrigue, in 1963 there was observation of 'a continuing expansionist sentiment among Indonesian leaders' and the opinion was reported that Timor's eventual 'recovery' by Indonesia was a common belief among Indonesian leaders.[41] Such attitudes suggested Indonesian disappointment with the amount of territory apportioned to it upon independence and were related to its claim that neighbouring regions contained oppressed and enslaved peoples awaiting the freedom which Indonesian support could bring.

In November 1964 Canberra advised Washington of evidence that Indonesia may have been on the verge of taking some form of action against Portuguese Timor, using only the covert means which had already been planned. The document surmises that Indonesia may attack 'in response to a trumped-up plea for help'.[42] Adding to the intricacy, the introduction to *Australia and the Indonesian Incorporation of Portuguese Timor 1974–1976* comments that by the early 1970s Indonesia was no longer seen as a threat, and yet it alludes to Indonesia's willingness to 'subvert' the principles of self-determination in Portuguese Timor.[43]

Indonesia and Australia also adopted ambiguous positions on East Timor during the time when Suharto was president from 1967 to 1998. In May 1974 Australian ambassador Richard Woolcott stated that the Indonesians wished to avoid any appearance of having designs on Portuguese Timor which they feared could make neighbours suspect any political action as a desire to expand their territory.[44] But just one month later, the appraisal of the Australian Embassy in Jakarta was 'that Indonesian thinking on the possibility of taking over Portuguese Timor is well advanced, to the point of ascertaining likely local Indonesian reactions in the immediate area'.[45] Four weeks after that, it was known that a recommendation was to be made to President Suharto to 'mount a clandestine operation in Portuguese Timor to ensure that the territory would opt for incorporation into Indonesia'.[46] Australian officials were concerned that President Suharto might circuitously indicate to Prime Minister Whitlam that Indonesia was thinking of 'guiding developments in Portuguese Timor through covert activities',[47] thus making Australia complicit. Officials also knew that Indonesian thinking entailed the belief that it would 'not be difficult to influence the result of a plebiscite in Portuguese Timor'.[48]

Thus the Indonesian desire to incorporate Portuguese Timor strengthened in resolve over two decades, despite its many disclaimers. The purge of communists from Indonesia in 1965 and the heightened fear of communism in Indonesia and Australia fuelled this desire further and was used to give it justification. From the early years of the Indonesian Republic, therefore, Australia faced the dilemmas associated with opposition to a takeover by force yet maintained the desire to comply with what appeared the only way forward, given a realpolitik reading of Indonesian intentions. Australian authorities showed awareness of this situation but demonstrated the approach that was to characterize Australian responses in the decades to come. That approach was a reluctance to challenge Indonesian expansionism despite suspicions, even clear knowledge, of the planned manner of attaining it.

The Australian connections with the Indonesian invasion had thus been remotely established through prior realization of Indonesian desires since the 1960s. Occasional diplomatic reports and conjecture had not elicited from Australia any clear denunciation or warning about any consequences of Indonesian movement against the rights of the colonizing power Portugal. There was no statement concerning the possible effects of change, violent or otherwise, on the Timorese people, except for occasional references (in the context of global decolonization) to self-determination. Australian knowledge of Indonesian desires was evolving into support for the seizure of Portuguese Timor, an expression of the mimetic dependence on Indonesia which was to characterize future decades.

Indonesian covert operations before the invasion

Lack of any Australian challenge to the increasing clarity of Indonesian intentions indicated the existence of Australian compliance with Indonesia which deepened in succeeding decades. Such willingness to agree in action with Indonesian desires – despite statements of opposition to the use of force –compromised Australia markedly as Indonesian authorities strengthened plans to incorporate Portuguese Timor. In the 1970s the Indonesian government furthered the cause of its desired integration of the territory through a two-edged programme of political and military intrigue. This strategy progressively embroiled Australia.

Indonesian diplomatic overtures to Australia and Portugal in late 1974 and early 1975 accompanied a simultaneous but covert programme of destabilization of Portuguese Timor, taking advantage of internal Portuguese upheaval and its rapid withdrawal from its colonies. Having done little to prepare the Timorese people for these swift and extensive political challenges, Portugal was unable to address the unrest as the Timorese began to deal with the problems and possibilities which faced them. The duplicity of the Indonesian leaders was formidable. While calling publicly for Portugal to restore order in East Timor, they were privately pressuring Lisbon to accept their intervention, all the while quietly encouraging the disorder, infiltrating the territory and undermining Portuguese attempts at negotiation.[49]

After meetings between Portugal's president Costa Gomes and an Indonesian delegation in Lisbon on 14 and 15 October 1975, the Indonesian government reported that they had reached a consensus with the Portuguese on integration as the best outcome, while referring to the East Timorese people's right to a voice on their future.[50] At the very same time the Indonesian government's process of destabilization to influence Timor's new politicians to support incorporation was underway.[51] When it was apparent in early 1975 that Timorese resistance to that idea was too strong, plans for a military solution were set in train. The resulting campaign named Operasi Komodo included covert military preparations, complete with a rehearsal for an invasion on the beaches of Sumatra in February and the spreading of disinformation, particularly through Indonesian and foreign media.[52] An associated intelligence campaign, Operasi

Flamboyan, was devised and directed within the Department of Defense and Security from October to December 1975.[53] The Indonesian government lied about the presence of its troops on the border, claiming that any military in that area were Timorese fighting other Timorese. In truth, Indonesian troops were assembling in preparation for an invasion.[54] This Indonesian duplicity was echoed by Australia, as discussed in the following sections.

Australian involvement

Political compliance

The early release of the documents in *Australia and the Indonesian Incorporation of Portuguese Timor 1974-1976* has not quelled criticism but has demonstrated Australian policy in thrall to Indonesian desires. In addition, Prime Minister Gough Whitlam's influence on the invasion of Portuguese Timor displayed a style of leadership which demonstrated a lack of discernment and consultation and left a legacy which remains controversial. When elected in 1972 he took on the role of foreign minister as well as prime minister. Despite relinquishing the lesser portfolio in November 1973 he continued to control foreign policy closely and acted as foreign minister when his appointee Don Willesee was overseas.

An impossible Australian position regarding Portuguese Timor was formulated by Whitlam when he lay stress on a preference for integration, with 'obeisance' to self-determination.[55] This was later expressed as 'lip-service' by Richard Woolcott, the ambassador to Indonesia.[56] Foreign Affairs Minister Willesee, on the other hand, was more in favour of actual self-determination and worked to convince Indonesia that the outcome of such a process could be lived with and need not imply instability. Urging caution and the importance of giving time to resolve the difficulties, Willesee stated: 'Their (Portuguese Timor's) future should be decided by an act of self-determination recognized by the world.'[57] Nevertheless, Whitlam's approach prevailed so comprehensively over Willesee's that the Timor policy was not discussed formally, even in the Labor Cabinet.[58]

The extent of Australian involvement in the preparations for the invasion is clear in the record of two meetings between Prime Minister Whitlam and President Suharto in Indonesia, the first of which occurred on 6 September 1974.[59] The second took place in Australia on 4 April 1975.[60] During these meetings Suharto emphasized his concern for Indonesian and regional security and claimed that Indonesia, having 'no territorial ambitions', would not seek to colonize others and 'would never contemplate' such a thing as an invasion.[61] He told Prime Minister Whitlam that there were two alternatives: Portuguese Timor either became incorporated with another country or it became independent. The latter option was problematic in his view, as he felt the territory was not economically viable and would have to enlist external support. He voiced the fear that as the territory's only possible interest to others would be political, communist countries such as China or the Soviet Union might intervene. In that case, he said, Timor would become 'a thorn in the eye of Australia and a thorn in Indonesia's back'.[62] This attitude was the public rationale and private motivator for Indonesia to act, supported by Australia and the United States. Whitlam was of the opinion that Portuguese Timor should become part of Indonesia, while stating the view, as did President Suharto, that the incorporation should happen in accordance with the properly expressed wishes of the Timorese people.[63] Both leaders expressed support for the principles of decolonization. At the same time, both knew of the covert methods already underway to ensure that the actual Indonesian aspiration of annexation was realized.

Contradictory policies

Australian dependence on Indonesia is apparent in the 'romantic lie' of the documents which conceal the influence of the model, even while displaying it. This can be seen in the effect of such an effort in Australia policy: the production of an array of contradictions. It was believed that Australia's fundamental desire for security would be fulfilled by cooperation with the Indonesian quest to solve its problem with Timor. The question arises as to the effect this dependence on Indonesia had on Australian policies and operation. It is apparent from *Australia and the Indonesian Incorporation of Portuguese Timor 1974–1976*, as well as from subsequent historical commentaries, that the Australian policy of acquiescence to the Indonesian desire for control of the territory had two contradictory features. In the first place, Australia echoed Indonesia's proclamation of acceptance of the Timorese right to decide their future and publicly stated its belief in the right of all people to self-determination, in accordance with the international thrust towards decolonization and independence which became the norm after World War II. At the same time, however, the obvious desire of Indonesia to assimilate Portuguese Timor outweighed the importance of the principle of self-determination under Labor and Liberal governments alike. Prime Minister Whitlam's personal opinion was that East Timor should become part of Indonesia on the proviso that the people would choose that course of action in a process of self-determination. He told Suharto that he expected his view to prevail in government.[64]

Government cables indicate the Australian officials' belief that public interest was best served by the pragmatism of aligning policy with that of Indonesia.[65] The tempering of principles, it was stated, was required in some circumstances to serve long-term national interest, and that interest may require some short-lived frustration and disappointment.[66] Balancing these interests meant that the incorporation of Timor with Indonesia was found preferable to allowing the possibility of Timorese independence. This was based on a biased, pragmatic and ultimately incorrect judgement of Australia's long-term interests. It was the support of a larger power given to a colonizing power victimizing a smaller group. Australian dependence on Indonesia exemplifies the process of mimesis, that is, that desire is not autonomous but rather arises in relation to the other. In this case, the Australian support for Timor's integration increased as Indonesia asserted itself, mutually reinforcing each other's desire for 'security' despite the detrimental effects on Timor. The strategic reasons given to justify this support were a cover for this reciprocal relationship, which solidified both parties' overarching desires for security, territory and prosperity. Despite policies and statements upholding the principles of decolonization, both Australia and Indonesia imitated the exploitation which each one's colonizer had modelled to them. The domination, expansionism, rivalry and cultural ignorance obvious in the colonial practices of the British and Dutch, as well as the Portuguese, became apparent in the victimization of the Timorese people.

To maintain support for Indonesia, the Australian position was composed of two irreconcilable elements: that the Timorese people should be allowed to determine their future but that they should choose integration.[67] This contradictory reasoning appears in Woolcott's April cable to Foreign Minister Don Willesee:

> While we support the principle of self-determination and while we certainly could not condone the use of force, the prime minister still does not want to encourage the emergence of an independent East Timor and he believes that continuing public emphasis on self-determination, at this stage, is likely to strengthen pressures for independence.[68]

Testimony to the impossibility of meeting both requirements, neither Whitlam nor Suharto raised the problem of which objective would prevail in the likely event that the two opposite aims could not be reconciled, although both leaders voiced distrust of a process of self-determination.[69]

Such a weak policy burdened Australia with further dilemmas concerning the means which Indonesia was prepared to use to gain its desired outcome. In June 1975 Ambassador Woolcott voiced awareness of the extent of the force which Indonesia was considering when he alluded to 'the seeds of further trouble'.[70] Australian officials thence juggled an official policy of supporting self-determination while hoping for Timor's integration with Indonesia. This stance resulted in a position that when Indonesia invaded, the government would condemn the force used, but accept the outcome. The fence-sitting indicates Australian dependence on Indonesian desires and friendship. The maintenance of contradictions ensured that Australia remained in the orbit of Indonesian mimetic influence, and this in turn was preferable to assertion of Australian independence.

Placating Indonesia and the Australian public

As well as trying to balance contradictory policies, the Australian government also had to juggle Australian domestic expectations alongside Indonesia's preferences in the lead-up to the invasion. Whitlam hoped that proceedings towards Indonesia's desired option would take place without upsetting the Australian people.[71] Woolcott wrote to the head of the Department of Foreign Affairs Alan Renouf: 'It is worth recording – for limited distribution only – that the Prime Minister put his views on this subject frankly in the following way: "I want it incorporated but I do not want this done in a way which will create argument in Australia which would make people more critical of Indonesia." '[72]

Whitlam's nod to self-determination was an empty gesture and nothing more, yet such double talk was echoed when the coalition formed the government in December 1975. Foreign Minister Andrew Peacock expressed 'deep regret' at the Indonesian invasion, while in the same message acknowledging the 'gravity of the problems posed for the Indonesian government'.[73] Ultimately Canberra had to acknowledge that its policy of support for self-determination was incompatible with forced integration, so further manoeuvring was required. The introduction to *Australia and the Indonesian Incorporation of Portuguese Timor 1974–1976* summarizes the decisions officials took to play a double game.[74] They chose to pursue a course of outward non-involvement rather than openly favouring incorporation with Indonesia, while at the same time operating behind the scenes to moderate Indonesian fears of an independent East Timor. They also promised Timorese leaders that Australia would accept any result of a genuine act of self-determination.[75] Australian officials discussed alternatives with Indonesia.[76] They considered enticements for Portugal to remain.[77] They pondered the effects of any invasion on relations with Australia.[78] Yet none of these deliberations mitigated the implicit support given to Indonesia.

One of the most infamous statements associated with Australia's dilemmas regarding East Timor was written by Ambassador Woolcott. He pronounced the inevitability of a takeover by Indonesia:

> Basically, this situation is Portugal's – not Indonesia's – fault. Given this Hobson's choice, I believe Australia's interests are better served by association with Indonesia than by independence. I know that what I am writing is pragmatic rather than principled; but that is what national interest and foreign policy is all about, as even those countries with established ideological bases for their foreign policies have acknowledged. Let us not play the role of the naïve conscience of Asia, seeking to preserve our virtues by placing the fig leaf of self-determination – when we know it is unlikely to happen anyway – over the geopolitical realities of the situation. Inevitably Timor will be part of Indonesia.[79]

The statement is a supposedly hard-headed statement of foreign affairs policy but indicates the belief that the national interest is best served by values only when they are unchallenged or serve economic or political objectives. In other words, Woolcott advises subjecting cherished Australian independence to agreement with Indonesia for the sake of the 'national interest'. The same reference to pragmatism over principle was also used by Woolcott in a cablegram to Canberra one month beforehand, again preferring association with Indonesia rather than exercising independence, but in the context of the greater ease of negotiations over the Timor Sea border.[80] Australian independence was thus secondary to gaining the security believed to be afforded by such association and the benefits which would follow maritime border negotiations.

Despite its support for the Indonesian desire to subsume East Timor, the Australian government was subjected to indignities. It endured the ignominy of Indonesian accusations even while upholding the Indonesian position. Indonesian government officials summoned Foreign Minister Willesee on 7 September 1975 to protest alleged reports of Australian assistance to Portugal which they said, erroneously, was tantamount to recognizing FRETILIN as a de facto government, claiming that Australia was acting 'contrary to Indonesia's interests'.[81] Australia was accused of being the only country in the region that was unhelpful to Indonesia and the long-term good of the region and of being the victim of a duplicitous Portuguese plan.[82] Just days later, Australia was said to have refused to cooperate with Indonesia to restore law and order in

Timor.[83] Thereafter further complaints were issued by Indonesian officials to their Australian counterparts with anger and agitation. They referred to Australian street demonstrations as illustrations of Australian opposition. They accused Australians of fighting with FRETILIN. They denounced attitudes of the Australian media and the lack of concern for refugees in Indonesian Timor.[84] Hamstrung by Australia's underlying contradictory and duplicitous policy, its officials were reduced to discussing the political implications of food aid to Portuguese Timor.[85]

Such responses by Indonesia suggest a sense of paranoia in its desire to acquire the territory, and an irrational perception that Australia may pose an obstacle to its acquisition, in this way becoming a mimetic rival for the possession of the island. The Australian mimetic response was to agree, acquiesce and cooperate. The result was a policy direction distinguished by duplicity, compromise and complicity that caused disagreement in government and division in the population. It fundamentally indicated the domination of Indonesia as the model, the mediator, for the Australian desire for security. Ultimately, Australia's 1975 pragmatism and lack of principle brought serious challenges. Domestic disquiet continued at a consistent, if muted, level, and the relationship with Indonesia was challenged, for a time, when the Timorese eventually gained independence.

Complicity

Further complications ensued from the Australian entanglement in Indonesian desires. Australia was being drawn into complicity with Indonesia through Australian officials' knowledge of what was happening. Indonesian officials were informing Australians at the embassy in Jakarta by July 1974 that covert operations were underway in Portuguese Timor to manipulate Timorese opinion. Robert Furlonger, the then ambassador to Indonesia, wrote regarding the provision of such sensitive information: 'We are, in effect, being consulted.'[86] Ball and McDonald detail how Australia was repeatedly told of sensitive Indonesian actions by Indonesian officials as well as by persons in the Indonesian Centre for Strategic and International Studies (CSIS).[87] Furthermore, Australia was receiving information from the United States on the situation. Toohey and Wilkinson show that intelligence reports given to President Gerald Ford each day revealed 'that the US knew that Indonesia had been conducting a covert paramilitary campaign against East Timor for over a year before the full-scale invasion in late 1975'.[88] In September the United States knew that there was to be a three-pronged attack on the north coast involving two battalions attacking Dili and supported later by six thousand infantry who would drive in from West Timor.[89] On 14 October Indonesia planned to have the units move into Portuguese Timor in uniform but without insignia and using old Soviet weapons to evade recognition as Indonesian military.[90] Advice to President Ford clearly showed the Indonesian duplicity of denying intervention and placing responsibility on Portugal and the Timorese, while at the same time increasing covert operations in Timor.[91]

Australia was privy to much of this information as a result of intelligence-sharing arrangements with the United States.[92] Reinforcing advice from the US, Ambassador Woolcott relayed to Canberra his knowledge of the planning for the invasion, including numbers of troops, time and place of attacks and the fact that the Indonesians would be dressed as Timorese.[93] He dispensed with official reports of widespread FRETILIN control of Timor.[94] He wrote of Indonesia's determination to incorporate Portuguese Timor, regardless of any international criticism.[95] Official Australian imitation of Indonesian desires was clearly reflected in his reports: 'An example of the Indonesian Government's confidence that the Australian Government understands and is sympathetic with its objective of integration is the extent to which it keeps us informed of its secret plans.'[96]

Bill Morrison, the minister for defence in 1975, later said that having accepted so much information from Indonesia, Australia actually knew more about the situation than key Indonesian officials such as the foreign minister and the ambassador. Pretending not to know thus became a matter of protocol.[97] Australian mimetic dependence on Indonesia, corresponding complicity in its actions and the production of documents comprising a 'romantic lie' were comprehensive indeed.

Australian mimetic dependence

Imitation of Indonesian desires

Shared complicity in the invasion, even acknowledging the vastly different roles taken by Australia and Indonesia, indicates mutual dependence. Both nations reinforced each other's desires through imitation in the operation of mimetic attraction and dependency, Australia complying with Indonesia and Indonesia displaying the need for Australian acquiescence to its plans. Each nation also desired the economic benefits to be gained by an Indonesian takeover: Indonesia would control more of the archipelago, and Australia would enjoy easier negotiations regarding the resources of the Timor Sea.[98] The Indonesian desire to subsume Portuguese Timor became the desire of Australian governments as a means of maintaining a positive relationship with Indonesia and benefitting from consequent political and material security.

Crucial Australian decisions and actions during the invasion of Portuguese Timor betrayed not only the Australian imitation of Indonesian desires but also consequent imitation of Indonesian procedures. As has been outlined, Australian and Indonesian judgements on the future of Portuguese Timor were comparable, with both leaders voicing identical concerns. At the same time, each nation undertook positions which were internally contradictory. Indonesian diplomats pronounced on the necessity of international involvement, while covertly destabilizing the situation. Similarly, Australian officials declared support for Timorese self-determination but compromised that position with the precondition of integration. Thus, the 'rational' policy positions of each country were in effect merely a complex cover for underlying mimetic desires for security, territory and resources.

The Australian government's dilemma consisted of trying to mitigate public opposition while giving least offence to Indonesia. Choosing both positions resulted in ineffectual pronouncements about the violence of the Indonesian incorporation alongside declarations of understanding and support for Indonesian problems. In Girardian terms, these public Australian positions functioned unconsciously as 'myths'. They were used by the government to justify to the population the maintenance of support for the Indonesian desire to acquire Timor in the hope of possessing resulting security. At the same time they attempted to legitimize the means of that possession: the violent takeover of Portuguese Timor.

Moreover, the subversive Indonesian operations preceding the invasion were known to Australian officials via US intelligence and as a result of Indonesian disclosures to Australian Embassy staff in Jakarta. In spite of that, the Australian government allowed matters to take their course. One of the effects of this passivity in the face of Indonesian determination involved the deaths of the Balibó Five, a matter which has not yet attained resolution and which is detailed further in this chapter. The overarching Indonesian desire to incorporate Portuguese Timor, as well as the duplicitous methods used, was imitated by Australian docility and agreement, which assured the desired strategic, economic and political security. The act of violent acquisition of

Portuguese Timor produced a victim sacrificed to those ends: the Timorese people.

Mutual mimetic dependence

The similarity of desire between Australia and Indonesia resulted in a reciprocal relationship which blurred the distinctions between them. It appears to have been Woolcott's view that the overriding objective of Indonesian policy should be that of Australia, simply because it was Indonesia's.[99] Girard's insight applies: 'Internal mediation triumphs in a universe where the differences between men are gradually erased.'[100] Subsequent historical interpretations generally agree that Whitlam gave Suharto tacit encouragement to invade Portuguese Timor.[101] In this respect the Final Report of the Timor-Leste Commission for Reception, Truth and Reconciliation (CAVR) comments: 'For all his reservations, there is evidence that the views Whitlam expressed do seem to have strongly influenced the Indonesian decision that there was no alternative to incorporation.'[102] His reasons for supporting the integration of Portuguese Timor were the territory's supposed lack of political and economic viability and its vulnerability to the designs of more powerful states. In other words, his opinions were almost identical to that of Suharto, indicating the extent of official Australian agreement with Indonesian desires.

But despite evidence of Indonesian designs on Portuguese Timor over decades, Indonesian officials claimed that it was Australia which was the catalyst for their decision to invade. In October 1974 Frank Cooper, the Australian ambassador to Portugal, reported that Ali Moertopo, the head of the covert Special Operations project for Timor, had told him that a meeting between President Suharto and Prime Minister Whitlam in September had convinced Indonesia that integration of Portuguese Timor was the only solution:

> Ali said that until Mr. Whitlam's visit to Djakarta, they had been undecided about Timor. However the Prime Minister's support for the idea of incorporation into Indonesia had helped them to crystallize their own thinking and they were now firmly convinced of the wisdom of this course.[103]

These claims of 'crystallization' of the thinking of Indonesian officials after Whitlam's visit – and the suggestion that incorporation of Timor had only then occurred to them as wise – demonstrate the relationship of mimetic dependency between the two nations. The claim that Indonesian thinking had taken shape as a result of Australian support suggests Girard's observation that the model's determination to possess is strengthened by observing that the other shares the desire. Both nations desired a mutually beneficial relationship. While Indonesia certainly wanted to continue Australian investment, education services and trade, Australia's desire for a pleasant and profitable relationship with its nearest Asian neighbour – the most populous Muslim nation in the world, and one which at that time held the key to the lucrative Timor Sea – was at least as strong. The price both were willing to pay for remaining on good terms was the future of East Timor. So despite many months of preparation for armed invasion, Indonesia presents Australia as its model, the wise mentor, the avuncular sage, standing by with understanding of Indonesia's very difficult position.

Indonesia's concerns of negative reaction to an invasion may have been allayed but Australia was further subtly involved with the suggestion that the determination to incorporate Portuguese Timor was underpinned by Whitlam's attitudes and words. By claiming that the Australian prime minister's support for incorporation had helped the 'undecided' Indonesians to see the wisdom of such action, Indonesia reversed the roles of model and subject in mimetic dependence. It situated itself in the place of the desiring subject, with Australia as the mediator.

Thus the Australian mimetic dependence on Indonesian desires was complete enough to reflect itself back to the Indonesians, strengthening the mutual mimetic dependence. Girard refers to such reciprocity in stating that it is 'synonymous with the ability that humans have to increasingly imitate one another while at the same time completely misapprehending the fact that they are doing so'.[104] Both Australia and Indonesia became models for each other, their similar attitudes to the takeover of Portuguese Timor reflecting the shared desire for the mutually perceived good of shared political and economic interests. In the case of both nations the influence of the other resulted in similar effects on judgement, bearing out Girard's observation that once the mediator's influence is felt, the subject's judgement is paralyzed.[105] While Indonesia was the perpetrator of the physical invasion, Australia was deferential to its designs. Shared desires manufactured a shared judgement as to the future of the eastern half of Timor and its people.

The servility of the Australian support of Indonesian desires occurred in the events themselves but is mirrored in official accounts which the Australian government has made available for public consumption. As discussed, the official record in *Australia and the Indonesian Incorporation of Portuguese Timor 1974–1976* supplies evidence for these conclusions in the cables and other primary source material contained therein, exemplifying Girard's theory of the 'romantic lie'. Australian governments and their officials believed they were acting autonomously on behalf of the Australian people, taking independent decisions in the national interest, balancing the many and varied competing influences and thus ensuring Australian sovereignty and security. The communications express the policies of the Australian government as though they were the incisive and dispassionate product of policy realists.

Yet the text of the official record betrays a largely unwitting imitation of the model Indonesia. In realpolitik terms, while Australia was aware that it needed Indonesia and the United States for security in the face of the unfolding communist influence, in its historical record that dependency is veiled. Significant Australian historical documents demonstrate a similar Australian surrender of independent judgement in regard to historical decisions and actions. The policies and actions through which Portuguese Timor was sacrificed to regional concerns are recorded in a way which betrays the Australian inability to comprehend the scale of its dependence on the desires of Indonesia, and the terrible suffering in which it became complicit as a result. The Australian documentary record of its involvement in the Indonesian invasion is an example of the 'romantic lie' par excellence and testimony to the Australian mimetic dependence on its rival and model, Indonesia.

The die was cast. The invasion of Portuguese Timor began at dawn on 7 December 1975. Indonesian troops launched a massive attack on the capital Dili from sea and air, looting, raping and killing indiscriminately. Many civilians were killed, and many fled with FRETILIN forces into the mountains. Simultaneous attacks occurred in Baucau to the east and Liquiça to the west of Dili. Thus began the occupation of East Timor by Indonesia which lasted for twenty-four years. Apart from some subdued initial comments opposing the invasion which soon lapsed from official commentary, the Australian position on the Indonesian invasion grew steadily into one of support, as will be discussed in the next chapter.

Balibó

The official Australian documentary record concerning the deaths of the 'Balibó Five' is a disturbing example of the 'romantic lie'. The events again demonstrate the dependence of Australian governments on Indonesian good favour, and the record illustrates the lack of Australian perception of that dependence. The presence of Australia-based journalists in the border town of Balibó introduced the problem of the murders not only of Timorese but also of Australian residents and nationals. These deaths of Australia-based journalists exemplify how the Australian government sacrificed the lives of its own residents, alongside the many Timorese who died, for its coveted relationship with Indonesia and the benefits flowing therefrom. Discussion of the inquiries and the documentary record concerning the events at Balibó demonstrate the incapacity of Australia to acknowledge the force of its mimetic dependence on Indonesia.

Briefly, two of the journalists attempting to report on the Indonesian invasion of Portuguese Timor in 1975 were Australian citizens, Greg Shackleton and Tony Stewart. The other three were Australian residents, Gary Cunningham from New Zealand and Brian Peters and Malcolm Rennie from Britain. All were working for Australian media companies. The five were murdered and their bodies burned by the Indonesian military on 16 October 1975 in the Timorese border town of Balibó, to the west of Dili. A journalist operating independently, Roger East, was shot dead on the Dili wharf on 8 December, the day after the invasion. There was no Australian government challenge to Indonesia over the deaths of these men, its residents and citizens, murdered while carrying out the tasks of their employment. Moreover, the record indicates increasing rather than diminishing Australian compliance, as can be seen in the outcomes of the numerous investigations which occurred in subsequent decades. The responses of Australian governments and their agencies to the evidence complete the picture of abject subservience to Indonesian desires and the mob mentality of the invasion. The extent of that chosen subjection has resulted in a culpable variant of 'romantic lie', where Australian governments ignore and defy the outcomes of their own legal processes.

Girard's concept of the romantic lie presupposes some level of unconsciousness of mimetic dependency, as suggested in the discussion of the Australia-Indonesia relationship. The case of the Balibó Five, however, provides evidence for some awareness of this dependency in the strategic way that the Australian government sought to protect Indonesia and its official relationship with the Indonesian government. This awareness came about because complicity in the invasion required actions to obscure and minimize anything that could cause the invasion to be questioned. The Australian government thought it was pursuing a 'rational' policy, although in reality it was dependent on Indonesia for such policy. The way in which the Balibó Five deaths were handled signalled the tenor of Australian dealings with Indonesia in the subsequent twenty-four-year occupation, that is, neglect and obscuration of evidence to deflect attention away from a burgeoning moral insight: the innocence of the victims of Indonesian violence.

Inquiries into the deaths of the Balibó Five

Once the innocence of the scapegoated victim has been realized, it cannot be unseen. Understanding the immorality of victimization has led, over the centuries, to processes designed to dispassionately enquire into guilt and innocence, and thus the rule of law and judicial oversight are employed as humans make the arduous journey from the ancient mob response of scapegoating towards truth and justice. Such efforts played a role in attempts to determine accountability for these men's deaths. As will be shown, however, the strength of the 'romantic lie' is powerful against these notable advances.

The numbers of reports on the Balibó Five is substantial. In 1976 there was a report on the matter from the Australian embassy in Indonesia, followed two decades later in 1996 and 1999 by two reports by the National Crime Authority. The International Commission of Jurists held a colloquium on the matter in 1997, and there was an investigation by the United Nations in 2000. A classified report by the inspector general of intelligence and security was submitted to the Australian government in 2002.[106] In 2005 the CAVR Report stated that the five journalists were not killed in crossfire or as a result of an Indonesian misadventure in its attack on Balibó. It concluded that further investigation 'of the elusive truth of this matter' was required.[107]

Subsequently in 2007 the NSW coroner held an inquest into the death of Brian Peters that interviewed new witnesses, revealed previously unseen intelligence information, had the power to compel evidence and demonstrated a high level of judicial independence and impartiality.[108] The inquest found that Peters (and by association his four companions) was murdered by the advancing Indonesians to prevent the revelation that Indonesian Special Forces had attacked Balibó.[109] It concluded that the journalists were not accidentally killed, as had previously been stated in official explanations. The perpetrators of the murders were named as members of the Indonesian Special Forces, including Major General Benny Murdani, Colonel Dading Kalbuadi, Cristoforo da Silva and Yunus Yosfiah.[110] Murdani died in 2004 after a career as commander in Angkatan Bersenjata Republik Indonesia (ABRI) or Armed Forces of the Republic of Indonesia from 1983 to 1988 and in government.[111] Kalbuadi died in 1999, having been significant in the invasion and in his subsequent military career. Of the lower-level officers, Silva and Yosfiah returned to normal life, the latter having been promoted in the military and gaining high government positions in civil life.[112] After an eight-month inquiry by the NSW state coroner, the matter was formally referred to the Attorney General's Department, which charged the Australian Federal Police (AFP) to launch the investigation, commencing in August 2009.

For the next five years the AFP conducted the investigation. In the latter part of that time period discussions concerning jurisdiction and progress of the case, the status of witnesses and instances of Indonesian refusal to cooperate were undertaken in Australian Senate Committees.[113] Then suddenly, on 20 October 2014, the AFP, in a statement made in answer to a question asked by a reporter in the context of the thirty-ninth anniversary of the murders, announced that its investigation had ceased.[114] It claimed that 'all reasonable avenues' had been investigated and that as these were fruitless the investigation would be closed.[115] Thus the policing body of the Commonwealth of Australia decided to end the investigation despite the comprehensive and conclusive findings of the latest of the many investigations and the naming of persons of interest. While harm to the relationship between Australia and Indonesia may have been minimized as a result of this decision, the Indonesian nationals responsible for the murders of Australian civilians committed in the name of the Indonesian military outside a theatre of war have not been brought to justice.

Behind the decision of the AFP to cease investigation lies the same spectre of offending Indonesia which lay at the back of the Australian position regarding the invasion and occupation. Seen in the context of the extraordinary lengths to which Australian governments and their agencies have gone to ignore the findings of the coronial inquest, and in the clear lack of justice applied to the Balibó Five, their families and the Australian public, it is apparent that the subjection of Australia to the mimetic mediation of Indonesia remains formidably strong and deep. The Balibó Five saga shows that Australian actions, as well as the official documentation of those actions, reflect the presence of the mediator, Indonesia, and the complicity of Australia in support of Indonesia in violence. Successive Australian governments' failures to these residents, a situation which persists to the present day, indicate the depth of the Australian enthrallment by the model, Indonesia.

Claims to independence as well as concern for truth and justice regarding the deaths of its own citizens and residents were eroded for Australia in the face of the need to imitate its model and partner in security. An interpretation based on Girard's mimetic theory draws the veil away, showing the strength of the influence of mimesis. Australia is Indonesia's dependent partner, protecting that partner from accusations that could threaten its moral standing, even to the extent of declining to pursue justice for its own residents.

Challenges to the Australian 'romantic lie'

Munster and Walsh

Levels of unconsciousness and unanimity were detected by René Girard as features not only of the scapegoating mob responsible for victimization but also of the record of scapegoating events enshrined in myths. The erosion of the capacity of scapegoating to bring harmony in modern times is accompanied, however, by the current impossibility of an unconscious unanimity. There are enough people who can see through the lie. The efforts of writers, activists, journalists and others to present honest interpretations of facts have challenged official Australian attempts to conceal government dealings in the invasion of Portuguese Timor. One major episode of truth-telling occurred in late 1980. George Munster and Richard Walsh drew together selections of the written advice to governments given by senior Australian public servants in a variety of international situations, including that of Portuguese Timor. They attempted to publish them in a book called *Documents on Australian Defence and Foreign Policy 1968–1975*.[116] Within twenty-four hours of the publication of extracts in newspapers, the Commonwealth of Australia issued injunctions against the authors and distributors and succeeded in denying further publication via copyright law. Two years later Walsh and Munster published an abbreviated version as *Secrets of State* which contains the introduction to the banned book.[117] In it they describe examples of departmental advice given to government as 'widespread pretensions to official expertise' which resulted in their relief on occasions when such advice did not become policy. They stated that such fortuitous outcomes came about because the Australian government lacked both capacity and opportunity to influence events.[118] The truth of this judgement is borne out by the Australian unwillingness to confront Indonesia over its invasion of Timor. Australia did not intervene even when Indonesian plans were obvious, as has been discussed. Any potential and possibility for diplomatic challenge was overridden by its mimetic dependence on Indonesia which drove policy in regard to East Timor.

The government hoped that its 2000 publication of *Australia and the Indonesian Incorporation of East Timor* would allay the population's concerns at government decisions and actions regarding East Timor. Yet Walsh and Munster had demonstrated twenty years previously that that particular Australian policy was an episode of inefficient action flowing from incompetent analysis.[119] Referring to the invasion of East Timor they state that the Australian role was both ineffectual in opposing the invasion and complicit in encouraging it.[120] They mention a foreign affairs paper written in October 1975 which described the Timor problem as trivial compared with the importance of a good relationship with Indonesia.[121]

Munster and Walsh's books join those of other Australians critical of the Australian position on East Timor that show Australian government actions to have been unprincipled, self-serving and complicit. These publications demonstrate Australia's accommodation of Indonesian desires, decisions and actions in the scapegoating of an innocent victim, the Timorese people.

Moral insights in documents

Intriguingly, there are some slight allusions to a more moral and therefore realistic appreciation of the Australian dependence on Indonesia and to alternative policy approaches in the collection of documents of 2000 under discussion. These illustrate Girard's reference to 'chinks and cracks' in texts of historical persecution, through which the face of the victim was seen.[122] Among the most notable are comments by Frank Cooper, the Australian ambassador to Portugal at the time, who wondered whether government officials had all been so mindful of the overriding importance of the relationship with Indonesia that it had inhibited them too much in what they said to the Indonesians.[123] When considering the Australian government's move towards recognition of Indonesian sovereignty over Portuguese Timor two years later, he referred to his belief

> that our policies should not merely promote our national interests, but that they should also be based on certain moral principles such as respect for human rights and the settlement of disputes by negotiation rather than force. If the Government now decides to recognize what it has previously condemned the question many people will ask is not whether we can live with it but whether we can live with ourselves.[124]

Ambassador Cooper thus allowed the face of the scapegoated victim to peep from behind the mask with which Australian governments attempted to cover their complicity, inadequacy and dependence. Furthermore, a summary of the events in East Timor up to the UN ballot in 1999, in the Introduction to *Australia and the Indonesian Incorporation*, includes a distinctive paragraph which hints at some recognition of the enormity of the results of Australian dependence on Indonesian desires:

Almost twenty-five years after its integration with Indonesia, and after a formal vote to end that integration, East Timor remains a divisive and emotive issue in the history of Australian foreign policy. The complex and difficult policy issue has been overlain by individual tragedies: first the deaths of six Australia-based journalists in circumstances never fully nor satisfactorily explained; later the broader tragedy of a people suffering under a more repressive regime than the policy-makers of the 1970s could reasonably have envisaged; and, most recently, by acts of post-referendum brutality and destruction. The issue is further overlain, for many Australians, by guilt: a belief that a people close to Australia's doorstep have had their wartime kindnesses and suffering on Australia's behalf repaid by betrayal.[125]

The use of such words as brutality, emotive, destruction, divisive, deaths, repressive, tragedies, suffering, betrayal and guilt in this one short passage give it a flavour not found anywhere else in the materials in this book. It may be argued that the nature of government cables and policy statements are not the place for reference to human suffering. It is certainly the case that the vast majority of communications presented in these documents follow that lamentable line. But the fact that the introduction to *Australia and the Indonesian Incorporation* has referred to these human realities, even if in one paragraph only, expresses an unease with the general rationalizing tone of the remainder of the book. Moreover, it succinctly describes the failure of the Australian government and its policies regarding Timor: that Australian and Timorese lives were sacrificed to an immoral foreign policy that betrayed Australia's weaker neighbours and which did little to serve its integrity and good standing. The paragraph itself is a chink, a crack in the Australian mimetic mask.[126]

Conclusion

Australian government actions comprise one element of the events of the Indonesian invasion of Portuguese Timor, and the documents which recount the episodes are another. Both are subject to mimesis. Both demonstrate the Australian inability to see that its desire for security mirrored Indonesia's desire for security. The Australian desire for possession of a positive relationship with Indonesia echoed Indonesia's desire for expansion across the archipelago. The shared desire gave strength to opposition to the common enemy of communism. At the same time, however, the threat of communism was used by both powers as an excuse for the scapegoating of their inconvenient neighbours, the Timorese people, who could be blamed for providing the conditions for a potential incursion of communism in the region and therefore could be invaded and colonized under a cloak of justification.

The challenges to regional and global security, as well as domestic problems such as the dismissal of Whitlam as prime minister, markedly influenced Australian decisions affecting Portuguese Timor. Australian government actions leading up to the Indonesian invasion testify to contradictory policies, undue influence of Indonesian embassy officials, secrecy, passive compliance with aggressive Indonesian intentions and actions which imitated those of Indonesia. Fearful of upsetting the lucrative markets and cultural sensibilities of its neighbour, and of jeopardizing the hope of stability, security and future lucrative oil and gas projects, Australia squandered its own high standards. The obstacle to living up to those standards while pleasing Indonesia was the victim, Portuguese Timor. The half-island appeared as a political and geographical anomaly within the Indonesian archipelago and was perceived variously as a communist problem, an unstable threat and an economic opportunity.

The official written record shows Australia in thrall to Indonesia and ignorant of the force of mimesis operating in the relationship. It is a 'romantic lie'. The documents try to present Australian governments as autonomous entities, but they reveal Australia as dependent on Indonesia, lacking in the autonomy and fairness so prized as Australian characteristics. There is no appreciation of the effects on the Timorese people of that dependence. Indonesia's presence as mediator of the Australian desire for security and profit is therefore reflected in the documents but is not revealed.[127] The following chapter deals with the situation of mimetic dependence which continued for the next twenty-four years as Australian governments complied with Indonesian attempts to absorb the Timorese people, perpetuating the sacrifice of the Timorese people as victims.

5

The occupation of East Timor

Previous chapters have shown that East Timor fulfilled the conditions of scapegoating as described by René Girard, being considered expendable in relation to the conflict between Australians and Japanese during World War II and to the expansionism of Indonesia in the post-war years. In the latter case, prospects regarding the Timor Sea resources contributed markedly to the decisions taken by Australian governments.

In this chapter, the twenty-four-year Indonesian occupation of East Timor is discussed in the light of the policies embraced by successive Australian governments which continued to support the Indonesian government's desire to possess the territory. Throughout this time Australian actions demonstrated dependency on Indonesian desires regarding East Timor. These were expressed in a series of measures which included the continuation of contradictory policies. Hopes of consolidating regional supremacy and stability were coupled with the prospect of financial gain from the resources of the Timor Sea, and the pursuit of both advantages was argued to coincide with Australian 'national interest'. The Timorese people were therefore abandoned by official Australian policies in favour of what was perceived as the greater good in the achievement of a desire for security (initially against communists) and sacrificed to that end.

It will be demonstrated in this chapter that Australia's initial mimetic dependency on Indonesia at the invasion developed into an abiding complicity during the occupation. East Timor was the scapegoat of its neighbours not only at that time but also for nearly a quarter of a century after that. Significantly, it also continued to be the scapegoat of the texts presented as the official Australian history. The focus here is the official versions of events during the occupation, with an analysis of the most well-known massacre, that at the Santa Cruz cemetery in 1991. There follows a case study concerning Monsignor da Costa Lopes and ex-prime minister Whitlam. Drawing on Girard's criteria for the scapegoating process, this study is an example of attempts to address challenges to Australia's relationship with Indonesia by deflecting the focus onto a convenient and credible scapegoat.

The Indonesian occupation (1975–99)

The Indonesian occupation of East Timor lasted from the invasion on 7 December 1975 to the weeks following 30 August 1999, the date on which the Timorese people voted overwhelmingly for independence rather than for an offer of special regional autonomy within the Republic of Indonesia. Throughout this twenty-four-year period the territory was under Indonesian control, primarily through the presence of ABRI (*Angkatan Bersenjata Republik Indonesia* or the Armed Forces of the Republic of Indonesia) which consisted of the army, navy, air force and the police. In 1999 the police force was separated from the armed forces, leaving the military as the TNI (*Tentara Nasional Indonesia* or the Indonesian National Armed Forces) whose purpose was to achieve pacification and integration, the political objectives of the Indonesian state.[1] The methods used were designed to subjugate the population and overcome its resistance to Indonesian control, a regime of violence affecting every level of Timorese society. The armed wing of the resistance was known as Falintil (*Forças Armadas de Libertação de Timor-Leste* or the Armed Forces for the Liberation of East Timor).[2] It conducted a guerrilla campaign against the Indonesian military for the whole length of the occupation. There was a clandestine network throughout the countryside, towns and villages that covertly resisted the occupation, funnelled information to the international solidarity movement and supported the armed resistance.

Subjected to numerous forms of state-sanctioned violence, the majority of the Timorese people lived in fear. The presence of Timorese informers brought suspicion to relationships and interactions, sowing discord in communities large and small.[3] Further, ABRI paid and trained Timorese militias as an extension of its reach, terrorizing the population. Consistently supported by the Indonesian military, these groups exercised violence with impunity, thus depriving the people of the protection of law and the exercise of justice. The civil administration was also subordinate to the purposes of the Indonesian government via the military and the police, becoming another means of social control.[4]

Among the many studies of the recent history of East Timor, the official report of the Timor-Leste Commission for Reception, Truth and Reconciliation (CAVR) is the most comprehensive with regard to the occupation. It was commissioned by the United Nations Transitional Administration in East Timor (UNTAET) and presented its findings to the Timorese government and the United Nations in 2005. As part of its thorough investigation of all parties to the conflict in East Timor, it reports on the deaths and other violations committed by Timorese against Timorese from 1974 as well as on the Indonesian violence through to 1999.[5]

The CAVR Report advises that the number of conflict-related deaths from 1974 to 1999 was between 102,800 and 183,000, comprising an estimated 18,600 killings, most of which occurred between 1975 and 1980, with over 2,500 killings in 1999. The deaths of 84,200 people were due to hunger and illness caused directly by occupation-related events.[6] Using a variety of estimates, however, Sarah Staveteig proposes a higher death toll, citing a figure of 204,000 deaths due either to direct violence or to hardships, including large-scale displacements, forced upon the population by the Indonesian military.[7] It is unlikely that the actual death toll will ever be known. What is clear, however, is that an enormous proportion of the Timorese people died violently and from unnatural causes under the Indonesian regime. President Suharto held office for twenty-three of the twenty-four years of the occupation and thus held ultimate responsibility. Serious violations occurred during the first years after the invasion followed by a pattern of relatively low-level but consistent violence for the next two decades. The CAVR Report discusses the extrajudicial killings, intimidation, torture, arbitrary detention, sexual violence and political trials which were used to quell opposition, punish victims and terrorize the people.[8] Human rights abuses affected both individuals and groups. Massacres accounting for the deaths of hundreds of people each at Lacluta (1981), Kraras (1983) and at the Dili Santa Cruz cemetery (1991) have been documented, and in the case of the Dili massacre, filmed.[9] Indonesian military personnel, either acting alone or in collaboration with Timorese militias and auxiliaries, were found to have carried out the overwhelming number of killings, rapes and incidents of torture.[10]

The early years after the invasion saw tens of thousands of people fleeing to the mountains, but the military assaults against them as well as the impossibility of maintaining a food supply caused many deaths and eventually the surrender of large groups.[11] Massive dislocations organized by ABRI prevented access to farms and gardens and caused illness and starvation. Over half of the Timorese people experienced one or more displacements from their homes, lasting from short periods of one month to extended periods of time. The average displacement time endured by the Timorese people was approximately four years.[12]

The famines of 1978–9 caused the deaths of thousands of people and ensured that food production and distribution remained precarious throughout the 1980s.

Annual forced marches by the military known as the 'fence of legs' continued for at least four years, beginning in 1981.[13] This exercise was designed to flush out the resistance by forcing tens of thousands of Timorese males to march in lines ahead of soldiers. The Timorese returned to their villages debilitated after days and weeks in the human chains. Adequate crops were not planted during these times, resulting in widespread food shortages in the succeeding months.[14] Clandestine resistance against the occupation renewed and strengthened, however, despite the presence of Timorese informers and paramilitary groups.[15] The armed resistance engaged in combat with the Indonesian military and remained a viable guerrilla force for the whole of the occupation.

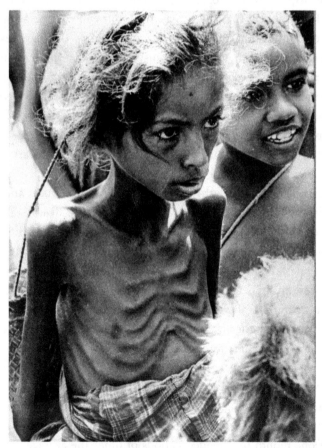

Figure 5 Starving Timorese children in Laga, East Timor, 1979. Subjugation of the people was attempted by forced displacement and the destruction of crops and livestock. Widespread famine caused suffering and death on a huge scale. © Peter Rodgers/*Sydney Morning Herald*.

Figure 6 Starving Timorese children in Laga, East Timor, 1979. © Peter Rodgers/*Sydney Morning Herald*.

Australian policy during the occupation

This chapter now turns to an examination of the Australian government's position with regard to the Indonesian occupation that amounted to the scapegoating of East Timor for decades. Australian government documents stated that the consistent official position was to uphold the Timorese right to self-determination.[16] This is countered by voluminous evidence to the contrary, as will be discussed. To begin with, the Australian voting pattern on the issue at the United Nations and continued military assistance to Indonesia demonstrated support for the Indonesian annexation that continued from 1975 to 1999. Gough Whitlam, the Labor prime minister in 1975, tacitly endorsed Indonesian claims to sovereignty. The Liberal-Country Coalition government under Malcolm Fraser (1975–82) publicly supported Indonesian claims.[17] When in opposition during those years the Labor Party condemned the annexation.[18] However, its government under Bob Hawke (1983–91) maintained the Australian government's support of Indonesia. The next Labor government under Paul Keating (1991–6) actively sought to strengthen the relationship with Indonesia and pursued closer ties with the Indonesian military. Keating extolled President Suharto's New Order government as beneficial.[19] He said that human rights should not get in the way of the relationship between Australia and Indonesia.[20] The succeeding coalition government led by John Howard (1996–2007) continued the policies of the previous decades. Howard described Suharto, the overseer of the Timorese oppression, as a national leader displaying skill and sensitivity.[21] His deputy Tim Fischer went so far as to describe Suharto as 'perhaps the world's greatest figure in the latter half of the 20th century'.[22]

A major political disruption of this consensus came when Laurie Brereton, the opposition spokesman on foreign affairs, succeeded in bringing a change to Labor Party policy regarding East Timor, which took effect at the party's national conference in 1998.[23] The resignation of President Suharto in May 1998 and the accession of his replacement B. J. Habibie accompanied growing agitation for change in East Timor itself. Increased international support for the Timorese people, particularly after the Santa Cruz massacre, included massive Australian resistance to government policy. However, it is clear that even after Suharto's resignation Australia's official position of favour towards the Indonesian annexation of East Timor was constant.

The coalition government only slowly began to read the writing on the wall. It moved towards accepting the increasing international consensus on the need for significant change, as shown in John Howard's letter to Suharto's successor, President Habibie, at the end of 1998. He suggested a development of the president's recent offer of autonomy which would include discussions with East Timorese leaders. Nevertheless, Howard emphasized in the letter that Australia's support for Indonesia's sovereignty over East Timor was unchanged.[24] He opined that an autonomy package spanning some years would allow time to convince the East Timorese of the benefits of such an arrangement within the Indonesian republic.[25] President Habibie reacted swiftly and unexpectedly to the letter and to the increasing international pressure by abruptly announcing an act of self-determination in East Timor. Finally, after the Timorese comprehensively rejected the option of autonomy within Indonesia in favour of independence in the United Nations referendum in August 1999, the Australian military undertook leadership of the UN peacekeeping force as the Indonesian military withdrew.

The relationship between the scapegoat and the text

As demonstrated in previous chapters, accounts of East Timor's recent history clearly depict it as the scapegoat of its neighbours. Girard's insights into scapegoating have a double application as victims inhabit the role of scapegoat both in the circumstances of their sacrifice and in the myths recounting the process. As discussed, Girard describes the scapegoating process as existing in the oral and written mythic representations of ancient persecutions and also in the documentation of cases of collective violence in more recent times. Modern texts of persecution mirror the ancient tales in that these texts have the same fundamental principle: the exoneration of the actions of those who participated in the killing or expulsion of the scapegoat – either as the mob or its supportive spectators. The World War II record of the Timor campaign has been shown to be a collection of texts of persecution. Documents relating to the 1975 invasion demonstrate that Australian texts are expressions of the 'romantic lie' through which the Australian mimetic dependence on Indonesia was obvious. This chapter focuses on Girard's claim that not only are the fortunes of scapegoats described in texts but the texts *themselves* can be the means of scapegoating victims.

Girard distinguishes between narratives in which scapegoating is clearly present in the plot and those in which the scapegoating principle is hidden. If the text itself is clearly depicting the misfortunes of a scapegoat, that is, as the visible theme of the work, the scapegoat is *in* the text. Such texts bear witness to the truth. On the other hand, the text itself may be the vehicle of oppression, where scapegoating can be detected as the operating principle of the text, but concealed. In this case the text itself is engaging in scapegoating, and the subject is undergoing persecution by means of the narrative. Here is found the scapegoat *of* the text.[26]

Girard's designation of a scapegoat *in* the text clearly applies to the range of publications which detail the facts of death and destruction in East Timor. Such texts demonstrate that the Timorese people were being persecuted by the Indonesian regime and present them as innocent victims resisting the interests of the powerful. In Girard's terms the role of scapegoat in the text applies to these narratives because East Timor is shown as possessing the characteristics of a victim.[27] Portuguese Timor fulfilled the physical criteria of one that is small and vulnerable.[28] Its supposed susceptibility to the influence of communism and the consequent threat to the region strengthened the case against the Timorese people. It is clear in this range of texts that in this interplay of geopolitical realities, the Timorese people were violently subjugated to the interests and fears of more powerful and predatory parties. They are easily seen in these accounts as scapegoats to be sacrificed to the perceived greater good of dominant powers.

East Timor: The scapegoat *of* the text

However, Girard's designation of scapegoat *of* the text is apparent in documents and commentaries issued by the Australian government. Texts that undertake the task of scapegoating have the concealed character of traditional myths, described by Girard as 'rationalizations or disguised accounts of an original act of violence, the truth of which the group needs to conceal or displace from itself'.[29] The official Australian need to ignore or disguise the violence done to the Timorese required the production of texts written from its own standpoint: that of a persecutor. The structure of such texts does not report the reality of the victim but becomes itself a means of victimization.

An example of East Timor as a scapegoat *of* the text appears in the government's account of its statements and actions at the end of the occupation. The narrative in question is *East Timor in Transition 1998–2000: An Australian Policy Challenge*, published by the Department of Foreign Affairs and Trade (DFAT). Its significance lies in its presentation to the Australian public of an official account of the Australian government's involvement in matters concerning East Timor from 1998 until August 2000. It devotes 160 pages to the changes in East Timor after the fall of President Suharto and the accession of President Habibie in 1998 and discusses the role of the Indonesian military and their Timorese militias. It is concerned with the Australian role in the referendum of 1999 and the United Nations Mission in East Timor, particularly with the humanitarian response and the establishment of the International Force for East Timor (INTERFET) which oversaw the initial restoration of peace and accompanied the United Nations in the preparation for independence in 2002. A further 112 pages of *East Timor in Transition* are annexes comprising selected Australian government and United Nations documents and letters.

Although brief, an initial chapter entitled 'The Historical Context' is the government's historical analysis of the Australian involvement in events prior to the referendum and forms the background for the remainder of the book. It is presented by the government to the Australian public in a readable and accessible form which requires little research capability to access. It can therefore be regarded as the government's preferred vehicle for popular information concerning the official Australian position. Information from other chapters in the book is used in this discussion where appropriate, but the concentration is focused on 'The Historical Context', providing a detailed appraisal of the government's own summary of its historical policies and actions. This examination finds that the chapter is composed of material and interpretation that is mostly characterized by lack of balance, and where embellishment, omission and deflection of blame are used to justify successive Australian governments' policies of support for Indonesia's occupation of East Timor. It exemplifies Girard's designation of the scapegoat *of* the text, as is now discussed.

It must be acknowledged at the outset that, contrary to the greater part of the content, there are two sentences in the 'Historical Context' chapter which recognize in a positive way the role of the East Timorese people in the final years of the occupation, namely:

> It (the separation from Indonesia) called for enormous discipline and restraint on the part of East Timor's pro-independence leaders in the face of serious provocation. Above all, it required the East Timorese people themselves to demonstrate inspirational courage and determination, in the face of violence and intimidation, to insist upon their right to exercise a choice about their future.[30]

Similarly, the foreword to the whole book acknowledges that the Timorese people 'achieved self-determination and have taken the first steps on their path to nationhood'.[31] These two instances are distinctive for their positive commendation of the Timorese people.

Authorship and balance

Regrettably, the remainder of 'The Historical Context' raises serious questions, the first of which concern the writers' conflicts of interest, and the lack of balance brought to the document as a result. The foreword to the complete book *East Timor in Transition* is signed by Foreign Minister Alexander Downer who gave the research task to Dr Ashton Calvert, the secretary of DFAT. According to Downer, Calvert 'put together a strong team of departmental officers who had worked on East Timor over the period'.[32] As Clinton Fernandes points out, the book therefore was not produced by DFAT's Historical Documents Project but by officers who had worked on the East Timor issues. Credibility thus appears not to have been a major concern when the policymakers themselves were charged with assessing their own work and publishing it as an official record.[33] As East Timor issues have affected Australian foreign policy in diverse and compromising ways, it is obvious that more independence and historical expertise in its authorship would have benefitted the production of this official Australian document. Those generating this document were personally involved with the issue, a fact that clearly has contributed to the bias, distortion and lack of balance that places it in the category of a 'text of persecution'.

The statement of the aim of *East Timor in Transition*, signed by Alexander Downer, is similar to that of *Australia and the Incorporation of East Timor* discussed in the previous chapter. This particular document is claimed to have been written as a full and balanced account of the Australian response to the immense foreign policy challenges of East Timor in the preceding two and a half years. It is claimed to be a balanced analysis of the major issues of the situation.[34] Underlining the assertion that balance was a main aim, it is stated that the writing team also drew from public sources in a balanced way, including from diplomatic reports and high-level exchanges that were integral to the formation of Australian policy.[35] While a single chapter could not be expected to comment on all the challenges which Australian governments faced during that period, the claims of balance which apply to the whole book should surely apply also to the presentation of the historical background. As the following evidence shows, the claim of balance in that chapter is groundless, and thus the credibility of the authors and the government is eroded as is the remainder of the book.

The account of the Australian involvement in recent Timorese history in *East Timor in Transition* is thus a vehicle for the continued scapegoating of East Timor by the Australian government. In trying to justify government actions, the account subtly positions East Timor as deserving of the Indonesian regime's repressive behaviour. East Timor becomes the scapegoat *of* the text.

The account of the Santa Cruz massacre

Embellishment and exoneration of Indonesian and Australian policies is vividly portrayed in the account in *East Timor in Transition* of the Santa Cruz massacre of 1991. It is outrageous in its bias and distortion of facts. The Santa Cruz massacre brought international exposure to the occupation. On 12 November 1991, a Catholic Mass was said in the parish church of Motael in Dili in remembrance of independence supporter Sebastião Gomes who had been killed two weeks previously. Hundreds of mainly young Timorese attended the Mass and immediately afterwards made their way to the Santa Cruz cemetery in a customary funeral procession, joined by others on the way. They displayed banners which they had been making in anticipation of a visit by Portuguese officials, calling for freedom and the intervention of Portugal and denouncing the Indonesian regime. At the cemetery, the Indonesian military fired on the crowd in a sustained attack, leaving many dead and wounded. A film of the incident was smuggled out to Britain, and its broadcast across the world became a catalyst for eventual Timorese independence at the end of the decade. The Indonesian government admitted to 50 dead, while the CAVR Report put the death toll at 271, with 250 listed as missing.[36] Hundreds of people were subsequently arrested and detained, and execution of the wounded was reported to have occurred over the following days.[37] There were trials of those involved in the massacre, but the penalties imposed on the perpetrators were minor in comparison to those given to organizers of the demonstration.[38] Many families have been unable to find the remains of their loved ones.[39]

Distortion

From the outset the facts of the Santa Cruz massacre are distorted in the 'Historical Background' chapter of the Australian government's *East Timor in Transition*. It states:

> When the much-anticipated visit of a Portuguese parliamentary delegation was cancelled by Portugal at late notice in October 1991 in protest over restrictions on their party, youths from pro-and anti-integration groups clashed in Dili, leaving one dead on each side. They were Sebastião Gomes from the pro-independence group and Alfonso Gomes from the pro-integration side.[40]

The 'restrictions on their party' refers to Indonesian displeasure at the presence of certain journalists of whom it did not approve.[41] The comment evades the problem of Indonesian strictures on journalistic freedom, and the responsibility for the cancellation is placed (at least in part) on Portugal. There is no mention of the role of the military or of provocateurs – of whom Alfonso Gomes, the anti-independence youth, was one. On 28 October the Indonesian military had mounted a raid on the Motael church. The church was the venue for pro-independence preparations for the visit of the Portuguese, with whom the Timorese youth planned to plead for assistance. Two died in the raid that day – the East Timorese spy for the military, and a clandestine activist, Sebastião Gomes Rangel.[42] The Australian document paints it as a clash between two Timorese sides, blaming internal Timorese rivalry while ignoring the larger oppressive Indonesian reality.

The account in *East Timor in Transition* of the actual massacre that occurred two weeks after this incident consists of five paragraphs. In the first two there is mention of two soldiers being stabbed by the demonstrators on the way to the Santa Cruz cemetery, yet a similar (although relatively minor) assault on one of the independence supporters during the march is omitted.[43] There is reference to the military's subsequent account and that of Indonesia's National Commission of Inquiry, which report on the demonstrators engaging in rock throwing, firing a shot, waving knives and throwing a grenade; however, the account adds the qualification that there was no independent corroboration of these acts.[44] The relatively lengthy inclusion of these minor unverified accusations against the demonstrators in the brief Australian account, alongside the omission or downplaying of the established facts of the subsequent violent Indonesian overreach, raises serious questions about the balance stated as one of the aims of the document.

There is a pattern in the chapter of giving such significant space to minor details while omitting more important features. Comparison of the document's treatment of the Santa Cruz massacre with that of the 1994 report on the event by a United Nations special rapporteur, Mr Bacre Waly Ndiaye, demonstrates this distortion.[45] Major conclusions of the Ndiaye report were that the demonstration was peaceful, the civilians were unarmed and claims of necessity and proportionality regarding the use of lethal force are unsubstantiated.[46]

Ndiaye considered all available accounts, including those provided by the Indonesian military, police and Commission of Inquiry.[47] Contrary to the Ndiaye report, the Australian document omits the non-compliance of Indonesian authorities to supply requested military reports on the incident.[48] It omits that security agencies knew about the demonstration days beforehand, that the military persons who were injured were not in uniform and that their injuries were sustained one kilometre from the cemetery and one hour before the killing of the demonstrators.[49] *East Timor in Transition* relates that gunfire was heard for two or three minutes, and then sounds of gunfire for another twenty minutes, while the Ndiaye report states that 'sporadic shooting was heard throughout the city and in neighboring villages during the rest of the day, and possibly during several days'.[50] The inclusion in the Australian version of the few minor instances of disruption by the demonstrators may be viewed as an attempt to give the 'balanced' account claimed as one of the aims of the document. It is obvious that emphasis on these unsubstantiated events, alongside omission of the more serious actions of the military, is clearly unbalanced.

The Ndiaye report presents a comprehensive sequence of facts, giving appropriate weight to the actions of both demonstrators and military during the procession and on arrival at the cemetery, whereas the Australian account merely summarizes the police and military accounts, mentioning the Ndiaye report only in reference to the numbers killed.[51] In the interests of the balance which the Australian publication was designed to address, it is unfortunate that details which excuse the military's response are included, while the greater number of details testifying to their disastrous overreaction are omitted.[52] Such omission serves to lessen the Indonesian responsibility for the violence in the eyes of readers unfamiliar with the facts. It contributes to the overall tenor of this official Australian government document as a text of persecution which confuses responsibility and deflects blame from Indonesia.

The third of the five paragraphs in the historical background chapter of *East Timor in Transition* detailing the Santa Cruz massacre is an account of the killings, arrests and subsequent deaths over following days, while the fourth paragraph relates the problem of ascertaining the exact number of deaths and gives a fair summary of the various opinions. Neither of these paragraphs attempts to soften the facts.

The fifth paragraph, however, continues the generally indulgent approach to the perpetrators of the violence. It maintains that the Santa Cruz massacre caused a reversal in an otherwise improving situation where 'goodness, tolerance, liberality, self-expression, a better deal and peace' were now unfortunately lost.[53] The chapter states:

> The shock and anger caused by the tragedy refueled the resentment felt by ordinary East Timorese towards the security forces and the failures of Indonesian rule. It extinguished the hopes of many that some good could come from Indonesia's administration. It marked the end of a relatively tolerant period in East Timor and the loss of influence of those who had championed the more liberal regime. It meant that the newfound right to self-expression was again lost and that the prospect for achieving a better deal for the East Timorese through peaceful means was as remote as had ever been.[54]

The whole thrust of this passage is in keeping with the Australian position that the Dili massacre was a terrible but unusual incident, an 'aberration', some sort of regrettable but freak occurrence. In reality it was yet another massacre, one involving at least 271 young people that gave even more shocking evidence of decades of injustice. The assertion of a breakdown of progress resulting from the killings insinuates some blame on the part of the Timorese. There appears to be no sense of irony in the statement that 'the newfound right to self-expression was again lost', when the massacre was Indonesia's response to a demonstration found by the United Nations special rapporteur's report to be orderly.

There were trials of those involved in the event, but the penalties imposed on the perpetrators were minor compared to those given to organizers of the demonstration. Ten Indonesian military persons were tried for disciplinary offences and were sentenced to prison for up to eighteen months. Most served time under house arrest and were released before the expiry of their sentences. East Timorese organizers of the protest, however, were jailed for at least five years, and some were given life sentences.[55] *East Timor in Transition* omits any reference to these grossly inadequate and unfair sentences imposed after the Santa Cruz massacre. Curiously, it refers instead to the trial and jailing of Indonesian soldiers who killed six civilians in Liquiça, an event which happened in 1995, four years after the Dili massacre. With breathtaking nerve, *East Timor in Transition* presents this later event as proof that progress towards justice was underway in cases of human rights offences by TNI personnel.[56] It highlights an event some years after the Dili massacre but omits the unjust treatment of Timorese connected to the massacre that is the actual subject of the passage. The focus is clearly to put Indonesia in the best possible light. It also suggests an effort to present evidence of improvements which might be seen to justify the political and diplomatic approach towards Indonesia taken by Australia over many years.

Bias and embellishment

The section following the account of the Dili massacre continues to read as an apologia for Indonesia.[57] One paragraph rightly points to the oppressive military presence as the cause of the Jakarta administration's inability to win over the East Timorese people. Yet there is a sense of frustration and a suggestion of blame in the mention of the antagonism of the young towards the incorporation of Timor into Indonesia, and the loss of Indonesia's hope that they would have been the generation which showed benefits of Indonesian rule.[58] The paragraph bemoans the realization that the post-1975 generation became Indonesia's single greatest liability.[59] The unwillingness of the youth to support Indonesia's aspirations in the territory is then blamed on FRETILIN (*Frente Revolucionária de Timor-Leste Independente* or Revolutionary Front for an Independent East Timor) which is accused of taking advantage of the youth in the development of its clandestine opposition.[60] The thrust of these statements puts the blame on the

Timorese. The paragraph applies the words 'effort', 'goodwill' and 'benefit' to the Indonesian involvement, while 'antagonism', 'liability' and 'clandestine' are used of the Timorese youth, clearly a biased use of language.[61]

There follows the statement that in the early part of the 1990s it was recognized that creative solutions, including a new and more sensitive approach, were needed.[62] A lengthy list of Indonesian proposals is claimed to have been designed so that the Timorese could exercise a greater degree of influence over internal affairs which, the paragraph states, were finally vetoed by President Suharto. The failure of the administration in the 1990s to advance any positive solutions is linked to the assertion that it was the security approach which lay at the heart of Indonesia's policy failure in the territory. This summation of the problem in the document is superficial and only partly true. The more fundamental problem, rather than lack of creative solutions, was the very existence of Indonesia as an illegal administering power in East Timor operating with brutality and impunity. The official Australian account of a highly significant event in the history of East Timor is one which manipulates facts to put those responsible for the killings in a positive light and to insinuate blame on the part of Timorese. East Timor is a scapegoat *of* this official Australian text.

The account of 1999

The events of 1999 are presented in ways which continue to excuse or absolve the Indonesian military and their militias of their violence, and thus the recounting of these events in the Australian government text reinforces the scapegoating of the Timorese people. The collapse of the long Indonesian occupation of East Timor occurred in the final months of 1999. Following Indonesian president B. J. Habibie's surprise announcement in favour of a plebiscite to ascertain the wishes of the Timorese people regarding their status, an agreement between the United Nations, Portugal and Indonesia on the process was signed in New York on 5 May 1999. After formal establishment by the Security Council in June, the United Nations Assistance Mission for East Timor (UNAMET) received enthusiastic international support, including from the Australian government.[63] Preparations for the referendum were undertaken swiftly, challenged by increasing military-inspired militia violence within the territory, as it became apparent that the vote would likely be in favour of independence from Indonesia.[64] International diplomacy tried to balance justice and appeasement as accounts of intimidation and massacres filled news reports.

Exoneration

In presenting that final stage of East Timor's gaining of independence in 1999, *East Timor in Transition* embellishes or dilutes accounts of the operation of Indonesian agencies. There is even a suggestion of heroism in the reference to the courage of the Indonesian leadership accepting international assistance to restore order.[65] Yet the CAVR Report describes the same situation thus: 'Frantic diplomatic activity took place ... to put pressure on Indonesia to fulfil its security obligations or consent to an international force to restore security.'[66] Furthermore, while *East Timor in Transition* states it was obvious that the TNI directed and supported the Timorese militias, it maintains that the extent and nature of the military's direction of the militia was impossible to determine and that there was no clear evidence as to whether the abuses were sanctioned or ordered by authorities.[67] Nevertheless, when UN Security Council members visited Dili on 11 September 1999, they found the situation to be calm, indicating a high degree of overall control by the TNI and demonstrating that security could be maintained when required.[68]

The influence of the TNI on the militias is documented in the CAVR Report.[69] It notes that militia groups had existed before Indonesia invaded but were increasingly recruited and controlled by the military, sometimes under duress, but often with the promise of money, drugs and prestige. Training intensified in 1998 and 1999, with the military attending militia inaugurations and providing arms. Australian claims in the chapter that the level of Indonesian oversight of the militias was impossible to determine are therefore questionable. Nevins claims that through agreements for intelligence sharing with the United States, Britain, Canada and New Zealand, the Australian government knew that the TNI – including its senior command structure – was responsible for coordinating the militia violence.[70] Toohey and Wilkinson's exposition of government knowledge of the invasion, and Collins and Reeds's revelations of pro-Indonesian bias in Australian intelligence services underline the knowledge which Australian governments have had over the decades concerning the East Timor situation.[71] Fernandes demonstrates that not only were the militias part of the Indonesian government's systematic campaign to deflect onto the Timorese blame for the mayhem but that the Australian government's repeated excuses and denials provided the military with welcome support.[72] That *East Timor in Transition* understates official Indonesian connections to the militias and omits the international pressure on Indonesia in favour of mention of its 'courage' are examples of the document's general tendency to portray the Indonesian government and its agencies in a positive light, regardless of their actions. The text continues to scapegoat the Timorese people.

Nevins comments that states are usually selective in the facts they present, preferring exaggeration of the good while ignoring poor decisions and outcomes.[73] *East Timor in Transition* is an egregious example of this tendency. Australia and particularly its foreign minister Alexander Downer are presented as increasingly concerned about deteriorating conditions in East Timor, initiating consultation with East Timorese leaders and applying consistent pressure to Indonesia.[74] Even as late as 1999, however, Downer was maintaining the traditional Australian government support for Indonesia, claiming that connections between the Indonesian military and the Timorese militias were not Indonesian government policy. He stated that any involvement by the military in abuses was the fault of 'rogue elements' and declared that the Indonesians had made clear to him that they would behave in a responsible way.[75] While Downer's statements may have been judged to be politically important to maintain Indonesian support of the Timorese referendum at the time, there is no admission in *East Timor in Transition* of this or that any historical Australian action, seen in hindsight, was deficient. There is nothing which approximates to the statement made by Gareth Evans, Australian foreign minister from 1988 to 1996, that the continued Australian training of Indonesian military helped only to produce 'more professional human rights abusers'.[76]

Australian support for the Indonesian position on East Timor (and its continued desire for Indonesian favour) is reflected in the Australian official record of the events. It is clear that the record exemplifies 'texts of persecution', where those responsible for scapegoating are exonerated and the victim continues to be blamed. East Timor is the scapegoat of the text of *East Timor in Transition*.

Australian complicity in the scapegoating of East Timor

Examination thus far of an official Australian history concerning the end of the Indonesian occupation has found that policy leaned consistently towards support of the Indonesian position, to the extent of distorting the facts. The Australian documentary record shows that East Timor was considered as a dispensable entity in the pursuit of other interests, the victim of Australian desire for the security offered by a compliant relationship with Indonesia. Remaining on good terms with Indonesia was seen to be crucial to Australia's interests.[77] Protection of good relations with Indonesia was paramount as had been the case for decades.[78] The maintenance of this position involved conspiracies against a vulnerable people in which deceit, hypocrisy and irresponsibility were employed.[79]

Key aspects of this Australian support for Indonesia include the swift bestowal of Australian de jure recognition of Indonesian sovereignty, strong support of Indonesia in the United Nations, continuance of military ties and conduct during negotiations over oil and gas resources in the Timor Sea. Significantly, the maintenance of two contradictory positions by Australian governments – that they supported Timorese self-determination even while concretely supporting Indonesian sovereignty – underscores that complicity throughout the occupation.

Recognition of Indonesian sovereignty

East Timor in Transition emphasizes the astonishing claims of Australian authorities that humanitarian concerns were the basis of government support of the Indonesian position. It states:

> In January 1978, the Minister for Foreign Affairs, Andrew Peacock, announced that the Government had decided to accept East Timor as part of Indonesia. Peacock said that the Government, like most Australians, deeply regretted that the events in East Timor since August 1975 had caused so much suffering, noting that humanitarian issues arising from the issue continued to be of major concern. Peacock said that the basis for this position was that Indonesian control was effective and covered all administrative centers.[80]

Following the internal discussions of the authorities of the time as contained in relevant cables, further reasons are advanced for Australian recognition of Indonesia's control, such as family reunion for Timorese refugees and the rebuilding of East Timor.[81] It was claimed that these issues required Australia to deal with Indonesian as the administering power. Therefore, Indonesian sovereignty was a reality with which Australia had to come to terms.[82] The document states:

> Both Coalition and Labor governments regarded Indonesia's control of East Timor as a reality that needed to be managed and considered that this was best done in the context of a strong bilateral relationship with Indonesia. With such a relationship, it was more likely that Indonesia would listen to Australia on the hard issues, including East Timor.[83]

East Timor in Transition thus depicts Australia as pursuing concerns for the good of the East Timorese people in a constructive and effective way as a result of the relationship with Indonesia.[84] Moreover, the document claims that Australia championed the human rights of the Timorese people to the extent of making concerns known at every level of the Indonesian administration, stating that 'the government's concerns over human rights violations were conveyed clearly and consistently to Indonesian officials, from the President down to the local military and police commanders on the ground in East Timor. It was also claimed that there was Australian pressure for troop reductions in the territory.'[85] Further, it states that concerning development assistance, 'Australia consistently urged the Indonesian authorities to adopt policies in East Timor that would promote the welfare of the East Timorese and, in particular, to promote and protect internationally accepted standards of human rights'.[86]

There is no evidence supporting these claims in *East Timor in Transition*. There are no references to any ministerial letters, statements, reports or discussions with the Indonesian authorities concerning these claims of efforts to protect human rights. On the contrary, the Australian voting record at the United Nations, the recognition of Indonesian sovereignty and the government's embellished historical account indicate that the human rights of the Timorese people were not a high priority, as discussed later. Significantly, the failure of any Australian government to actively champion the human rights of the East Timorese people is not admitted but simply deflected onto Indonesia: 'Australia had hoped for more influence than it was ever able to achieve.'[87]

United Nations: Australian voting and argument

One of the factors which contradict claims of respect for the Timorese people's human rights was the Australian governments' consistent upholding of the Indonesian incorporation of East Timor in the United Nations. Between 1975 and 1982 the United Nations General Assembly annually condemned the violence and called for an act of self-determination to be held in East Timor. Australia voted in favour of the resolution in 1975, abstained for the next two years and voted against the resolutions for the following five years.[88] *East Timor in Transition* omits to mention the Australian voting record. Instead there is a statement which places responsibility on other states and the United Nations itself, noting that the General Assembly adopted resolutions on East Timor each year from 1975 to 1982, 'although by a declining majority of votes'.[89] Admission of the Australian government's lack of support for East Timor was thus minimized and deflected onto others.

In March 1982, ex-prime minister Whitlam visited East Timor for three days, reporting on his return that all was well in the territory.[90] Later that year and a few days before the annual United Nations General Assembly vote on resolutions regarding East Timor, he appeared before the United Nations Special Committee on Decolonization, and stated: 'It is high time that the question of East Timor was voted off the United Nations agenda and ceased to preoccupy and distract the nations of Southeast Asia and the Pacific.'[91] Thus the man who had been prime minister and in control of the foreign affairs portfolio in the time leading up to the invasion attempted to conceal the effects of actions for which he had more responsibility than any other Australian. In his status as a high-profile ex-prime minister held in great esteem by large sections of the population, he had the means to influence the Labor government of the time. Instead, he chose to continue to support the policy that disregarded the rights of the Timorese people, treating their concerns as a distraction.

Military assistance to Indonesia

Australian government claims of concern for the Timorese people in *East Timor in Transition* are further challenged by the continuing military assistance provided to Indonesia by Australia for the greater part of the occupation. The CAVR Report notes the Whitlam government's initiation of a defence cooperation programme with Indonesia in July 1972, providing aircraft, training and intelligence cooperation, was renewed and increased by the Fraser government in 1975. That aid was provided on condition that it not be used in East Timor or for internal repression.[92] It is intriguing that such a stipulation was made and that it was seen to be necessary to make it. It is also offensively laughable in view of the Australian knowledge of the violence already wreaked on the Timorese people. Obviously the weaker partner in the relationship, Australia proved to have little control over Indonesia's use of aid, military hardware and training.[93]

After the Dili massacre the United States and some members of the European Union introduced partial embargoes on the provision of arms and military training to Indonesia.[94] Despite suspending some forms of aid at this time, Australia still emerged as the Indonesian military's leading provider of training.[95] For the years 1994–2000, an average of two hundred Indonesian defence personnel received training each year. In 1993 Indonesia's Special Forces Command (Kopassus) began training in Australia.[96] Australian claims that such training helped to sensitize trainees to human rights was proved wrong in East Timor.[97] *East Timor in Transition* makes no mention of the levels of Australian military aid to Indonesia during the time that East Timor was under Indonesian military control. On the contrary, it is stated that there was Australian pressure for troop reductions in the territory.[98] Even accepting that this occurred, there are again no references provided or any indication as to the content of such pressure.

Contradictions

One of the more astounding tasks of *East Timor in Transition* was that, once again, the Australian government attempted to explain the contradictory Australian position of support for the principle of Timorese self-determination while facilitating its opposite – agreement with Indonesian sovereignty. *East Timor in Transition* maintains that Australia's position was always that the people of East Timor had the right to self-determination.[99] That assertion of constant Australian support for the East Timorese people's right to decide their own future was not supported by Australian government practice throughout the twenty-four-year occupation, as has been detailed. It was also not supported by the letter of Prime Minister Howard to President Habibie dated 19 December 1998. In this letter Howard states: 'It has been a long-standing Australian position that the interests of Australia, Indonesia and East Timor are best served by East Timor remaining part of Indonesia.'[100] The Australian government's claim in *East Timor in Transition* that Australia consistently upheld the Timorese people's right to self-determination is false.

Clearly, government efforts to maintain two opposite positions simultaneously are a feature of the history. Such efforts were on display at the time of the 1975 invasion, as discussed in Chapter 4, when Australian lip-service to self-determination accompanied support for the seizure of East Timor. Little change from that position appears in this 2000 account of Australian involvement in East Timor's fortunes under discussion. The maintenance of such a contradictory position resembles that of the Indonesian government's claim of support for a peaceful Portuguese decolonization of Timor.[101] This claim was made three days before the invasion, with its troops standing ready for attack. Similarly, the Australian government claimed it had always supported the principle of Timor self-determination while actively facilitating Indonesian sovereignty. Indonesia and Australia resembled each other. Both were two-faced.

Timor Sea resources

Behind the Australian recognition of Indonesian sovereignty lay an element of mimetic desire by which Australia imitated Indonesian desire for territorial expansion through plans to profit from the resources of the Timor Sea. The documents clearly link that recognition to negotiations over the maritime resources. De facto recognition of Indonesian sovereignty occurred after the invasion and was followed by official de jure recognition in January 1979.[102] In 1985 official acceptance of the sovereignty of Indonesia over East Timor was confirmed.[103] Alongside these diplomatic moves were consistent statements expressing Australian desires and plans concerning the Timor Sea resources. In 1974 the Australian government considered the 'geo-political sense' of having Portuguese Timor incorporated into Indonesia. This would assist in confirming 'our seabed agreement with Indonesia' thus encouraging Indonesia towards further discussions on maritime arrangements.[104] At the same time, it was stated:

> We should be careful not to be seen as pushing for self-government or independence for Portuguese Timor or for it to become part of Indonesia, as this would probably be interpreted as evidence of our self-interest in the seabed boundary dispute rather than a genuine concern for the future of Portuguese Timor.[105]

In August 1975, on the eve of the invasion, Richard Woolcott offered the advice that the closing of the gap in the sea border (which had been agreed in 1972 with Indonesia) could be more easily negotiated with Indonesia than with Portugal or an independent Portuguese Timor.[106] Following the invasion, *East Timor in Transition* reports the motivation of Australian authorities to recognize the Indonesian incorporation of East Timor. Although the invasion is lamented, the incorporation is stated as being connected to maritime boundary negotiations:

> On 15 December 1978, Peacock signaled that Australia would give *de jure* recognition to the Indonesian takeover, with the commencement of negotiations over the delimitation of the seabed boundary between East Timor and Australia early the following year. Peacock said that Australia had to face the realities of international law in conducting seabed negotiations and that this did not mean the Government condoned Indonesia's method of incorporating East Timor.[107]

It must be recognized that the Timor Gap Treaty signed with Indonesia in 1989 was a breach of the obligation for states to not recognize territory acquired by force.[108] Yet legal opinion exists that reference to East Timor in the treaty as 'the Indonesian Province of East Timor' constituted one of the highest forms of de jure recognition.[109] *East Timor in Transition* defends the Australian position by pointing out that some thirty other nations also recognized Indonesian sovereignty over time, either explicitly or by signing treaties which recognized the entity 'Indonesia' as defined in Indonesian law.[110] Nevertheless, none of these nations negotiated with Indonesia over material benefits relating to East Timor as did Australia. The force of Australia's legal recognition of an annexation constantly regarded as illegal by the United Nations is thus cushioned in *East Timor in Transition* by association with other nations' lesser acts of recognition, all of which, however, lacked the particular legal ramifications of Australia's de jure recognition. The ramifications of the long-running Timor Sea saga continue at the time of writing. Revelations of predatory and illegal Australian actions to exploit the sovereign maritime assets of the Timorese people are increasingly coming to light.[111]

The dependency of Australia on the Indonesian desire to subsume East Timor extended to imitation of tactics and willingness to present inconsistency and contradiction as acceptable policy. The voting record at the United Nations and continued military assistance demonstrate Australian subservience to Indonesian desires, serving Australian need for regional security. The negotiations over the Timor Sea signal the Australian awareness that complicity in persecution and dependency on large power can be very profitable indeed.[112]

Features of scapegoating in Australian complicity

Crisis, crime and criteria for the scapegoat

In order to demonstrate the Australia-East Timor relationship with regard to Girard's insights into scapegoating in greater detail, a case study is now analysed. It concerns Monsignor da Costa Lopes, the Catholic Church's apostolic administrator of East Timor from 1977 to 1983.

Girard identifies consistent features, or stereotypes, that recur in the mythic representations of ancient persecutions and in modern cases of collective violence. Firstly, in these accounts of persecution, there are social crises which threaten the peace and stability of communities. Secondly, accusations are made against a person or group to identify a crime, which is interpreted as the origin or exacerbation of the crisis. Thirdly, some person or group displaying suspect features is blamed, becoming the scapegoat upon whom is heaped responsibility for the crime. Scapegoats are usually chosen because of their credibility as victims, and those whose marginality serves to protect the accusers. Since the scapegoat caused the crisis, he/she/they must then be held accountable to restore equilibrium. The three initial stereotypes of persecution are the 'crisis', the 'crime' and then the 'criteria' for the selection of the victim. The killing or expulsion of scapegoats is the fourth of Girard's stereotypes, that is, the unanimous collective 'violence' done to the victim to reinstate communal stability. The fifth is the peace or order that is established or restored following the scapegoating violence, resulting in sacralizing the victim.[113] In a general sense, one can identify these features in the East Timor situation from the 1970s:

1. A security crisis caused by communism and Portuguese colonization had arisen.
2. Accusations were made that the East Timorese could not be self-governing and were supportive of communism.
3. Certain features about East Timor (marking it as marginal and blameworthy) were identified or supposed, such as its small size, communist leanings and inability to be politically and economically self-sufficient.
4. Violence was perpetrated against East Timor by the Indonesian government, supported by Australia and the United States, supposedly to prevent a communist threat.
5. A semblance of order and control was established in East Timor although it was protested against and resisted.[114]

More specifically, Girard's categories of 'crisis', 'crime' and 'criteria for the choice of the victim' are observable when considering the high-profile public incident in Australia relating to East Timor which involved Monsignor da Costa Lopes, the former Australian prime minister Gough Whitlam and the starvation which was decimating the Timorese people at the time.

Case study: Monsignor da Costa Lopes

Crisis

Monsignor Martinho da Costa Lopes had been appointed to administer the diocese of Dili in 1977.[115] Rather than include the diocese in the Indonesian Bishops' Conference upon the resignation of Bishop José Ribeiro, the Vatican undertook direct control and appointed Lopes as apostolic administrator.[116] He held the post until his forced resignation in 1983.[117] During his tenure, famine took hold in Timor in the late 1970s and early 1980s as the Indonesian military attempted to gain control of the territory.[118] In an effort to weaken their resistance, ABRI forcibly moved people and deliberately destroyed their crops, livestock and food stores, thus depriving them of the means of subsistence.[119] The CAVR Report notes that the people were denied access to food and the sources of food.[120] In particular, the forced displacement into crowded resettlement camps resulted in starvation and death of appalling proportions, especially in 1978 and 1979.[121]

International aid agencies received reports of famine as early as April 1977, and a visit by foreign ambassadors in September 1978 raised further awareness. However, humanitarian relief was controlled solely by the Indonesian military which refused entry to agencies until September 1979.[122] Such access was granted once the military believed that the bulk of the population was under control and that the resistance was significantly weakened.[123] By that time, three hundred thousand people (55 per cent of the population) were found to be seriously malnourished.[124] Delegates from the International Red Cross described the situation 'as bad as Biafra'.[125] News and photos of the starvation stirred Australian agencies into action which included ongoing discussion of Australian policy.[126] While the ensuing aid programme relieved the famine considerably, the long-term effects on the Timorese population were immense.[127] The huge death toll in such horrendous circumstances brought further individual and communal sorrow and trauma. The social upheaval of continual displacement, threat and starvation for political purposes violated the people's rights, traditions and lifestyle.[128]

Subsequently Bishop John Gerry, the secretary of the Australian Bishops' Conference, wrote a letter to Monsignor Lopes on 11 November 1981 asking for information and advice concerning the situation in East Timor.[129] Bishop Gerry specifically enquired about the social and political situation, types of assistance required and the stand the Australian church agencies needed to take, referring to the usual famine over the New Year during the usual 'hungry months' of November–February. Lopes's reply on 19 November 1981 described the Timorese situation as 'tragic', wrote of atrocities committed in Lacluta where he claimed that five hundred Timorese were killed and referred, as Bishop Gerry had done, to the expected famine.[130] The publication of the contents of Lopes's letter moved Australian and international agencies to prepare to gather and send aid to the territory as they had done so recently in the late 1970s.[131] Dormant popular opposition to the Indonesian invasion surfaced again in sections of Australia in the face of further news of famine, fuelling antagonistic sentiment towards government policies. It was in this context that Gough Whitlam and the journalist Peter Hastings undertook a three-day visit to East Timor to survey the situation. They gave a press conference in Jakarta on 5 March 1982, before returning to Australia. As will be detailed, Whitlam then launched a ferocious verbal campaign of attack against Monsignor Lopes which lasted for months.

The genesis of the visit illustrates the crisis inherent in the Australia-Indonesia relationship in regard to East Timor. During the press conference, Whitlam refused to say on whose invitation he had made the trip, claiming that while he and Hastings travelled with the Jakarta representative of the International Red Cross, he did not know how the arrangements were made.[132] Whitlam later admitted, however, that he was briefed by the Centre for Strategic and International Studies (CSIS) and that he called on President Suharto and the acting foreign minister in Jakarta before returning to Australia.[133] Pat Walsh (from ACFOA, the Australian Council for Overseas Aid, and later an advisor to the CAVR) maintained that the visit was at the invitation of the Indonesian government as a way of weakening an Australian Senate Inquiry into East Timor which was to be conducted around that time. He referred to reports that Indonesian embassy officials in Canberra were unnerved about the forthcoming Senate Inquiry.[134] Such sensitivity no doubt signalled to the government that the desired equilibrium in the relationship with Indonesia could again be at risk. Walsh also maintained that a further reason for the visit was to discredit Lopes, a move designed to throw doubt on the adverse reports on the situation emanating from the Timorese Catholic Church and to erode the Timorese people's confidence in the church and its 'focus for nationalist sentiment'.[135] A weak senate report and doubtful accounts of the situation in East Timor would lessen the newsworthiness of Timor, thereby averting a further crisis in the relationship with Indonesia. As a self-styled 'elder statesman', Whitlam would also benefit from a reduction in negative accounts of the outcome of the Indonesian incorporation in which he had played an influential part.[136] Such a social crisis required a resolution with an appropriate scapegoat, thus diverting attention from the complicity of the Australian state in the outcomes of the Indonesian annexation. The scapegoat was Monsignor da Costa Lopes.

Crime

Australian governments had already failed dismally to address the real crime – the treatment of the Timorese people – demonstrating that the maintenance of the relationship with Indonesia remained more important to them than Timorese lives. Along with the media, the government was satisfied to comment on the tragedy of a possible impending famine without reference to the cause. Whitlam, too, averted his gaze from the system which had already decimated the people and which threatened another famine. He had evaded the consequences of his short-sighted approach to the Timorese question when in office, neglecting to use his considerable political strengths and the international standing of Australia to attempt to mediate. In this instance he chose to address the mention of famine and atrocity in the letter by Monsignor da Costa Lopes rather than the cause of the problem. The tenacity of his denunciation ensured that, far from being a catalyst for further investigation of the possible famine, public focus was pointed towards the letter and its writer, who was painted as villainous and malign.

At the press conference in Jakarta on 5 March, Whitlam discussed Lopes's reply to Bishop Gerry's suggestion of the expected famine. Throughout the interview he repudiated the claim of such an event and accused Lopes of knowing about negotiations for adequate Australian assistance when he wrote to Bishop Gerry. Whitlam stated: 'I cannot understand or explain how the Monsignor came to send that misleading and cruel letter, or why in a word the Monsignor perpetrated this wicked act.'[137] In an ABC interview later that month Whitlam repeated his claim that Monsignor Lopes was a liar and declared that he suffered from an identity crisis. That judgement flowed from Whitlam's view that the Monsignor could not accept that Indonesian rule was more beneficial to the Timorese than Portugal's.[138] Yet Whitlam signalled the real cause of the crisis as he apportioned blame when he wrote: 'This alarmist, inaccurate letter to the Australian Bishops ... has done a great deal of harm to relations between the Australian and Indonesian governments, and the Australian and Indonesian peoples.'[139] Further, he alluded to social disquiet as a result of the letter in Australia, and blamed Lopes:

> The Monsignor has distressed hundreds of thousands of Australians who responded generously when the last news came out over two years ago about a famine in East Timor and the effect that that had on the health, now and for the future, of so many of the population. And one expects that humane, charitable people in Australia would have responded to his assessment.[140]

Thus Whitlam attributed to Lopes the crime of falsely warning of starvation, thereby precipitating damage to the relationship between Australia and Indonesia and causing Australians distress. The fundamental crime of the atrocities committed by the Indonesian military against civilians – including politically induced starvation – was ignored.

The language Whitlam used in a series of interviews and in an article he wrote for The *Bulletin* in March 1982 is extreme. Describing Lopes's letter as 'cruel' and 'wicked', and its writer as 'malicious' and 'mendacious' as well as a 'liar', is extraordinary.[141] Such language is not only immoderate or intemperate but irrational when seen in the context of the actual state of peril, prolonged suffering and violent deaths of people to whom the letter refers. Whitlam's actions and statements are aptly interpreted by an insight of Girard's: 'It is undeniably and universally true that the less rational the persecutors' conviction the more formidable that conviction becomes.'[142] For months Whitlam pursued the matter. His denouncement of the bishop's supposed crime was equalled only by his lavish praise of the system responsible for the situation of the Timorese people:

> I am convinced that what the Indonesian Government is doing in East Timor … is visibly beneficial … There's no denying the evidence of one's eyes. There are new schools, including secondary schools, there are new or reconstructed hospitals and dispensaries. There are now many more kilometres of asphalt road, and there is proper provision for increasing the amount of food.[143]

Visibly beneficial as a few roads, hospitals and schools may have been, the unreported and therefore invisible forced labour, massacres, rapes and starvation occurring concurrently with Whitlam's visit place his musings in perspective.[144] Despite the effort to extol the Indonesian occupation and thereby redeem his own part in its genesis, Whitlam's excessive language of accusation betrays him as collaborating with persecution. In hindsight Girard's insight is apposite: such conviction is not convincing enough to hide its character and the scapegoating mechanism from which it springs.[145] Whitlam was embroiled in a crisis in which he had played a leading role. He attempted to diffuse the crisis by diverting attention away from the famine and occupation with the accusation of the crime of false reporting. His visit to Timor and consequent statements denying the oppression reveal him to be compromised by his own past, producing a series of 'texts of persecution' – modern-day myths – found in the transcripts of the interviews he gave and in his writings.

These texts are not important simply in regard to Whitlam's record but because they became a means of diverting attention away from Australian complicity with the main cause of the famine – the illegitimate colonizer, Indonesia. For instance, while admitting some Indonesian 'bungling', a *Sydney Morning Herald* editorial in January 1982 extolled Jakarta's 'enormous and largely unremarked efforts ... in the fields of health, education and agriculture'.[146] It referred to the danger posed by 'Australia's nagging, relentless criticism of the Timor affair'.[147] The editorial declared that the 'real point at issue is that East Timor has become a running ulcer in Australian-Indonesian relations'.[148] Thus Monsignor Lopes's claims about possible starvation became a vehicle for media support of government policy on East Timor, exoneration of Indonesian rule and belittling of public criticism. No doubt such reports were comfort for Mr Whitlam and for those who fully accepted the incorporation of East Timor as being the best situation for all concerned. Sections of the Australian press and government were also willing, as was Whitlam, to champion Indonesian rule in Timor. As evidence they broadcasted the limited experience gained in their rare and brief visits.[149] Therefore, with the media focus on the credibility of Monsignor Lopes's claims, any Australian responsibility regarding the underlying causes of the problem was ignored while East Timorese people were again blamed for causing disruption to the Australia-Indonesia relationship, even as they starved.

Criteria for the selection of the victim

The third of Girard's features of persecution is that of the reasons for the choice of a particular victim. The credibility and marginality of traditional scapegoats are fulfilled in the selection of Monsignor da Costa Lopes. While foreigners, the poor, someone with a physical difference such as colour of skin, or ethnic or religious minorities are obvious targets for scapegoating, Girard adds another marginal group to the list: a rich or powerful person or a leader.[150] Monsignor da Costa Lopes matches well some of these criteria. He was the leader of an insignificant group, while also being a non-white foreigner to a mostly white Australia. He was the de facto spokesman for the Timorese while also being the official leader of the Catholic Church in East Timor, the only institution which existed there at that time besides the Indonesian military. His was a place of privilege and power, which he used to advocate for a beleaguered people facing extraordinary threat to their culture and lives. Under Monsignor Lopes's leadership, the church symbolized succour and hope to the Timorese. As its increasingly outspoken leader, he became a focus for the Timorese and a target for the Indonesians and their supporters, including Australians. His stand for his people and their welfare in the exercise of his office marked him out as a threat, one who would not comply with the accepted norms of behaviour required either by the Indonesians or the political expediency of Australian governments.

Additionally, the process of scapegoating Lopes included discrediting his opinion and experience as well as attacking his authority. For example, his comments from the pulpit on the people's suffering were denigrated by Whitlam as 'what he described as a homily'.[151] Whitlam always used inverted commas – 'the Bishop' – when referring to him, thus underlining his lesser status as an apostolic administrator despite his work and responsibilities being identical to that of a bishop.[152]

Violent scapegoating and peace restored

The continuing disturbance in Australia over the Lopes affair points to substantial underlying guilt and anger concerning the Timor situation. Distracted by Whitlam's attacks, the media concentrated more on the words of Monsignor Lopes than on the issue of possible famine to which he was referring, to the extent that the ACFOA requested a retraction by the *Sydney Morning Herald* concerning claimed misreporting of the monsignor's words.[153] Australian unease was thus sublimated into more academic questions concerning the truth or otherwise of a narrow range of statements. Nevertheless, Lopes's warnings about famine were vindicated, with, for example, a 1984 report that stated 'the threat of widespread famine ... is intensifying'.[154] Yet after Whitlam's criticism of him and the adverse publicity given to Indonesia as a result of the monsignor's words, Indonesian military personnel pressured the papal envoy to Indonesia to advise the Vatican to remove Lopes, and in 1983 he was forced to resign.[155] Girard's fourth feature – violence – is here evident; the scapegoating of Monsignor da Costa Lopes was complete. The accusations were primarily conveyed through the media and backroom politics, but the effect was a coerced and violent expulsion. As a result, the relationship between the Australian and Indonesian governments was rescued from a crisis and restored, for a time, as harmonious and ordered. Lopes's experience clearly demonstrates Australian complicity in scapegoating East Timor, particularly by the government and media, to support Indonesian occupation.

Girard comments on the case of Alfred Dreyfus that has some parallels with Monsignor da Costa Lopes.[156] In 1894 French army intelligence found that military information was being conveyed to the German government. Captain Dreyfus was accused of selling state secrets via a handwritten note that had been discovered in the German embassy in Paris and given to French authorities. His trial, held in a closed court, was peppered with false claims, forged documents, wrong handwriting analysis and unsubstantiated accusations. Despite this, seven judges unanimously convicted him of treason, and he was sentenced to life imprisonment on Devil's Island. New evidence emerged that found that a French army major was the real culprit, but it was suppressed. Dreyfus was then accused of additional charges, based on other forged documents. After some years he was exonerated and served France with distinction in World War I. French society was deeply divided over the affair for years. It is clear now that Dreyfus's status as a Jew was the catalyst for the huge opposition against him. Girard states that those against Dreyfus were caught up in a myth, a false accusation that they confused with truth, their anti-Semitic prejudice successfully blocking out the clear facts of the case.[157] Those who supported him were few to begin with but were able to see that the facts were essential to the truth of the matter.

In the case of Monsignor Lopes, the texts of the various letters were misrepresented, there was threat to the stability of the Australian relationship with Indonesia and an influential ex-prime minister was at pains to vindicate past decisions. Lopes represented the Timorese people who were enduring Australian disapproval by governments that fawned on their oppressors, a media with apparently more pressing interests and a population increasingly desensitized by official inaction and lack of information. The facts of the politically induced starvation were concealed except when rare glimpses were seen. Lopes was unjustly accused, victimized and, like Dreyfus, exonerated only after years had passed (although not before his death).

Conclusion

The bedrock of Australian policy in the region for the twenty-four years of the Indonesian occupation of East Timor was the desire to cement a positive relationship with Indonesia and to gain financially from the Timor Sea, to the detriment of both the Timorese people and Australian integrity. That policy generated official Australian responses to massacres, famines, the Timor Sea resources and UN resolutions that were clearly unprincipled and culpable. Australian government publications on the events of the occupation have since sought to minimize negative opinion of Indonesia and Australia. They are 'texts of persecution'. Their claims to balance are undermined by selective and distorted use of evidence in support of Indonesian policy and the maintenance of a relationship beneficial to Australia. These publications, official historical documents of the Commonwealth of Australia, are texts that continue to scapegoat the Timorese people.

6

Collapse and resurgence

The end of the Indonesian occupation

This chapter reflects on influences that contributed to the end of the Indonesian occupation, including political shifts in Australia. Using aspects of Girard's conclusions about violence, it interprets elements of the non-violent responses of the Timorese people to the situation that was engulfing them.

On 30 August 1999, the Timorese people voted for freedom from Indonesian rule with a registered voter turnout of 98.6 per cent. Despite intimidation and violence they delivered the extraordinary result of 78.5 per cent in favour of independence. Once the result of the vote was announced by the UN on 4 September, violence against the population dramatically increased. The unarmed UN staff withdrew to the UN compound in Dili, while Timorese across the districts who had worked for the UN were left to the mercy of the militia. The fury of the Indonesian military and their Timorese proxies resulted in over 1,500 deaths and the decimation of the infrastructure.[1] Killings, looting and burning accompanied the forcible removal of 150,000 people to West Timor. Difficult international diplomacy accelerated, involving Australia and the United States. After weeks of destruction, these negotiations resulted in a UN intervention which took the form of the International Force for East Timor (InterFET), authorized and dispatched under the leadership of Australian major general Peter Cosgrove. InterFET arrived in East Timor on 20 September 1999, three weeks after the ballot, and at its height comprised five thousand Australian troops among eleven thousand from nations across the world. On 25 October, the Indonesian Parliament annulled the 1976 incorporation of East Timor as its 27th Province. The UN then established a Transitional Authority (UNTAET) charged with the task of assisting East Timor towards building itself as a nation.[2]

There were no Australian InterFET deaths as a result of the military aspects of the intervention. Residue of the diplomatic tensions between Australia and

Indonesia remained, including some distrust. However, trade, investment, education and military cooperation continued or soon resumed, and Australian prime ministers and Indonesian presidents subsequently engaged with each other on state visits. The alliance between the governments of the two nations weathered the storms of 1999 and the relationship re-established itself. In contrast, the effects of the occupation on the Timorese people – the victim – were devastating, adding substantially to the numbers of people traumatized, tortured or murdered throughout the previous decades. It is sobering to reflect on the Australian mimetic dependency that continued to exist as the Indonesian regime in East Timor collapsed, and on what influence Australia had on that change.

Political motivations for change

Indonesian relinquishment of control of East Timor arose in association with complex international and internal political realities. The reversal of Indonesian policy precipitated major changes in the bipartisan Australian support of the Indonesian occupation, forcing a complete turnaround in Australian policy. Chief among the causes of the Indonesian change was the demise of the Suharto regime in 1998 in association with the Asian financial crisis. The democratic reforms of Suharto's successor President B. J. Habibie then introduced major changes affecting the status of East Timor. Compliance with Indonesian preferences had been the hallmark of the Australian side of the relationship, which suggests that in whatever way Indonesia chose to deal with East Timor, either by giving special autonomy to the territory or jettisoning it, Australia would feel obliged to agree. The Australian government largely followed Indonesia's lead, a move which, in the end, had the added political benefit of ameliorating a situation which had been causing Australian domestic dissent. (Australian civil society's opposition to government policy is discussed later.) Noting new policy openness in Indonesia under President Habibie, the Australian government was able to shift policy in favour of East Timor while avoiding overt destabilization of its relationship with Indonesia.

Changes in Australian policy

Prime Minister John Howard wrote of his realization early in 1998 that the new president looked on Timor as 'a costly drag'. This realization influenced subsequent coalition policy. Howard was also aware of the growing appetite of the Australian population for a resolution to this problem, noting that the president had a new attitude on an 'old and troubling issue'. He claimed that foreign policy needed to embrace such opportunities and so drive change.[3]

Whether the 'old and troubling issue' would have been addressed by the Australian government had there not been a new Indonesian president with new attitudes is a matter of conjecture. The situation was fraught with political and regional dangers for the Howard government. On the one hand was the desire to continue to build a positive relationship with Indonesia, and on the other the increasing domestic dissent over Timor was offering electoral provocations. The government's key policy objectives in the first part of 1999 regarding East Timor showed that maintaining a positive relationship with Indonesia was paramount. That aim was more important to Australia than the future of East Timor. Any outcomes which put the relationship with Indonesia in jeopardy were to be avoided.[4]

Retaining the advantages of the friendship of Indonesia, however, regardless of Timorese matters, was complicated by the new challenges of relating to a changing government under President Habibie. Additionally, Australia had to consider its relationship with the powerful military bloc which, despite Habibie's reforms, retained many seats in the Indonesian parliament and exerted major influence.[5] In fact, the Australian government's own preference was for East Timor to remain part of Indonesia, a desire expressed as late as 1998–9, proof of official Australian willingness to allow the occupation to continue. This was illustrated by Prime Minister Howard after President Habibie offered an autonomy package to East Timor in July 1998 that signalled an impending change.

Howard wrote to Habibie in December of that year, reiterating Australian support for Indonesia's sovereignty and stating that the interests of all concerned were best served by East Timor remaining part of Indonesia.[6] Howard suggested that Habibie avoid a quick decision on self-determination by arranging for the deferral of a referendum on East Timor's status for many years.[7] It is probable that Howard's mention in the letter of the Matignon Accords in New Caledonia may have implied that Indonesia's occupation of East Timor resembled French colonialism.[8] Thus it could well have been judged by Habibie as an affront to Indonesia's long-claimed opposition to colonial rule and therefore as an insult. One month later, Habibie announced the staggering decision that the Timorese would be offered a choice between autonomy within Indonesia or independence.[9]

In keeping with past practice, Australia attempted to maintain the appearance of support for Indonesia. At the same time, however, it endeavoured to avoid anything that might jeopardize the means by which East Timor could repudiate Indonesia, thus honouring the other prong of the Australian contradictory stand, that of support for Timorese self-determination. Such a position required similar duplicity to that of previous years, where excusing, explaining or ignoring Indonesian practice in East Timor absorbed Australian governments. In some circles, similar positions may be accepted as unavoidable political realities. Where human lives are at stake, however, the raw practice of victim sacrifice by dominant groups should be named for what it is. The Australian contradictions are demonstrated in relation to the attacks by the Indonesians and their militias against independence supporters, where the Australian government repeated excuses for Indonesian actions. Despite overwhelming evidence to the contrary, the Howard government claimed that the continuing violence did not result from official Indonesian or military policy. It was said to be the work of 'rogue elements'.[10] Australian government support for Indonesian policies and actions continued, ensuring that East Timor was consistently seen as an obstacle to the Australia-Indonesia partnership. East Timor was the 'pebble in the shoe',[11] the cause of the crisis and thus the victim.

A major development which influenced government and emboldened the solidarity movement was the reversal of Labor Party policy. Labor changed its position at its National Conference in January 1998 in favour of 'a process of negotiation through which the people of East Timor can exercise their right of self-determination'.[12] Thus the coalition government had to juggle – without bipartisan support – its compromised policy in the face of two challenges: that of the speed of the Indonesian changes with which the Australians officially did not agree, and that of political and popular championing of the Timorese cause that was now supported by the parliamentary opposition. Howard's change of tactic flowed from the need to stay in tandem with movements in Jakarta, accompanied by the realization that Australian bipartisan consensus was collapsing with Labor's increasing agitation regarding East Timor's status.[13]

It is clear that both Prime Minister Howard and Foreign Minister Downer planned their next moves to support East Timor's independence not from principle but to remove the main obstacle to a better relationship with Indonesia.[14] Thus changes of policy did not indicate any fundamental change in the relationship with East Timor. Officially, that relationship continued to be an expression of the Australian dependence on Indonesia, regardless of the reversal of policies required to maintain that dependence. The change in Australian policy was in large part a realpolitik set of decisions made to ensure the continuance of a positive relationship with Indonesia that required deference to the immense Indonesian political changes. The Australian decisions involved calculations that the best way to remain in favour with Indonesia in the long term was to steer alongside the shifting political and economic landscape, even though those shifts included internal Indonesian conflicts, for example, regarding the political influence of the military. The Australian government thus found itself manoeuvring policy in line with the major developments in Indonesia, even though that meant risking short-term relational strain.

It can be seen that the victimage mechanism which had governed the Australia-East Timor relationship for decades was played out to the end. The plight of the victim East Timor was subordinate to the status and prospects of the perpetrators of the violence. The Australian desire had been to secure its relationship with Indonesia, a desire which had required complicity in the invasion and occupation of East Timor. Australia was now embroiled in a complex situation in which, again, it was the Timorese people who suffered. The alignment of Australian policy with that of Indonesia in this massive political switch can be interpreted mimetically. Indonesia's sudden desire, under President Habibie, to rid itself of East Timor drew the classic subject response from Australia, imitation of the desire of the model. That mimetic response was a continuation of the Australian position of the previous twenty-four years: imitation of the Indonesian policy.

In this regard, the insights of Ricardo Roque are instructive. He writes of certain phenomena of mimesis operating in the relationship between colonizer and colonized, using the prior Portuguese administration of East Timor as an example. He describes how the Portuguese incorporated Timorese customs and law into their own systems as a strategy of control. He reads this as the attempt by a colonizer to master the world of the colonized by becoming similar to it, which is an expression of mimesis.[15] Thus the Portuguese forwarded their desire to control the colony by engaging certain actions and behaviours modelled by the Timorese. To a significant extent, Timorese laws and customs thereby became models which the Portuguese imitated for the attainment of the harmony they desired for the colony. There was a reciprocity in this process. On the one hand the Portuguese saw they could incorporate indigenous rules into their colonial justice system, thereby increasing their power.[16] But on the other hand the recognition by the authorities that such incorporation was necessary to maintain good order testifies to a type of control exercised by the Timorese. In Roque's view, the Portuguese assimilation of many Timorese codes of behaviour was a practical admission that territorial control could be exercised only through Portuguese dependence on the Timorese model.

An intriguingly similar mimetic dependence can be identified in the relationship between Australia and Indonesia, even though a strict colonial relationship did not exist. Here, the Indonesians take the role of the model. The incorporation of East Timor, and the policies enacted to retain that control, fed into the overarching desire of Australian governments for regional security and for the profits generated through trade and investment in Indonesia. Just as the Portuguese depended mimetically to a great extent on harnessing and observing Timorese custom for their own ends, so also Australian policies towards East Timor constantly imitated those of Indonesia. As a declining power, Portugal still retained a sense of its status as European and clung to the historical stability and growth afforded by that description, yet the manipulation of Timorese systems was required to retain power in its far-flung outpost. Similarly, Australia, inheriting British structures and claiming associated virtues, found subscription to the policies of Indonesia essential for the maintenance of the trade, investment and security benefits of the association. Roque describes Portugal's approach to Timorese law and custom as the practice of governing others by using those very others' perspectives.[17] The Australian approach to Indonesia during the invasion and occupation can be described as endeavouring to placate its Indonesian neighbours through similarly capturing and upholding their perspectives.

Roque reports that Portuguese administrators even went so far as to recommend that the Portuguese suspend their horror of savage practices and tolerate even the most gross forms of Timorese justice, such as trials and executions of those accused of being witches.[18] In much the same way, the evidence of Indonesian atrocities against the Timorese was ignored, disbelieved or concealed by Australian administrations for decades. Roque sees this as the operation of the mimetic faculty: the powerful human fixation on behaving, and hence even becoming, like someone else.[19]

The question arises as to what extent the Howard government desired a just outcome for East Timor. Publicly, government pronouncements consistently upheld the practice of supporting Indonesia's position. Nevertheless, it is true that in the name of Australia, the Howard government responded to the changing circumstances in Indonesia in a manner which was ultimately positive towards East Timor's prospects of freedom. Such support was viewed by many in Indonesia as unwarranted interference and put some pressure on the relationship, as has been noted. However, there had been no initiative on East Timor's behalf on the part of Australian governments throughout the twenty-four-year occupation, even by way of mild diplomatic challenge, as is clear from official historical documents. Instead, political manoeuvring in the late 1990s was largely in response to changes which the Indonesian administration had itself so unexpectedly set in train.

Timorese inspiration

Alongside the intricate political manoeuvring of regional and world powers another powerful force was exerting influence. The inspiration provided by the Timorese people was a relentless, large-scale and, in the end, irresistible foil to the calculations of the global political chess game. It was characterized by non-violence, lack of revenge and openness to reconciliation. Two reflections flow from consideration of these forces using a Girardian lens. First, the suffering of the Timorese gave them the position of 'judge' of all involved in the historical events. As a paradoxical consequence, the humanity of everyone involved was offered the opportunity to be restored, regardless of their roles. Thus the Australian-Timorese history can be fruitfully understood as one in which the 'forgiving victim' provides a compelling way of interpreting violent relationships. Second, the example of 'positive mimesis' (in Girard's terms) provided by the Timorese posed a challenge which led many Australians to turn towards the victim and so attain a more humble and realistic view of their nation. These reflections will be expanded on in Chapter 7.

The inspiration provided by the Timorese people to the rest of the world was crucial to their eventual freedom. The Timor-Leste Commission for Reception, Truth and Reconciliation (CAVR) Report states that civil society's interest responded to the initiatives of the East Timorese people, not the other way around.[20] The courage of the Timorese people and their political and religious leaders was crucial in providing the leadership which inspired many nations to act.[21] Timorese youth movements worldwide were notable in initiating large, decentralized networks of activists. Particularly after the Santa Cruz massacre of 1991 non-violent international protests, including in Indonesia itself, became formidable.[22] Some of the actions were peaceful sit-ins or protests in the view of visiting dignitaries or in foreign embassies.[23] The leadership of Timorese expatriates contributed significantly to these movements and to the final resolution.

An event consequential to the cooperation between the Timorese and their supporters was the greater accessibility of East Timor from 1989 when

Indonesia considered that the people were sufficiently 'Indonesianized' to allow an opening of the territory.[24] The CAVR Report notes that the following few years saw numerous foreign individuals visiting East Timor, as many as three thousand between 1989 and 1991. They contacted the resistance and gave material support to the people, and as a result of the new flow of information, international interest was rekindled.[25] Far from advancing Indonesia's preferred outcome of wide acceptance of its claims to domination, however, this relative openness provided more evidence of the oppression of the people. The refusal of the Timorese to capitulate ensured that worldwide support, while at first relatively small, was never extinguished and grew solidly in the 1990s. The Timorese people's long years of suffering and their relentless resistance provided the impetus for the stirring of the world's conscience. The situation was seen for the unjust oppression it was, and the people were increasingly recognized as the innocent victims of immoral political alliances and intrigue.

As Indonesia reeled from its political, social and economic upheaval in 1998–9, the Timorese people capitalized on the signals of imminent change. Large peaceful gatherings in East Timor itself in the latter half of 1999 were broadcast widely as the world's media gave more time and space to the Timor question. Danger existed in these displays as Timorese leaders were more easily identified. Religious gatherings too were risky but expressed the unity of the people and contributed to their strength.[26]

Non-violence

One of the most crucial aspects of the Timorese resistance was its non-violent nature. This feature was consistent across the civilian population and lasted throughout the occupation. As the situation became better known, the Timorese non-violent and non-retaliatory stance demonstrated the people's position as innocent victim. In their study *Why Civil Resistance Works*, Chenoweth and Stephan investigate 323 violent and non-violent campaigns between 1900 and 2006, finding that resistance campaigns based on principles of non-violence were nearly twice as successful as those which tolerated violent means.[27] The authors cite the liberation of East Timor as an example.[28] However, they claim that East Timor's non-violent resistance occurred after a failed violent campaign, a futile insurgency.[29] While it is true that the armed Timorese resistance, Falintil, was not successful in military terms, Chenoweth and Stephan's conclusion omits the symbolic role played by those Timorese who remained in the mountains as a fighting force, thus assisting the hope of freedom to inhabit the Timorese imagination. Neither do the authors refer to the extraordinary events of 1999 where, on the advice of the United Nations, Timorese fighters were ordered by their leader Xanana Gusmão to remain in cantonment areas even while they could see the capital Dili burn. Without any means of ascertaining the fate of their loved ones, these soldiers displayed the discipline that allowed the international community to recognize that the violence of 1999 was all coming from the Indonesian military and their militias, and proving that Falintil was not responsible for the conflict.[30]

While violent action was employed by the armed wing of the resistance throughout the oppression, the overall East Timor story remains a significant example of the power of non-violence and even within the armed resistance itself at the climax of Indonesian occupation. Surely one of the proudest claims the Timorese people are able to make is that during the twenty-four-year occupation not a single Indonesian civilian was murdered by a Timorese.[31] This fact takes on extra significance in the light of the official transmigration programme beginning in 1980 through which the government resettled people from densely populated areas of Indonesia, thus increasing the number of Indonesians in East Timor.[32] Explanation of these extraordinary features of the Timorese resistance necessarily entails understanding the intersection between the Christian faith practised by a growing number of Timorese during the occupation, and the dogged resistance to that occupation staged by the Timorese over nearly a quarter of a century. This was expressed through and within the growing Timorese membership of the Catholic Church.[33] It was the church that was able to provide some means of support and protection to help the people confront their terrible losses and the violence which confronted them daily. Christianity in East Timor was of singular importance in the resistance to the occupation.[34]

As the only local institution operating among the Timorese, the Catholic Church was in solidarity with the people, providing physical support and avenues of resistance. Significantly, the church was a primary mainstay of Timorese community, defending and promoting those aspects of culture which go to the heart of identity, particularly language.[35] The church became a major focal point of resistance to the other main institution, the Indonesian military. Refusing to leave the people to the mercies of the invaders by withdrawing to some other-worldly realm, the church endeavoured to support them in their endurance and non-violent patience. In so doing, the church developed an 'ecclesial counter-politics', in William Cavanaugh's words.[36] As a result, people found within the church the depth of meaning which enabled them to unite themselves with the passion and resurrection of Jesus, recognizing themselves as victim with their non-violent risen Lord. In their resistance to oppression the Timorese people imitated Christ. They found strength in the Christian faith which a large proportion of them embraced during the occupation.[37]

Lack of revenge

The non-violent nature of the Timorese resistance was accompanied by an ongoing willingness to forego revenge. While Timorese people have shown little appetite for retaliation against the Indonesian people, the Australian use of Timor for its own protection during World War II and its compliance with the Indonesian occupation did not result in widespread calls for Timorese revenge against Australia. This is not to deny that the Timorese harbour strong feelings about foreign occupiers. It expresses once again the courageously non-violent resistance movement which flowered both within East Timor and among those who had escaped the territory. It was not abuse and threats which the Timorese took to Australian rallies but doves of peace and calls for freedom.

The actions of the Timorese people are all the more remarkable when considering that the international community has not pursued the normal channels of justice that apply in other circumstances.[38] Whether the international and Australian responsibility for the crimes against the Timorese people will be shouldered, and regardless of how much time that may take, Timorese decisions have already had the consequence of absorbing and restricting violence. Given the mimetic nature of humans, Girard maintains it is absolutely necessary not to resist evil with evil.[39] He argues that this highly ethical command indicates the only possible way to break free of the vicious cycle of mimesis and violence.[40] The Timorese people have achieved great success in ensuring that vengeance has been curtailed and that the spiralling nature of revenge and aggression has not been allowed to take control.

The reciprocal nature of revenge exemplifies its mimetic character. The mechanism involves the blaming and punishing of another, with the likely result that the other will retaliate, only to be met by an answering violent response. In regard to East Timor this cycle of revenge has not eventuated. This has occurred not only because of Timor's weak geopolitical position but also because of the hard spiritual lessons learned over twenty-four years of Indonesian occupation, and over four hundred years of the 'benign neglect' of Portuguese colonization. The willingness of the Timorese to suffer in the cause of justice and their unwillingness to avenge themselves were key. This contrasts markedly with the capitulation of nations to violent mimesis which is apparent in history, of which the twentieth century stands as a most devastating example.

Mimetic theory, according to Girard, claims that rather than violence being part of politics, it is politics which is part of violence.[41] It is the endemic nature of violence in the human approach to relationships which is misunderstood, resulting in its constant use. Despite the outcomes of violence over millennia, that is, the deaths and destruction arising from it, the human race has yet to learn that violence begets violence. Summarizing Girard, Hodge notes that political systems have failed to understand the nature of violence as arbitrary, reciprocal and escalating.[42] In his final book Girard describes the ultimate solution to violence: adopting the behaviour recommended by Christ, that is, to abstain completely from retaliation.[43] This was the path taken by the Timorese people in response to the violence of their victimization.

The authority of the victim as judge

According to Girard, the victimization of the innocent is a human construct upon which has been built all religious and cultural systems.[44] His insight that such a basis for human systems is now unveiled as a lie by the Gospel accounts of the death and resurrection of Christ is significant. Acceptance of that recognition requires change in one's perception of the world. If accepted, the criterion for relating to the world can therefore no longer be human institutions and their value judgements but the 'recognition of the innocent victim'. It is indeed momentous to claim that this principle carries greater weight than the authority of political institutions purporting to ensure national security or national interests.

Earlier parts of this book have shown that giving due weight to the moral claim of the victim was a fundamental struggle that occurred in Australia during World War II and over decades of Indonesian occupation. The Australian treatment of the Timorese victim during those periods remains a scar on the psyche of the Australian body politic that has been sought to be suppressed by revisionist histories like those examined earlier. This scar has come about because of the affront that the recognition of the victim represents: it undermines and upends conventional morality, politics and cultural logic. The logic of politics – which generally involves sacrificial judgements to maintain order and security – is thus fundamentally challenged. In effect, Australians are summoned by the history of East Timor. The subpoena must be answered; a judgement is sought. James

Alison refers to the subversion of the idea of 'judgement' throughout the Gospel of John, culminating in the realization that 'it is by being crucified that Jesus is the real judge of his judges'.[45] As a development of this insight, an obscure scriptural debate of little apparent importance provides an entry into reflection on this concept regarding the Australia-East Timor relationship.

At one point in the Greek text of the nineteenth chapter of St John's Gospel a curious enigma occurs. The scene is the judgement seat of Pontius Pilate, the Roman governor. Jesus of Nazareth stands before him, having been scourged and crowned with thorns. The process of unconscious scapegoating is underway, with the political and religious leaders joining with the crowd in baying for the blood of the innocent; a unanimous chorus of condemnation. Even Jesus's companions, infected by the contagion of blame, have denied him and fled.

The text reads: 'Pilate had Jesus brought out, and seated himself on the chair of judgement at a place called the Pavement, in Hebrew Gabbatha' (Jn 19.13). In this text there is a grammatical anomaly concerning the object of the verb 'to sit'. There has been debate over interpretation of this word among a minority of scholars, who point to the possibility of the verb being transitive, so making Jesus the one who is seated. As the syntax is inconclusive, the question arises, 'Does Pilate sit or does he seat Jesus on the judgement seat?'[46] Some scholars suggest that the biblical narrator may have been deliberately ambiguous so that either interpretation of who sat down is possible.[47] Regardless of the cause or intention of the minor grammatical oddity, the irony of the scene suggests a profitable reflection and gives an insight into the meaning of power, authority and judgement. It is linked to Jesus's earlier response (in the same scene) to Pilate's assertion of power over life and death, where Jesus had indicated that authority comes from God. 'You would have no power over me if it had not been given you from above' (Jn 19.11). Thus the whole trial is given a 'cosmic perspective'.[48] Jesus then proceeds to make his own judgement as to the relative guilt of those involved: 'that is why the one who handed me over to you has the greater guilt' (Jn 19.11b). Jesus, the defendant and witness, indicates where the ultimate authority to judge lies in this cosmic drama. At the same time, he is also judge and brings down a verdict of guilty on the whole process.[49]

This disputed minor point serves to illustrate the import of the full Gospel narrative of the passion and death of Jesus Christ: the hasty trial of a perceived rabble-rouser in a provincial backwater is inverted to reveal its universal application as the trial of the innocent victim who reveals the innocence of all victims. As Girard states, 'The protective system of scapegoats is finally destroyed by the Crucifixion narratives as they reveal Jesus' innocence, and, little by little, that of all analogous victims.'[50] A single verb ironically contributes to the larger and unique perspective that the accused victim, Jesus, is divine judge and, from his place as victim, passes judgement on the court.

However unlikely the moment, this incongruity between victim and judge throws light on the meaning of the Timorese people's place in the relationship with Australians. In this moment of recognition, the Timorese as victims ironically came to be the judges of Australia's complicity with Indonesian persecution. Their claim on the conscience of Australians challenged the political mythology that led Australians to believe that supporting Indonesia was the only politically effective and expedient action to pursue. Occupying the place of the victim, they possessed the credibility to be able to see through the violence which had decimated them and which unveiled the inhumanity of their persecutors. The unique perspective of the 'victim' was theirs.[51] Through the magnitude of their suffering the Timorese people took their place on the judgement seat, with complete authority to judge.

The Timorese people were sacrificed to their neighbours' concerns which were considered greater than their lives or those of their children. Throughout the invasions by Australia, Japan and Indonesia and subsequent occupations they were ignored insofar as their desires or interests were concerned. They were the subject of intense speculation only insofar as their geographical placement afforded their neighbours some material prospects or strategic advantage. They were treated as pawns in political games of rivalry and the pursuit of security. Their contributions to the welfare and success of Australian soldiers in World War II remain treated with an official silence bordering on contempt. Their Indonesian murderers were cajoled and fawned upon. They were abandoned, excluded, belittled or ignored. They suffered the classic treatment meted out to scapegoats, and for decades 'lacked a champion'.[52] Having done nothing to merit such treatment, the Timorese people displayed the most important feature which marks the scapegoat: innocence. Such treatment gives to the victim the status of 'judge' of those whose insecurity and fear arise out of the mimetic dependency inherent in the brutal game of international politics. As Alison states, it is the very position of the victim *as victim* that bestows the authority to judge.[53]

Timorese forgiveness – expressions and criticisms

But what does this judgement consist of? This is the most pertinent, demanding and consequential question. Alison argues that it is the approach of the 'forgiving' victim towards the perpetrator that is the ultimate judgement. The status of East Timor as a victim of larger powers – but one which has demonstrated forgiveness – is rare in the world arena. Reflection on the Timorese response as the 'forgiving victim' is provocative.

As discussed, the forgiveness demonstrated by the Timorese was specifically expressed in their non-violent resistance and lack of revenge. The scapegoating of East Timor would appear to be a minefield for revenge, yet the general tendency in the Timorese people has been to demonstrate a willingness to forego retaliatory violence. The Timorese forgiveness can profitably be seen not only as an alternative to the non-existent application of justice to the criminality they endured but also as a response of an entirely different order.[54] This distinctive response received the commentary of Sergio Vieira de Mello, the UN special representative during East Timor's transitional administration (1999–2002). António Guterres, who assumed the role of secretary general of the United Nations in 2016, stated in 2010 that de Mello had marvelled to him at the capacity of the Timorese people to forgive and had commented that he found it the most surprising aspect of the whole situation. He told Guterres that despite having been witness to a number of global conflicts, he had never seen anything like it elsewhere.[55]

The orientation towards forgiveness evident in the attitudes of the Timorese people has been demonstrated by significant leaders. Xanana Gusmão and José Ramos-Horta – both of whom have had the roles of president and prime minister – have introduced concepts of forgiveness into the political dilemmas associated with their recent history.[56] They have advocated publicly for amnesties and spoken of reconciliation.[57] They have presented concepts of reconciliation and forgiveness, rather than retributive and adversarial justice, for the restoration of peace and harmony and for assisting the people to embrace once again their own dignity and identity.

It is clear that this immensely difficult task has serious risks. Where a wrongdoer refuses to acknowledge the wrong done, the effort to forgive can seem useless.[58] It can also be interpreted as a forgetfulness, even a betrayal of the past and of those who suffered.[59] While acknowledging these threats, Robert Schreiter discusses forgiveness as both a gradual process and a decision.[60] Forgiveness can hardly be an immediate response to violence, but the arrival at a decision to forgive signals that the violated one intends not to be controlled by the past. 'Forgiveness is an act of freedom.'[61]

This aspect of forgiveness was captured in a 2006 film made about the life of Xanana Gusmão who became president upon the restoration of Timor-Leste as a democratic republic in 2002. In the film, an attitude of openness and willingness to forgive is shown in his reception of Eurico Guterres, the notorious leader of the Aitarak militia, whose trial in Indonesia was shown footage of him calling for independence supporters to be killed. Additionally, there were scenes showing Xanana embracing Wiranto, who had been commander of the Indonesian military during the last two years of the occupation. The film also shows Xanana greeting his Indonesian jailers enthusiastically and opening his arms to the Timorese man who betrayed him to the Indonesians in 1992. He speaks poignantly of the power of forgiveness for personal peace of mind and liberation and for release from the desire for revenge.[62]

Both Xanana Gusmão and José Ramos-Horta have spoken of the criticism they have received as a result of their public appeals and personal example that urged the Timorese people to engage in forgiveness for the decades of oppression.[63] The decision to forgive has been described as an effort by Timor-Leste to promote bilateral relations with Indonesia by relinquishing judicial processes.[64] It has been remarked that any accountability which had already been achieved in Timor-Leste was undermined by political decisions such as to commute sentences and release people from prison, putting at risk the rule of law and necessary confidence in the judicial and political systems.[65] Similarly, other criticisms are made of Timor-Leste for not pursuing violators and for granting amnesties in the light of the commitments it undertook in signing all the core UN human right conventions. While realizing the importance of a positive relationship with Indonesia (and indeed Australia), some see the price paid for those relationships being denial of justice for the Timorese victims.[66]

However, the recognition of forgiveness as essential to the future existed not only in the view of the Timorese leaders. The violence in which Timorese was pitted against Timorese occurred during the internal conflicts of 1975. These were exacerbated by accusations of collaboration and in the experience of loss and suffering without redress throughout the occupation. The CAVR Report details the successful Community Reconciliation Program which began to provide avenues for justice and reconciliation soon after the Indonesian withdrawal. Efforts towards the settlement of past divisions and the reintroduction of peace into communities were highly successful.[67]

In order to begin to respond to the violence and trauma of the occupation, many Timorese communities responded with their own efforts at truth, reconciliation and forgiveness. One example was an event at Suai on the Timorese south coast on Christmas Eve 1999, where the residents re-enacted the massacre of 6 September that occurred just after the result of the vote for independence was announced. The central element in the re-enactment was the opportunity for the survivors to tell the victims' story.[68] It was not used as an opportunity to call for vengeance but rather to begin a process of truth-telling and healing. It was an example of Xanana Gusmão's explanation that the Timorese seek reconciliation before justice. While not forgetting the past, reconciliation is seen as pre-eminent. 'We advocate a reconciliation process whereby there is justice but which eschews revenge, resentment or hatred.'[69] Additionally, numerous instances are recounted of Timorese responses to extreme violence which illustrate a general pattern of a forgiving attitude among the people.[70]

This capacity of the Timorese people for forgiveness was acknowledged at the Dili Massacre Commemoration Mass at St Mary's Cathedral, Sydney, on 12 November 2000, in the presence of a Timorese choir that was in Australia at the time. Fr Tony Doherty, then dean of the cathedral, said: 'The response of the Timorese people to violence has been beauty and grace.' This statement was a poetic expression of a major Timorese accomplishment. In saying all this there is no attempt to idealize the Timorese people or to try to give the impression of the existence of an entirely pacific or positive situation. It is clear that there were actions of vengeance after 1999, and there remain long-term effects of trauma and the prevalence of domestic violence, all of which witness to the complex situation that still exists among the Timorese people.[71] However, a formidable array of actions and attitudes of the Timorese people have provided startling contrasts to this legacy. They have already succeeded in the extraordinary achievement of emerging from an unjust and brutal oppression in a forgiving manner, refusing to focus solely on the wrongs done to them. They have sought to embody what Girard has advocated in the conclusion to his book *The Scapegoat*: 'The time has come for us to forgive one another. If we wait any longer there will not be time enough.'[72]

By engaging in a process which values and enacts forgiveness, the Timorese people have given witness to the abstinence from retaliation which Girard sees as the only solution to violence in the world, a violence which if not renounced 'will lead straight to the extinction of all life upon the planet'.[73] Demonstrating in detail the disastrous nature of human violence in modernity, Girard identifies the 'escalation to extremes' as the tendency for human beings to imitate the violence with which they are confronted, resulting in more and more violence.[74] What the Timorese have done by refusing to retaliate and choosing to forgive is to go against this violent trend. Despite some mixed results following independence, they have attempted to release themselves from retaliatory violence and its consequences with singular success and in so doing have become a unique exemplar for humanity.

Reconciliation

A further reality to be explored in relation to the forgiveness demonstrated by the Timorese people is that of reconciliation, a possible outcome of forgiveness. Reconciliation can occur as a result of the forgiving victim's capacity and willingness to restore not only their own humanity but also that of their persecutors.[75] Examples of attempts to incorporate forgiveness as a major element towards restoring harmony through reconciliation are discussed by Robert Schreiter concerning South Africa at the end of the apartheid era. In Schreiter's experience, forgiveness given freely is an invitation for the wrongdoer to repent so that a new relationship can emerge. The reconciliation needed to restore harmony is not a substitute for liberation from the evil done; rather, it requires an end to the oppression.[76] It cannot be done in haste or by glossing over the enormity of the violence. There must be recognition that perpetrators of evil usually whitewash their actions in order to evade the consequences.[77] Neither does true reconciliation resemble a programme of mediation or negotiation or of other tools of management.[78] In the Christian understanding, reconciliation is essentially a gift – firstly a gift of God – whereby the victim is being brought by God to forgive. In God a victim can discover the existence of his or her capacity to forgive and the willingness of God to enable such forgiveness.

Robert Schreiter writes compellingly of this reality. The victim suffers, the perpetrator tortures, the life of each is utterly changed. The violence robs both the victim and the perpetrator of a measure of his or her humanity. Only the victim has the power to forgive in this situation; the evildoer cannot forgive themselves. Forgiveness of the perpetrator does not guarantee a change of heart – but neither does punishment. The extreme difficulty of forgiveness appears beyond a human being, yet it can happen. If the victim can allow the grace of God into their abused and shattered life, they can find the capacity to forgive and not take revenge. In response to this, the perpetrator of the evil has the opportunity to repent, and if that opportunity is accepted, he or she draws on the capacity to begin rebuilding his or her own humanity.[79]

Thus Schreiter presents the insight that in the process of reconciliation, 'forgiveness precedes repentance'. While people normally expect that evildoers must first repent and make reparation, he states that the true Christian understanding works the other way around. In the realization of God's freely given forgiveness of our own failings and trespasses, we are prompted to repentance.[80] We ourselves cannot earn forgiveness – it is graciously given.[81] However, just as forgiveness cannot be earned, neither can it be required.[82] No one has the right to tell the Timorese people, or anyone else, to forgive. This was compellingly expressed by a religious sister in the documentary *A Hero's Journey* when she stood in the aisle of the church at Suai, still red from the blood of those who had been massacred there in 1999.[83]

Nevertheless, it is this perspective of the 'forgiving victim' that Xanana Gusmão and other Timorese leaders embraced in the aftermath of the oppression. Theirs may have been politically and strategically astute moves, but they were not merely so. Their leadership and example expressed the religious and cultural imagination that looks beyond the endless and self-perpetuating cycle of revenge and leads towards reconciliation. In representing the Timorese people, they evaded the trap into which so many peoples have fallen – that of nourishing past wounds, even to the extent of becoming vengeful perpetrators themselves.

Conclusion

The end of the Indonesian occupation came swiftly. The contradictory policies of Australian governments that juggled obeisance to Indonesian desires while pretending to promote the rights of the Timorese people collapsed as Indonesia itself ejected East Timor from the republic. The effects on the Timorese people of the last weeks of the occupation were devastating, adding to the numbers of people tortured and murdered, traumatized and dispossessed throughout the previous decades.

The recorded actions and sentiments of the Timorese people are evidence of the possibility of human beings resisting oppression and winning freedom through non-violent means. Astoundingly, this triumph is accompanied by the Timorese rejection of retaliation and becoming 'forgiving victims'. Obviously, Timorese society has deep divisions and retains levels of social violence requiring redress and healing. However, the people have demonstrated an ability to forgive that opens the space for reconciliation. That capacity sought to reconcile with their oppressors, including with the Australian government which was complicit during the Indonesian occupation. This willingness to advocate for the truth and seek the good of their oppressors, rather than destroy them, was integral to the Timorese resistance and flowered in the extraordinary inspiration that they offered to the rest of the world.

7

Solidarity and conversion

In the Girardian perspective, the recognition of the basic lie of scapegoating and its associated myths, ancient or modern, can transform perceptions of the self and of the foundations of cultures. Changes in understanding of the bases of these identities and any consequent modification in behaviour constitute the 'conversion' of which Girard writes.

Girard's initial insights into mimetic desire concerned certain novelists who saw that human desires are borrowed from others, leading to rivalry and conflict. He realized that it was growth in the novelists' understanding of themselves which was reflected in later novels. Such perception of mimesis was described by Girard as a 'conversion'.[1] The ability of the great novelists to recognize the previously unconscious influence of relationship, rivalry and conflict in their own mimetic desire indicated a growth in self-knowledge, a reversal of inaccurate notions of themselves, a type of collapse of their prior understanding of themselves as autonomous individuals who possessed control over their object-orientated desires.[2] Girard's insights assist in an understanding of Australian actions from World War II to 1999 as demonstrations of the effects of mimesis on humans. National insecurity and fear in reference to external 'enemies' arose as a result of unhealthy forms of mimetic dependencies on others which entailed the sacrifice of a near neighbour and wartime friend. The unveiling of the suffering victims in East Timor in whose oppression there was Australian complicity gradually brought about an Australian 'conversion' towards the victim.

The events of the late 1990s can be perceived as incorporating an Australian 'conversion' in regard to East Timor that significantly affected changes to official government policy and action. A Girardian interpretation of the relationship at that time reveals the presence of a cardinal insight of mimetic theory, that is, the recognition of the innocence of the victim. An extraordinary political and social transformation was enabled by the perception of a vast number of Australians that the East Timorese nation and people were the persecuted victims of violence – violence which was supported by Australian policy – and were virtuous and even Christ-like in their reactions to such violence. This perception permeated Australian civil society and politics with ever-increasing urgency, motivating and sustaining the advocacy of the solidarity movement that was integral to the eventual success of the Timorese resistance. Application of René Girard's insights to the Australia-East Timor relationship now turns to interpreting the responses of Australian civil society towards the close of the occupation as a type of 'conversion'. The relationship between the official Australian change of policy in the late 1990s that enabled a practical government response, the influence exerted by ordinary Australians on that change and the lack of accountability for the crimes against humanity which had been committed throughout the occupation all invite reflection.

This chapter discusses how Australian civil society both influenced and was affected by events concerning the Timorese people. First, the principled and long-standing efforts of Australian solidarity groups, to which the inspiration provided by the Timorese people was crucial, are considered as part of the international movement of support of East Timor. Second, the advocacy of civil society is seen to have reached a critical mass as the violence against the Timorese people became the focus of media and government attention, revealing the Timorese people as victim, not only of the military regime, but of decades of Australian collusion. Discussion focuses on the influence of civil society on government decisions, concluding that political manoeuvring merged with popular outrage to cause momentous regional change. This indicated a movement towards the victim by the Australian people, and thence government, that contributed to a major change in the relationship with East Timor.

This change provokes important questions: How did an issue which had been of concern to relatively few for many years evolve into a formidable influence on Australian government policy? To what extent did the actions of civil society affect policy? What influence did the Timorese people have on Australians and their nation? How does a Girardian analysis throw light on Australian actions?

Civil society

Support for the Timorese cause – expressed, for example, in levels of dissent concerning the Indonesian occupation – was generated and advanced by the actions of civil society groups and actors who kept the Timorese cause alive in the public imagination through consistent advocacy. Australian solidarity movements were integral to this international civil society movement. Support for the Timorese people took many years to grow and consisted of the efforts of a small number of dedicated citizens across the world who worked to make the suffering of the Timorese people known.[3]

Civil society is the locus and the means by which private individuals and groups promote shared beliefs and interests.[4] Such shared interests can serve the general good or be designed to benefit a minority. These groups can contain a variety of ideological positions, such that they do not necessarily speak with one voice, and indeed, it is the diversity of vision and values in these groups that gives them strength. Of its nature civil society is pluralistic since no one group claims to represent the whole.[5] Sets of shared values give civil society the basic principles which enable people from various geographical and philosophical bases to transcend their limitations for the common good. Motivated by concepts of justice, civil society can exercise the key democratic function of challenging the structures of power, particularly on behalf of those who suffer disadvantage. In the context of shared appreciation of universal human rights, both religious and secular groups and individuals can unite for common purposes. Support for East Timor demonstrated the values of justice, resistance, unity and compassion. The Timor-Leste Commission for Reception, Truth and Reconciliation (CAVR) Report identified particular characteristics of this civil society solidarity, which included non-violence, favouring principle over strategy, cooperating with government and business when appropriate, being non-party-political and welcoming contributions from many people.[6]

International support for East Timor

Civil society's support for East Timor on a small scale existed throughout the occupation, but the 1990s saw an upsurge of concern. The international publicity surrounding the Santa Cruz (Dili) massacre in 1991 brought the issue of Timor forcefully into the public domain. Seminars and conferences linked people from a range of nations who worked together and established solidarity groups to share information and devise strategies for the support of East Timor.[7]

Gatherings of some influential persons continually called on Indonesia to observe the United Nations resolutions on East Timor and challenged governments to cease arms trade with Indonesia. Support groups were established and strengthened in various nations, including Portugal, Britain, the United States, Japan, the Philippines, Canada, New Zealand, Ireland and in Indonesia itself. Amnesty International and other NGOs consistently issued reports about the human rights situation in East Timor, while solidarity groups such as the influential East Timor Action Network (ETAN) continued support for East Timor for decades.[8] In 1994 the Asia-Pacific Coalition for East Timor (APCET) was established, coordinating solidarity across Asia, despite opposition from the Indonesian government and some other ASEAN nations.[9] Importantly, it challenged the notion that East Timor had no support in Asia.[10] Despite limited memberships, networking among such groups increased their effectiveness.

Once the relative openness of East Timor after 1989 allowed the entrance of foreigners, the non-violent resistance of the Timorese became better known. As a result, increasing numbers of people across the world organized to support them and protest against the repressive Indonesian occupation. The growing international support was substantially motivated by the moving evidence of the victimization of the Timorese which gradually began to seep out of the territory.[11] There was also a shift in various governments during the 1990s, particularly as the US administration finally took a sympathetic interest in Timor in the late 1990s, acknowledging its tardiness in providing the leverage which its position in the world could have given had there been the political will.[12]

The terrible spectacle of the 1991 Santa Cruz massacre was a turning point in public consciousness regarding Timor, influencing the international solidarity movement markedly. The filming of the atrocity by Max Stahl was crucial to international understanding of the situation as it was the first time that visual evidence of the Indonesian military oppression victimization of the Timorese people was widely broadcast.[13] The testimony of two American journalists present, Allan Nairn and Amy Goodman, also helped to bring the facts to light.[14] The worldwide transmission of the images of the Timorese fleeing the bullets in the cemetery vividly displayed the victim targeted by the persecutor. The stark horror of the incident recorded on film is a faithful presentation of persecution and attests to the ingenuity of Girard's analysis of the victim mechanism.[15] The subsequent denials and minimization of the massacre were incapable of concealing the truth of the unadorned film – the violent persecution of the victim.

One of the most notable international acts of civil resistance to the violence in East Timor occurred in Britain in 1996, where four women disabled a British Aerospace Hawk aircraft.[16] They prepared their action over months and, after damaging the airplane, they left a statement of opposition to the use of such equipment in East Timor, providing a video of the bombing of Timorese villages using British-made aircraft and weapons. They then surrendered to the authorities. Significantly, at their trial they were found not guilty, as their intention in destroying property was to prevent worse destruction. This incident and trial again showed the intensifying recognition of East Timor as the victim of powerful forces, particularly among Western nations. Describing civil society's contributions to the resolution of the conflict at the independence celebrations in May 2002 in Dili, the UN secretary general Kofi Annan stated that its support was critical.[17]

The culmination of the involvement of international civil society was seen in the oversight of the UN-sponsored ballot undertaken by nearly 2,300 observers, the majority from non-government organizations. The CAVR Report notes that they stood for a great many citizens from numerous countries who saw in the ballot the outcome of the Timorese people's epic struggle that they had supported. The ballot demonstrated to all 'the importance and capacity of principled people's power in world affairs'.[18]

The growing international consensus on the status of East Timor testified to the increasing triumph of the principle of the innocence of the victim. Girard contrasts the present-day preoccupation with victims with the disregard towards them detected in ancient times:

> Our society is the most preoccupied with victims of any that ever was. Even if it is insincere, a big show, the phenomenon has no precedent ... Examine ancient sources, inquire everywhere, dig up the corners of the planet, and you will not find anything anywhere that even remotely resembles our modern concern for victims. The China of the Mandarins, the Japan of the samurai, the Hindus, the pre-Columbian societies, Athens, republican or imperial Rome – none of these were worried in the least little bit about victims, whom they sacrificed without number to their gods, to the honour of the homeland, to the ambition of conquerors, small or great.[19]

It is true, states Girard, that the modern world makes more victims than ever before, but at the same time it is one that saves more victims than ever before.[20] He attributes the solicitude for victims to the dawning realization of the innocence of the scapegoat. For Girard, this 'timeless moral imperative' arose from the Gospel.[21] It is universal, even if often observed in the breach. It is unrelenting, if gradual. It was evident in the response of so many people worldwide to the victim, East Timor.

Australian solidarity

While part of the international movement of solidarity, Australian support of East Timor took on a particular significance and tone compared to that of other nations, especially given its proximity and historical connections to East Timor.

The Australian people are forever marked by the fact that their governments' involvement had contributed to the widespread death and suffering of the Timorese people in two different historical eras. The realization that tens of thousands of Timorese died as a result of their harbouring of a few hundred Australian soldiers during World War II was, and remains, a heartfelt and singularly poignant element which can evoke feelings of shame and guilt. Understandably, the subsequent complicity of Australian governments in the Indonesian invasion and occupation were interpreted by many as a complete betrayal of proven friends. A growing number of Australians therefore felt an unparalleled responsibility towards the Timorese people. This was highlighted by the solidarity movement and was an ongoing point of sensitivity, as evidenced by the protests of 1990s in favour of the Timorese.

The shared history of the two peoples motivated increasing numbers of Australians to take the Timorese situation to heart. Many personal links were established between Australians and Timorese, including the almost ten thousand people born in East Timor who were living in Australia towards the end of the 1990s. Almost all of those had escaped from the Indonesian regime.[22] With such a strong Timorese presence in the community, Australians had further cause to play a prominent role among the international supporters of East Timor and rose to the occasion. The CAVR Report states that Australia was 'the principal centre of international civil society support' at the time of the invasion.[23]

Thus, the gradual yet relentless appreciation of the revelation of the victim mechanism influenced Australians regarding East Timor. Political bipartisanship and public apathy could not withstand the truth of the scapegoat and fell away as the collective awareness of the victim grew. A singular example of an Australian 'false imaginary' was revealed.[24] The hidden stories of Timorese heroism on behalf of Australian soldiers enthralled new audiences. The Balibó Five atrocity was recalled with frustration and anger and the invasion and occupation found publicity again. Australians were once more faced with episodes showing their nation as a false friend rather than as the champion of the underdog. Some of the courageous and compassionate actions arising from that realization are now briefly described.

Solidarity groups

Of the dozens of solidarity groups operating in Australia during the occupation, there were some that were specifically formed to address the East Timor situation, while others were existing associations that took up the East Timor cause, in keeping with their rationale.[25]

The people involved were characterized by their determination to uphold the right to self-determination of the Timorese people and raise awareness of the unjust situation in Timor. The cause demonstrated that people could work with others across cultural, political and religious divides for a greater good. Non-violence was taken as a given.

Solidarity groups emerged from different experiences and backgrounds, demonstrating the broad nature of the movement. An important group was the 2/2 Commando Association. Remembering the loyal service of the Timorese people towards them in 1942, its members worked to support the people materially and advocate for justice. Another was the Australia-East Timor Association (AETA) which was formed in 1974 to support self-determination for East Timor. Active in Melbourne and Sydney, its members lobbied governments on behalf of the Timorese people for decades. Additionally, certain trade unions lent valuable and consistent support, and many other groups continually expressed concern about Australian policy.[26] A variety of other partnerships and circles across Australia established themselves as years passed, also calling for justice and providing succour.[27] Some of the associations continued for years, while upon independence others ceased operation or were subsumed into other groups.

Those who were members of such groups and supported East Timor reflected the diversity of Australian society: activists, teachers, taxi drivers, nuns, academics, doctors, journalists, homemakers, bishops, aid workers, human rights advocates, lawyers, mums and dads, priests, nurses, politicians, dentists, ministers, trade unionists, students, soldiers and others. A number of church groups across the country used their structures effectively to educate Australians and support the Timorese. The strength of all these advocates flowed from involvement in a variety of ways on a diversity of fronts, many networking and lobbying in Australia and internationally.[28] Compassion towards the victim was expressed particularly through advocacy for justice, practical aid and efforts to make the situation known to the outside world.

Advocacy

The support groups across Australia worked diligently to influence political decisions relating to the Timor question during the occupation. Letters to newspapers strongly criticized government policy from the beginning. Four returned soldiers of the 2/2 Commandos wrote to the *Sydney Morning Herald* a few months before the invasion in 1975 expressing their grave concern at the events unfolding in Portuguese Timor, fearful that Australia would 'turn tail and allow avoidable disaster to occur'.[29] Similar opposition to government policies continued to be expressed throughout the next quarter century. Articles for newspapers and journals, and the production of newsletters and periodicals became sources of information and education for sections of the community, although their pursuit by the large mainstream media outlets was generally inadequate to the situation. Access to information increased in the 1990s and significant materials were published by organizations such as the Melbourne-based East Timor Human Rights Centre, Oxfam, Caritas Australia, AETA, the East Timor Relief Association (ETRA), Minority Rights Groups International and Diocesan Catholic Commissions for Justice and Peace. Support groups also lobbied politicians and church leaders. These and other groups developed opportunities for public speaking at schools, church and civic groups, service clubs and rallies to raise awareness. Particularly towards the end of the Indonesian regime they were involved in large demonstrations, marches, prayer vigils and services.

A number of individuals were outstanding in their support during the occupation years, only a few of whom are mentioned here. One covertly entered the territory to interview people, including Timorese resistance fighters.[30] The opposition of others to the Australian government made them subjects of Australian Security Intelligence Organisation (ASIO) surveillance.[31] Moreover, members of the families of the Balibó Five mounted consistent advocacy on behalf of the Timorese and against the Indonesian invasion and occupation, which gave Australians their own collective connection to the destruction of life in Timor.[32]

Welfare and aid

As well as advocacy, the material needs of the Timorese people were of concern to their supporters. Among the first examples of solidarity was that undertaken by the Australian Council for Overseas Aid (ACFOA) which negotiated shipments of food aid to the territory some days before the invasion.[33] Church agencies such as Catholics in Coalition for Justice and Peace (CCJP) gained valuable information through their networks and disseminated it to raise awareness. Difficulty of access to the territory after the invasion prevented sustained welfare projects, as the whole of East Timor was closed to the world for fourteen years from 1975.[34]

Despite this, a small band of activists, accompanied by a returned soldier of the 2/2 Independent Company, attempted to get food and supplies into East Timor in the early years of the occupation. A customs vessel intercepted them in September 1976, and they were found guilty of attempting to take guns and drugs into East Timor. One described the guns as 'four Darwin-registered shotguns' while the drugs consisted of Vegemite and a large amount of the antimalarial Camoquin, paid for by Community Aid Abroad. Malcolm Fraser was the prime minister at the time and personally ordered that charges be laid.[35] International assistance was given for a time when news of the famines of the late 1970s was broadcast, but the process was compromised as the Indonesian military controlled distribution. The 1990s saw greater opportunity to provide material assistance, and especially after independence some Australian groups implemented beneficial programmes, many of which continued for years. Such assistance paved the way for current focused programmes of support in which Australians continue to engage with Timorese partners through official aid channels and local government, NGOs and civic and church groups.

Although Australian governments began to contribute to the Timorese people's welfare after the referendum and independence, the most critical Australian assistance to the Timorese population was provided when they needed it most, that is, during the occupation. It was civil society which provided that inadequate but heartfelt succour, through personal support, political advocacy and welfare. Australian citizens cooperated to alleviate human suffering and attempted to educate others as to the injustice of the situation but were relatively ineffective in the face of the blanket control of the Indonesian regime. Significantly, they conducted their advocacy in defiance of Australian governments.

Communications

Alongside material support and agitation for justice, a courageous Australian civilian communications effort occurred early in the occupation. A few staunch trade unionists, a parliamentarian and a couple of other intrepid Australians (including one who had tried to deliver food in 1976) assisted the Timorese by receiving and transmitting FRETILIN (*Frente Revolucionária de Timor-Leste Independente* or Revolutionary Front for an Independent East Timor) radio messages. This communication was the Timorese resistance's only link to the outside world, as at that time the Indonesian military prevented entry into and departure from the territory. The broadcasts from the mountains of Timor reached Darwin via a radio with two crystal-controlled frequencies, one for reception and another for a two-way link.[36] The Timorese resistance was thus able to appeal for support and describe the deteriorating situation under Indonesian rule. These 'Radio Maubere' messages were relayed for two years to FRETILIN members internationally, as well as to the United Nations, the media, other support groups and governments.[37] Although members of the public came to listen to the broadcasts, including a Catholic bishop, a future governor general, various Darwin residents and some Timorese people, support was not forthcoming from visitors in positions of power.[38]

In 1976 the Australian government began to try to seize the privately owned equipment. The activists countered their few successes by replacing the transmitter and continuing to send abroad the reports of the people's situation, for two years evading Australian authorities to maintain the links with the suffering Timorese. The Indonesian military then gained control of the Timorese end of the radio link in 1978, and apart from a brief

Figure 7 Laurentino Pires and Rob Wesley-Smith speaking to Timorese resistance via 'Radio Maubere', late 1975. For three years clandestine radio was the resistance's only means of supplying accurate information to the outside world. Australian authorities managed to seize the equipment twice, but the activists replaced it and continued to relay broadcasts until the Indonesian military gained control of the Timorese end of the link. © Rob Wesley-Smith.

re-establishment in 1985, the valuable support, which allowed the voice of the Timorese people to be heard, ceased.[39] This courageous and sustained effort to make public the dire situation of the Timorese had the effect of providing some information to the outside world but also remains testimony to the lengths to which both Indonesian and Australian authorities were willing to go to conceal the truth.

Solidarity groups and, indeed, the whole Australian population were denied reliable information on the Timor situation not only by being prevented from communicating with those in Timor, for example, via Radio Maubere, but through government silence about the atrocities and destruction to which it was privy as a result of significant technological capabilities.[40] The Australian Broadcasting Corporation, through its avenue Radio Australia, which transmitted beyond Australia, was pressured by government concerning news on East Timor. Ambassador Woolcott told Radio Australia to lessen its coverage of East Timor to reduce offence to Indonesia.[41] The Australian ambassador Thomas Critchley in Jakarta advised that it was better to say on radio 'since East Timor became part of Indonesia' rather than 'the invasion of East Timor'.[42] Clearly, efforts of Australians to assist the Timorese by making the facts of their victimage known were impeded by government pressure. The innocence of the scapegoat was to be concealed at all costs.

Political action and Australian solidarity, 1999

The atrocious situation in East Timor became clearer internationally during the 1990s, and the conversion towards the victim continued inexorably. All sections of the media became more focused on events in the last terrible months, and the world was thus summoned by verifiable images and texts to witness the suffering of the victim. The dangerous days in September 1999 after the announcement of the outcome of the UN-administered ballot dominated news and commentary outlets. Images of the capital burning, footage of people being killed by machete-wielding militia and stories of desperate people escaping to the mountains or to the Dili UN compound presented graphically the revenge being meted out to the Timorese who had had the temerity to vote for freedom. There were reports of the displacement at gunpoint of over one hundred thousand people from Dili across the border into camps in West Timor.

Figure 8 Timorese students at a rally in Dili in June 1998. Walk-outs from universities and schools in the latter part of the occupation were a formidable means of resistance showing the Timorese people's determination to be free. Photographer: Charles Dharapak © AAP.

Members of the public took to the letters' pages of both conservative and liberal newspapers to express their increasing concern as well as their recognition of the culpability that had played on the Australian conscience for years. On Tuesday, 7 September 1999, the Murdoch newspaper the *Australian* ran eleven letters with the headline 'Time to Get Tough with Indonesia'.[43] On the same day, Fairfax's *Sydney Morning Herald* published twenty-four letters under the heading 'Act to Stop the Slaughter'.[44] Many letters called for the Australian government to intervene militarily while a few opposed that view. Most letters placed the responsibility for the deaths in Timor onto the Indonesian military and accused the Australian government of cowardice and complicity not only in the wake of the referendum vote but throughout the occupation. Widespread voice was thus given to the case which the solidarity movement had kept alive for decades.

On Monday, 13 September 1999, the *Sydney Morning Herald* in its 'Postscript' column described the public's reaction to the bloodbath in Timor on 4 September when the result of the referendum was announced:

> The letters response to East Timor last week was quite overwhelming. To date there have been something like 1,000 responses. The only way to give vent to the feeling was to run extended sections of letters on the issue every day, including today.
>
> Readers were shocked, angered, saddened, appalled by the terrible, terrible story. But what was almost palpable was the frustration and impotence expressed by so many. Correspondents wanted something, anything, done to relieve the suffering they were exposed to through daily news reports from Dili. And there appeared nothing much they could do at all. Letters attacked the Government, specifically the Prime Minister and the Foreign Minister, for what the writers saw as hand-wringing inaction. Others concurred with their caution and restraint ... But what angered readers most, it seemed, were the policies and the politicians whom they saw responsible for a quarter of a century of 'appeasement' that they saw as leading to the events of today.[45]

The extremity of the Australian response was reported similarly through all major media outlets, indicating that the media's usual political leanings were put aside in deference to the unparalleled surge of feeling for the Timorese. The moral and political superiority of the victim over all other considerations was thus exemplified. On 9 September 1999, the *Australian* printed a list of actions by which some Australians across the nation expressed their anger and frustration at the carnage. It included a petition from prominent institutions calling for an armed peacekeeping force; damage to the Perth Indonesian consulate requiring police guard; graffiti on the Melbourne Indonesian consulate; protesters on the streets in Melbourne, demonstrations in Darwin with flag burning; invasion of the Department of Foreign Affairs and Trade (DFAT) offices in Brisbane; plans for a national day of protest; trade union actions disrupting movements of goods by sea and air, and delaying of passengers; and plans to ban Indonesian goods.[46] A photograph of the words 'Shame Australia!! Shame' written on the front of Parliament House Canberra appears in the newspaper.[47] Interestingly, information on rallies and prayer services in every capital city is given, as well as the contact information for protest to the Indonesian president, heads of Indonesian military and the secretary general of the United Nations, indicating that the media had taken an unprecedented role in supporting civil society efforts.[48]

Girard's notion of the concern for the innocent victim was thus on widespread and passionate display during September 1999. The influence exerted by the Timorese people's faith, courage and non-violence was demonstrated vividly as the popular Australian support for them grew. An essential stimulus for this response was the increased access of the population to information concerning the situation. The visual and descriptive accounts of the atrocities being visited on the Timorese introduced a relatively new reality: access of the Australian nation to factual information about what was happening. As the extremity of Timorese suffering was more widely seen, Australians responded with anguish. The moral imperative of responding to the suffering of the victim was coupled with the sense of responsibility arising from the historical relationship with East Timor, particularly the memories of Timorese service and loyalty in World War II, the resentment at the unresolved Balibó Five question and the shame of the unacknowledged betrayal of Timor since the invasion. Australian feelings of guilt at the injustices brought upon the victim enabled the population to identify the perpetrators of the scapegoating, and they denounced their government accordingly. The Australian people thus made the choice of standing with the victim rather than engaging in forms of vacillation or apathy which would have again rendered them as part of a persecuting mob.[49]

As a powerful institution within Australian civil society, one with fundamental international bonds and natural religious affiliation with the Timorese people, the Catholic Church played a major role in the fortunes of East Timor in the form of two dimensions that operated within it. In each of the church sections of hierarchy and laity there were people who championed the cause of the Timorese people and those who did not. These differing responses were significantly affected by the political and philosophical influence of communism and the role it played in East Timor's fortunes. In this regard, the Australian Catholic Church's overall response resembled that of others worldwide: resolute and courageous in some quarters, suspicious and tardy in others. As Patrick Smythe so poignantly reports, it was the silence of many in the international church which caused so much grief to the suffering Timorese. They described it as 'the heaviest blow'.[50] Nonetheless, the strength of the church's relationship with East Timor provided it with particular opportunities and responsibilities towards the people, and it made significant contributions to the success of the civil society movement of support.

Figure 9 Various religious sisters at a demonstration in support of East Timor on 11 September 1999, including Tess Ward OLSH, Rosita Kiss RSJ, Therese Carroll RSJ and Irene Macinante RSJ. All sections of Australian society were represented in actions supporting the Timorese people as the occupation collapsed. Private collection.

Convergence of the political and the moral

Critical mass

The climax of the turning towards the innocent victim was seen in ordinary people's determined championing of the Timorese people and the heightening of public outrage through the increased publicity in the late 1990s. While the numbers of Australians who properly understood the Timorese story had remained relatively low over the years, those who had awareness were often highly motivated, enabling them to respond swiftly and with credibility at moments of crisis, particularly during the events of 1999.

The consistent claims of activists of the brutality of the repression were revealed in 1999 as credible, leading to an increase in the numbers of those repudiating the treatment of the Timorese and critical of government policy. The 'tipping point' was finally reached. Such a watershed moment occurs when the opinion of an unyielding and consistent minority overrides an initial majority opinion.[51] Studies propose that when 10 per cent of a population are committed to a cause and are persuasive and invulnerable to opposing views, they form a critical mass which permeates the whole, contributing to major change.[52] Thus, influenced by a cohort of persistent activists and armed with ever-increasing information, the numbers supporting the Timorese cause grew exponentially. The phenomenon of 'courage breeding courage' was evident, a process particularly compelling to witness when those engaging in acts of solidarity were very ordinary people, usually described as law-abiding, even conformist.[53] In government circles it was believed that 90 per cent of Australians judged that Australia had done the wrong thing by the Timorese people.[54] Alexander Downer himself stated that during his time as foreign minister no other foreign policy issue had captured the interest of the Australian public more than East Timor.[55]

Accounting for change – political or popular pressure?

There are various assessments of the influence of popular pressure on the Australian government's decision to intervene in East Timor in 1999, even so far as to lead the military International Force for East Timor (InterFET) in the September of that year. Some commentators see government action arising primarily from public pressure while others discount such influence. Some believe that the decision to send in Australian troops was a result of massive protests.[56] Others believe that Australian involvement in favour of East Timor independence lacked the strength to force a change of policy, given Howard's demonstrated ability to withstand public opinion.[57] The example of the 2003 public opposition to the invasion of Iraq is cited, which saw not tens of thousands, as with East Timor, but hundreds of thousands of Australians taking to the streets in vociferous but ineffectual condemnation of going to war.[58]

Nevertheless, it remains true that the nearly unanimous support for East Timor – in the midst of overwhelming violence in East Timor in September 1999 – demonstrated the Australian population's clear identification of the Timorese as innocent victims who deserved liberation. This unprecedented upsurge of dissent certainly influenced the government as it scrambled to support Indonesia by complying with its policy reversal on East Timor.

There are fundamental links between moral motivations for action regarding East Timor and the political motivations already discussed. The international intervention, including by Australia, is seen as resulting from an unusual alignment of events.[59] Indonesia's financial collapse in the late 1990s and heightened dependence on international agencies was coupled with the end of the long Suharto era and the weakening of the military hold on Indonesian institutions and agencies. These developments influenced the change of policy on East Timor in Indonesia and, as a result, in Australia. In addition, the presence of many journalists and observers witnessing the mayhem after the 1999 ballot was crucial in bringing to international attention credible and widespread evidence of what was occurring, thus highlighting the role of civil society actors. It is clear that activists and increasing numbers of ordinary people were among those who strongly influenced the outcome by keeping the media's attention on Timor and agitating for intervention.[60] Pivotal to the intervention was the work of non-government organizations and church networks that influenced their governments, rallying populations around the world, particularly in Canberra and Lisbon.[61] This shows that international solidarity was at least as important as political concerns for the decision to allow the ballot.[62] Also crucial was the courage of the East Timorese people, the personal commitment to the process of UN secretary general Kofi Annan and the fact that Habibie's proposal for a referendum served his desire to win the much needed support of the international community in addressing the mounting Indonesian financial crisis and its effects.[63] The international community's desire to avoid a repeat of the recent humanitarian disasters endured by the innocent victims of Rwanda and Srebrenica was also vital.[64]

The situation in East Timor was indeed a matter of morality to which people worldwide and in Australia responded with courage and compassion, actively affecting government decisions. Yet the view that humanitarian concerns were responsible for moving the people and the government is countered by asking why such concerns did not triumph when they were made known in previous decades.[65] For example, the death toll in East Timor was far greater during the starvation of 1977–9 than in 1999 and was attested by the photographic evidence of journalists.[66] The Santa Cruz massacre of 1991 had been filmed and was seen worldwide, yet that information in itself did not cause sufficient condemnation to bring about change of policy. It can be concluded that the tipping point was reached when the wider geopolitical realities of upheaval and policy change in Indonesia converged with the willingness of the international community to act. Contributing markedly to this climax was the work of civil society through the solidarity movement that prepared the ground for decades for a political response to the suffering of the Timorese people. Together, these finally broke political will and forced change. Moral considerations linked with an uneasy historical conscience, driven by concern for the Timorese as innocent victims, worked with extraordinary geopolitical realities to bring resolution.

Girard's anthropological insights revealed the victim mechanism as the foundation and bulwark of societies. The human capacity to lay the blame for crises on some expendable entity and thus restore a semblance of harmony spawned societies built on victimage, held together by myths of dominance, exceptionalism and otherness. As demonstrated in the case of East Timor, 'the revelation' of the innocence of the victim can have an opposite and unprecedented effect: the capacity to unveil the inherent violence of political power and structures and to bring about unimaginable change.

Australian 'conversion'

Recognizing the global political and economic influences that led to the significant changes in East Timor's fortunes over decades provides a valid but partial understanding of the history of the Australia-Timor relationship. Application of Girard's insights adds a different clarity, by identifying in the Australian response the mimetic components of what Girard calls 'conversion'. James Alison states that an anthropology flowing from an understanding of the force of mimesis is first and foremost an anthropology of conversion.[67]

There are two sides to the conversion process: seeing the victim, and realizing one's part in the scapegoating process. Many Australians embraced this twofold conversion, showing the capacity not only to see the victim but to see through the Australian violence and the cover-ups and lies which supported it. In recognizing that reality, the deficiencies of Australian history and self-appraisal were obvious. Instead of the 'loyal mate' of popular lore, Australians recalled that they had abandoned those who had been loyal to them. The images of courageous battlers and diggers gave way, for a time, to the realization that Australian fear of losing the patronage, security and economic potential of larger powers contributed to the sacrifice of their weaker neighbour. Australian independence was the dream but dependency the reality. In 1998 Hamish McDonald quoted former diplomat Bruce Haigh: 'We think that we're so terrific, but in terms of moral courage inside the bureaucracy … it's non-existent.'[68] In parliamentary

Figure 10 A gathering of two and half decades worth of Australian prime ministers, foreign ministers and other officials. A fine example of one task of a political cartoonist: exhibiting the emperor's new clothes. © Peter Nicholson https://nicholsoncartoons.com.au/.

speeches as Australian InterFET troops entered East Timor a few politicians acknowledged the betrayal, the appeasement, the mistakes and the acquiescence of previous Australian policies.[69]

Australian ignorance of Indonesia, its misplaced trust in America and the underestimation of the East Timor challenge were described as delusional.[70] In turning towards East Timor and recognizing the victim, Australians saw through the violence and knew victim and victimizer more keenly than ever before.

Australians were summoned by the Timorese. We did not see them as they were, as the victims of our fear and insecurity. When we looked at them at all, it was as an obstacle to our self-protective desires, within which we wove an image of ourselves as victim. Because we did not see their face, we could not see our own. We produced the 'false imaginary' of victimhood, nourished by fear and

Figure 11 Australian foreign minister Alexander Downer giving advice to Timorese prime minister Mari Alkatiri in 2004. Much of the Australian political attitude towards East Timor and the United States over decades is depicted here. © Geoff Pryor/The Canberra Times

oblivious of the mimetic desire and rivalry through which we hoped to gain protection, security and wealth. Once the true face of the victim began to be seen, however, the Australian desire for the emergence of its own true self had some space and scope. The conversion entailed in the Australian recognition of the Timorese people as victim expressed itself in the shouldering of responsibility towards them. Countless Australians turned and saw the other, the victim: the tortured man, the raped woman, the fleeing family, the starving child.

On reflection, Girard's mimetic theory has made it possible to see through the violence, but in the process we too have been seen and we have been 'seen through'. Reflection on the Australian contribution to the relationship reveals the ease with which a 'false imaginary' can grow to dominate, ultimately mocking human ideals. The prevalence of the 'romantic lie' in Australian notions of self-identity is stark. Projections of supposed virtue onto a history laden with evidence of self-serving deceit, as demonstrated in the relationship with East Timor, can only be maintained by ever deeper lies, secrecy and denial. However, alongside the tendency to retreat into fanciful notions of blanket excellence is the equally available call to 'conversion'. Australian exemplars of decency, goodness and courage abound. We can choose to be gazed at by the Timorese people – the very ones whom we so often ignored, exploited and victimized. We can choose to be gazed at by them, and changed, converted, if we have the courage. Scrutiny of Australian history regarding East Timor through a Girardian lens proves to be a potent force in determining 'who we might be as much as who we think we were'.[71]

The interpretation of the relationship between Australia and East Timor in accordance with Girard's insights into the victim requires the recognition of one's own 'complicity in the murderous order of the world, and therefore of the degree of one's blindness'.[72] Hence condemnation of the actions of Australian institutions requires one to be aware of one's own complicity as an Australian, a citizen, an elector, a beneficiary of government policies. Consequently, a reality to be considered is the easy willingness of Timorese supporters, including the writer, to point the mimetic finger at others while ignoring or excusing personal lack. Here lies also a means of intense moral scrutiny and honesty for the Timorese themselves as they reflect on their own violence towards each other.[73]

An integral part of 'conversion' is the challenge that the texts of persecution themselves can be read with mercy, sorrow, and forgiveness, rather than accusation and resentment.[74] The very call to show mercy can present problems, however. For if one 'shows mercy' to the Australian texts, is not the culpable manner in which much of the violence is recorded being condoned?[75] In relation to accountability for crimes against humanity, a situation which applies to the Timorese history and to Australia's involvement in it, this is a deeply perplexing question. The application of justice to situations of violence, domestic or national, is humanity's attempt to come to terms with the violence of scapegoating. The gradual understanding of victimization has moved nations to place retributory violence against malefactors within the hands of the state, thus weakening the power of private or random acts of scapegoating, vendettas and rivalries. This can be problematic, however, because of the abuses of state power worldwide. The state reserves to itself the right to commit violence, for example, to declare war or to punish wrongdoers. This very power contains dangerous possibilities, as in certain circumstances states turn on the very people they are established to protect.

The Timorese people experienced many state-based forms of 'justice' in their recent history that were deeply unjust and violent. In this regard it is also obvious that the usual forms of international justice have not eventuated for the Timorese people.[76] The absence of accountability for the crimes against humanity committed against them raises questions not only of justice, but of impunity and its detrimental effects on possible future victims.[77] Many concerned supporters of the Timorese people worldwide remain dismayed at the lack of application of justice as a scandalous affront to those who suffered and died, to the hard-won systems of justice worldwide and to those who supported the pursuit of Timorese freedom. Despite pressure, the UN Security Council decided against establishing an international criminal tribunal, accepting Indonesia's assurances that it would bring any perpetrators to justice.[78] Flawed international investigations, the general unwillingness to risk offending Indonesia and the complaints of activists have, however, coalesced into a vacuum. Among the reports of investigating bodies, the extensive suite of CAVR recommendations alone is practical.[79] The absence of accountability for crimes against the Timorese people exacerbates the victimage mechanism which has governed so much of their recent history. It implies that the truth of the Timorese persecution has not yet been fully acknowledged by those who perpetrated or supported it. The resulting impunity can ultimately lead to a situation in which other victims 'can be exposed to violence without fear of reprisal'.[80] This risks a dangerous situation which elsewhere has all too often been filled by private vengeance.[81]

Despite the injustice, the response to the violence that the Timorese people themselves have applied is mercy. This has opened a space for an alternative form of justice – a properly purified justice – that recognizes the universal claims and rights of the victimized and oppressed. Whatever the inner workings of politics in that movement, the fact remains that mercy and forgiveness rather than revenge and retaliation have characterized the Timorese people's management of their recent history. Violence has not had the last word.

Questions such as those concerning the lack of accountability for gross abuses have no easy answer. Denouncing reprehensible acts rather than attacking (in whatever form) the persons responsible is essential to prevent mimetic retaliation which can only repeat and escalate violence.[82] The Timorese people have manifested themselves as part of the slow, inexorable growth of humanity towards universal mercy, a mercy shown by Christ through the revelation of the scapegoating mechanism.

Struggling with the truth of the victim

The application of mimetic theory to other political and social situations presents other challenges. First, those who see themselves as championing victims can fall into the trap of concealing their own violence, masking it under the language of non-violence and concern for the suffering.[83] It is a subtle temptation in the pursuit of justice for the victim, a temptation which draws one towards making the guilty ones into victims. Having once been found out and blamed as scapegoaters, the hunters can become the hunted.[84] Those wanting to avoid this regression into violence require the conversion that acknowledges the endemic nature of scapegoating in all of humanity. They need to be willing to reflect on their own imitative motivations and take conscious steps to imitate Christ or Christ-like figures. Girard states: 'We have to acknowledge our mimetic nature if we hope to free ourselves of it.'[85]

Second, whilst humanity is more conscious of the process and effects of scapegoating, reversion to mythic narratives still occurs. To our violent political realities lesser entities are continually sacrificed, including other humans. This is described as remythologization, in which mythic self-aggrandizement and exoneration of the powerful is again claimed, at the expense of victims. Some societies express this by weaving mythologies with religious overtones. Others – with Australia as a prime exemplar – endow 'national security' or 'national interest' with an equivalent aura. Regardless of the genesis of such remythologization, the cultural solution to violence that it generates is invariably the use of more violence. Girard declares that we have moved from times of structured warfare to an era of 'security', where we imagine we can deal with disputes and conflicts just as we deal with sickness, that is, with increasingly modern tools.[86] The resolution of conflicts which threaten security remain violent, thus demonstrating that we continue to invite violence into us. We choose this rather than understanding what we actually have the capacity to do: to renounce violence.[87]

It is apparent that national security can become the overarching goal to which all else must be sacrificed. This discourse of security was, of course, the main driver in the Australian complicity with Indonesia's invasion and occupation of East Timor. It was believed that security could only be achieved through relationships gained at the expense of Timor. From the standpoint of the scapegoat mechanism this was true, because rather than seeking for honourable peace between neighbours, Australian governments settled for the unstable, exposed and temporary notion of security that emerges from doctrines of realpolitik. This security was the god of Australian foreign policy to which the Timorese were sacrificed.

The attempt at ancient scapegoating dressed in modern clothes has been demonstrated in the investigation of Australian government historical documents. A record is presented there that displays an unawareness of the depth of Australian dependency on other nations and blindness as to the effects of its actions on the Timorese people. The casting of Australia as the 'saviour' of 1999 while concealing prior complicity in the victimization of

Timor reasserts the myth of fearless, loyal Australians dealing fairly with a regional problem. The forgetfulness of the general Australian population, aided by government reluctance to admit the official scapegoating of the Timorese people, and a media which is often compromised and sometimes malignant, is an attempted remythologization. It may introduce elements of comfort but is incapable of obliterating the extent to which Australia scapegoated the Timorese.

Promotion of the myths that exist in the official Australian documentary record regarding East Timor does not augur well for wider Australian relationships. Resistance to the forgetting and concealment of Australian policy and action in Timorese history is an essential part of the rejection of remythologization. The Timorese saga presents Australians with an opportunity to judge present international policy in the light of past errors. It signals probable effects on other weaker neighbours if fairness, loyalty and independence continue to be claimed as national characteristics without a balanced and honest appraisal of Australian history.

Learning from the Timorese people's anguished historical journey would require that the Australian nation remember truthfully the dire situation of the victim and its complicity with the oppressor until the eleventh hour. It would mean sloughing off its projected caricature: looking good, expecting ovations, but all the while ludicrously oblivious of its dependence on others. It would mean shouldering the responsibilities which genuine relationships demand: truthfulness, honest dealing, recognition of rights, respect. It would require remembering the Timorese as the friends we said we would not forget instead of maintaining chronicles which form an Australian 'romantic lie'. Conversion can be a long process.

'Your friends do not forget you'

Australians and Timorese are neighbours geographically, but history has brought the added depth of friendship. The relationship of 'friend' is crucial in its positive recognition of responsibility towards the other. The extraordinary friendships that exist at grassroots levels demonstrate the best of the Australian responses to the Timorese people. Terry Veling's limpid reflections on Emmanuel Levinas's insights are compelling in regard to the fundamental responsibilities of such fellowship. The face of the neighbour becomes the face of every other. As I face the neighbour, I face the world, and the whole of humanity faces me 'in the eyes that look at me'.[88]

Face to face, relationship is irrevocably established, and in that reality, the mutual relationship arises from which all ethical systems flow.[89] Yet the basis of responsibility is personal. Humanity is continually threatened when this personal focus is concealed or ignored. Collective structures are in constant danger of ignoring the very reasons for their existence, that is, the personal, face-to-face nature of human relationship and responsibility.[90] The reality of the widespread relationships between many Australians and Timorese people is best described as friendship, but true friends are faced with the task of revealing the inner workings of systems which victimize one or other party. This task has been undertaken by many ordinary Australians who worked to erode the structures of oppression and expose their lies.[91]

Failures of our social structures are rightly laid at the door of the human refusal to recognize the basic responsibility inherent in relationship.[92] Girard sees this responsibility in terms of our fundamental connection to and reliance on the 'other' in the formation of our identity.[93] This primary responsibility is exemplified in the history of the relationship with East Timor. Australian actions are answerable to a particular 'other' who been grossly disadvantaged. Such answerability is not general, but particular, and is underscored because of the gaze of East Timor, the eyes that look at us. This book has attempted to see East Timor from an Australian point of view. The process has revealed, however, that the eyes of the Timorese are looking at me, at us. We are faced with the questions of the other, the Timorese people.[94]

Such interrogation examines me and my whole nation. Especially as scapegoat, this Timorese face calls Australians to account. An Australian willingness to be faced by the other introduces elements of the existential conversion which Girard saw as necessary to the realization of the influence of mimeticism.[95] That conversion involves the erosion of the self as rival and the nurturing of the other-centred self, leading to true self-awareness and the embracing of responsibility.[96]

Positive mimesis

Imitating the good

Mimetic theory presents cogent explanations for the rivalry and violence inherent in the scapegoating mechanism, the mimesis which leads to conflict.[97] However, Girard also recognized the reality of human imitation that leads to the flourishing of the good through the formative power of example.[98] Positive mimesis provides the possibility of behaviour that builds community and reins in violence. The non-retaliation and forgiveness of the Timorese towards those who victimized them places them in the position of a model of non-violence and non-revenge to the whole world. They constitute an exception to Girard's lament that 'positive models have become invisible'.[99]

Many Australians have found a positive model in the Timorese people on a number of levels. Apart from non-violence and absence of revenge, the courage of the Timorese during World War II and throughout the occupation is formidable. Similarly, their desire for independence remained, despite the array of measures taken in language, education and culture to 'Indonesianize' them. The Indonesian oppression sought to envelop the Timorese, presenting capitulation to the desires of the regime as the inevitable solution to their suffering. However, the truth of the situation – its injustice – was recognized as the means of this fundamental affront to their identity. Paradoxically, a series of traits often claimed as describing 'Australian' was demonstrated for many years by the Timorese people: courage, loyalty and aspirations to true independence. It is compelling to reflect that in the midst of the challenges that the nation of Australia faced over decades concerning East Timor, it was the Timorese people who reflected to us the bulk of the content of our 'social imaginary'. While many individual Australians showed these same characteristics when championing the Timorese cause, it is difficult to apply them to Australian institutions as a whole in this matter. The documentary record is witness to the fact that such features characterized Timorese actions during the historical events, whereas they cannot be said to describe the Australian part of the narrative. The positive mimetic example of the Timorese provides a model to Australian consciences; it provides a mimetic mirror of the kind of people so many Australians aspire to be.

Conclusion

The main inspiration for the Australian solidarity movement within the worldwide civil society support for East Timor flowed from the Timorese people themselves. The Timorese were seen to be truly innocent victims – both as scapegoats sacrificed for the 'good order' of the Indonesian regime and as morally upright persons who acted peacefully and virtuously against enormous injustice – which served to heighten their appeal to the consciences of Australian citizens. There were years of advocacy on the part of a small but growing number of Australians opposed to the political inertia of successive governments. Then in the wake of the 1999 referendum and its brutal aftermath, there was a huge

Australian outpouring of anger, grief and support of the Timorese. Pressure by individuals and solidarity groups evolved into massive demonstrations across the country, demanding that government do something to prevent the horror which was engulfing the Timorese people. The frustrated impotence of more and more Australians was expressed forcibly in the media and in the streets as the Timorese people were clearly seen for what they were: the victims of powerful, self-interested forces. This increased popular feeling was accompanied by the turnaround of the Australian government as it grappled with the swift changes in regional politics and gave way to a convergence of political and moral realities. The morality of championing the victim was seen for a time as more important than other considerations, leading to influence on a changing political scene which those in power were unable to resist. In its status as innocent victim, East Timor undertook the role of judge – but offered forgiveness as the door to a new relationship with Australia.

Australian civil society's support for the Timorese people at the end of the Indonesian occupation, interpreted through Girard's insights, reveals the influence of the revelation of the innocence of the victim. Greater Australian self-knowledge can arise from the 'conversion' accompanying the recognition of complicity in the oppression of its neighbours. All facets of the perception have come by way of seeing through the window of the inspiration given by the Timorese people, who themselves have seen and experienced 'transcendent violence' but also 'transcendent love'.[100] Exploring the history of the Timorese people in that context may explain their willingness to bestow mercy, however incomplete and halting those efforts may be in the many challenges that face them. In Girard's thought, in seeing and receiving that transcendent love, we begin to know the deception that is human violence.[101] As did Jesus Christ, the Timorese have shown that the only lasting triumph over that deception is mercy: extending forgiveness and friendship to those who caused them suffering.

Afterword

I began this book hoping to be a witness for humanity in the 'mangled mess' of human life as I wrote about two peoples whom I love: the friendly, inscrutable Timorese, and my own sprawling and dogged fellow-Australians. My initial desire was to try to understand why Australia, particularly through successive governments, was complicit in the oppression of the Timorese people. I wanted to understand the flawed political rationales. This journey, using Girard's theories, has shown that by scapegoating East Timor and officially recording events in a way which continued the persecution, governments and sections of society rejected – for notions of Australian security – the Timorese claims to their own identity. Australia thus contributed to immense human suffering, before turning, for one glorious moment, to recognize the Timorese people as the scapegoat.

The discovery of René Girard's mimetic theory has provided a means of understanding why my nation, Australia, has treated East Timor the way it has. The concepts of mimetic rivalry and the victim mechanism have provided ways to approach and understand the forces underlying the way Australian politics contributed to Timor's scapegoating for 'national security'. I have applied Girard's insights into the manufacture of myths and 'texts of persecution' to provide a critique of the Australian historical record around East Timor that challenges the rationales for Australia's actions. Significantly, it is clear that recognition of the victim can generate a reversal of scapegoating – a conversion – which for Australian civil society meant to 'see through violence' and stand in solidarity with the victim.

Three interrelated features of Girard's theses, then, have been used to interpret the relationship between Australia and East Timor: the scapegoated victim, texts of persecution and conversion. These features have been used in a particular way to show that the Timorese were sacrificed by Australia and other world powers. The dynamics of the sacrifice were in some ways peculiar to the particular context of international politics. The instances of violent attacks against the scapegoat were accompanied by decades of repeated and accumulated acts that subjected the Timorese to violence, oppression and marginalization, all of which were tolerated by Australian security policy and alliances. This interpretation, using the new and fresh approach of a Girardian reading of human actions, has provided a way of analysing international politics and relationships amongst nation states, showing how such relationships can involve the sacrifice of weak nations such as East Timor. The book has shown how history and relationships can be interpreted from the lens of the victim and how that perception is necessary to understand how victimization can be overcome through 'conversion'.

However, the experience of 'conversion' carries with it a responsibility of remaining true to the insight, of shouldering the tasks required by the gaining of greater self-knowledge and of nourishing a deeper sense of duty towards those who have suffered. It is axiomatic that once something has been seen, it cannot be unseen. Greater clarity now accompanies the history of the relationship between Australia and East Timor as it continues to be assembled for future generations. That history requires reflection and discernment in pursuit of the truth, particularly about the subsequent association between the two nations in the extraordinary events concerning the resources of the Timor Sea.

Australian policies, decisions and actions regarding the maritime negotiations with Timor-Leste in 2004 pose serious questions. How have Australian governments responded to allegations of espionage? Has Timor-Leste remained a scapegoat of Australia? Are other associated scapegoats apparent? Have there been adverse effects on the Timorese people as a result of the Timor Sea negotiations? Have there been any effects on the concept of Australian 'national security'? Have there been any effects on relationships with other regional neighbours? How have Australian governments managed their responsibilities in relation to their intelligence agencies and the separation of powers? Have official documents been used as 'texts of persecution'? Have these subsequent events undermined the 'conversion' of 1999?

These and other questions summon Australians to set forth once more on the journey to 'conversion' in relation to Timor-Leste. The process entails further scrutiny of history in order to come to a deeper self-knowledge and a more genuine commitment to claimed values, so as to 'determine who we might be as much as who we think we were'.[1]

Appendix: René Girard at a Glance

Scott Cowdell, Chris Fleming and Joel Hodge

Note: Terms in UPPERCASE are defined in the glossary.

René Girard (1923–2015) was a French American thinker and remains an *immortel* of *l'Acadé mie française*. He honed a remarkable account of human culture and religion over fifty years of research across the humanities and social sciences. He began with modern realist fiction in the 1950s to uncover a novel account of human DESIRE as *mimetic* (see MIMETIC DESIRE). He went on to engage with foundational texts in anthropology, sociology and ethnography in the 1960s, venturing a new approach to culture and religion that recalls the socio-psychological phenomenon of esprit de corps, in terms of an ersatz peace that SCAPEGOATING a victim introduces to human communities. He then set out an alternative account of religion, seen to emerge in the Judeo-Christian scriptures.

Human desire, for Girard, is desire 'according to' the desire of another. Our desires, in other words, are borrowed from and stimulated by the desires of others. What Girard terms 'mimetic desire' (or 'triangular desire') means that the *subject* of desire imitates the desire of the *model* of their desire for an *object* of desire (see also MEDIATION). From Shakespeare and Cervantes to the great nineteenth-century novelists (Stendhal, Flaubert, Proust, Dostoevsky), a psychology is revealed in which the mimetic influence of others proves to be the true unconscious. Girard offers his own simplifying account of Freud's major conclusions to demonstrate the power of his approach, while, following Dostoevsky and Nietzsche, he explores various pathologies of the modern self.

These pathologies centre on the distortion of desire into envy and rivalry, in which the subject seeks to acquire the object of desire from the model/rival. The subject risks being *scandalized* by the rival whenever his or her desire becomes a stumbling block to the fulfilment of the subject's desire (see DOUBLING). In such rivalry, the dependence of the subject/self on the other's desire is heightened yet repressed in increasingly unhealthy and obsessive ways, to the point that the object's value decreases as the subject advances in obsessive competition with the model/rival, resulting in the madness described by Dostoevsky and Nietzsche. This pathological stage of MIMESIS is a manifestation of what Girard calls METAPHYSICAL DESIRE, in which the desire for being that underlies mimesis becomes clear. In this stage, the object eventually drops from view altogether and obsession with the model/rival becomes all-consuming. The subject in effect seeks the being of the model/rival. Explicating this state of thraldom allows Girard to theorize what he calls PSEUDO-MASOCHISM and PSEUDO-SADISM, along with self-destructive addictive behaviours, as mimetic phenomena.

Meanwhile, in the social context, the accumulation of mimetic rivalries risks wider mimetic contagion and disorder, threatening social breakdown. Girard argues that the mimetic escalation towards catastrophic violence in the proto-human group is contained by scapegoating, which founds and then maintains human culture. The contagion of mimetic violence comes to be focused on an individual or group arbitrarily chosen by the social whole, becoming a scapegoat upon which social chaos is focused and hence discharged. According to Girard, archaic cultures that manage by these means to survive their own violence show a common pattern in their myths, in which a violent crisis suddenly and miraculously gives way to peace and order. This change occurs as the hostile desires of 'all against all' suddenly become the murderous desires of 'all against one'. Through this victimization, the community returns to peace and to differentiation around the slain victim. This victim is made SACRED and divinized by the mob, which transfers responsibility for the crisis and its resolution onto the victim – the two sides of the sacred (the destructive and the saving) that constitute Girard's original account of Rudolf Otto's *mysterium tremendum et fascinosum*. Religion is the part of culture that emerges from this single-victim mechanism to encode its beneficial effects in PROHIBITION, MYTH and RITUAL.

Girard sees archaic religion emerging naturally in the evolutionary process as a necessary evil, containing rivalry's potentially catastrophic escalation by the memory of primal cathartic violence that scapegoating represents. Rooted in the management of our unfocused and unstable desiring, religion's targeted, culture-founding violence is both recapitulated and revivified through ritual (especially by sacrificial rituals), justified in myth and safeguarded by prohibition and taboo – these latter elements regulate relationships and establish boundaries to avoid further mimetic rivalry and violence.

Yet, in the Judeo-Christian vision that comes to its climax in Jesus, Girard argues that religion overcomes its origins: the innocence of the victim is revealed, the scapegoat mechanism is exposed and human desire is shown to be distorted and diverted from its true source in God the Father's gratuitous and self-giving love. Through analysis of many biblical texts, and especially the Gospels, Girard argues that the biblical revelation can be figured precisely thus: as a revelation from outside conventional human religion and culture that lifts the veil on human violence and distorted desire.

He does this through a distinctive hermeneutical approach that first identifies the common structural characteristics of mythical and biblical stories: (1) the presence of crisis, (2) the identification of a victim, (3) vulnerable characteristics associated with the victim (e.g. disfigurement or disability), (4) the climactic and unanimous violence of SURROGATE VICTIMAGE and (5) the restoration of order and peace that follows this scapegoating violence. Then, on the basis of these structural commonalities, Girard identifies significant differences in the content and trajectory of mythical versus biblical accounts, showing that while archaic myths endorse the violent mob, the biblical narrative reveals and champions the victim's innocence.

In this way, according to Girard, the victim-making engine of all religions and cultures is sabotaged by the Bible, setting history on a secularizing path towards modernity. For Girard, this is Nietzsche's death of God properly understood: the collapse of religion's social function and the release of a dangerous instability evident in today's most pressing global challenges.

Glossary of Key Girardian Terms

Scott Cowdell, Chris Fleming and Joel Hodge

Note: Terms in UPPERCASE are defined within this glossary.

Apocalypse/apocalyptic: Although present in his work on METAPHYSICAL DESIRE from the 1960s onwards, the theme of 'the apocalyptic' assumed increasing importance in Girard's oeuvre. Harking back to the etymology of the Greek term *apokalypsis*, apocalypse concerns the 'disclosure' of something – a 'revelation' or 'unveiling'. The term itself has biblical roots, and Girard's interest in it concerns the revelation of violence. Here Girard emphasizes violence as that which threatens human order and security because of its contagious nature, and he also emphasizes the extent to which this revelation itself further undermines human order and security. That is, the biblical uncovering of human violence – the laying bare of SURROGATE VICTIMAGE – *itself* destabilizes culture and society. By desacralizing the principal mechanism by which humans have attained unanimity and social cohesion – SCAPEGOATING – human communities are thrown into chaos that, in the short and intermediate terms, can exacerbate rather than ameliorate violence. In this situation, Girard argues that the internal logic of mimetic violence plays itself out as the mimetic and contagious nature of violence generates an 'escalation to extremes' that leads to destruction. Although Girard argues that his concept of apocalypse remains utterly faithful to the biblical tradition, it runs counter to a widespread understanding of apocalypse as divine violence against humanity.

Desire: Girard acknowledges that while humans have evolved biological appetites that operate at the level of instinct, it is the further evolved capacity for MIMESIS that most fully accounts for the dynamics of human desiring, whether or not any particular desire builds on or directs a biological appetite.

Doubling: In Girard's schema, conflictual MIMESIS is characterized by 'doubling', which refers to the progressive and mutually reinforcing dedifferentiation of subjects that occurs by virtue of an intensification of mimesis. That is, mimesis encourages, through positive feedback, an increasing symmetry between antagonists, which emerges despite increasing attempts at differentiation; it tends towards the erasure of significant differences between individuals – those differences that mark their socio-psychological identity and position within a particular cultural order.

Mediation: For Girard, whose conception of DESIRE is not object-oriented, desire is always mediated via a third party (a model or mediator) through a process of MIMESIS. There are two primary ways in which such mediation occurs: externally and internally. External mediation (*mediation externe*) occurs where the model or mediator is historically, socially or ontologically distant from the subject such that conflict over the object of desire is precluded. Conversely, internal mediation (*mediation interne*) occurs where the desiring subject's object of desire and their model's object of desire overlap and thereby become a pretext for rivalry or 'conflictual mimesis'. In this instance there is a mutual convergence on a desired object, and the model is designated a 'model-rival' or 'model-obstacle'.

Metaphysical desire:	Metaphysical desire (*le desir de metaphysique*) is an attraction to the very being of a mediator. In metaphysical desire, the object is merely a means by which the desiring subject can attain or absorb the mediator's (imagined) autonomy, uniqueness or spontaneity. Metaphysical desire is particularly evident when the object of desire is honour or prestige directly and not just one of their concrete markers.
Mimesis/mimetic desire:	The idea of 'mimesis' is at the centre of Girard's thinking. The etymology of the term can be traced to ancient Greece (μίμησις; *mimesis*), from μιμεῖσθαι (*mīmeisthai*), 'to imitate', and it has served a variety of purposes in theoretical discourse since at least Aristotle. In Girard's thought it refers to imitative desire (*le desire mimetique*). For Girard, desire is itself imitative: we desire what we desire because we imitate – consciously or not – the desires of others. Girard has called this a 'mimesis of appropriation' (*une mimésis d'appropriation*). The other main area in which Girard sees mimesis operating is in SCAPEGOATING. Here, the form of imitation observed is that of members of a crowd or populace converging around a victim or group of victims. Girard has dubbed this a 'mimesis of accusation' or a 'mimesis of antagonism' (*une mimésis d'antagonisme*). Girard's conception of mimesis can be traced back to his very first work, *Deceit Desire, and the Novel*, where he posits a distinction between novelistic (*romanesque*) versus romantic (*romantique*) works; where the former reveal and demythologize the mimetic nature of social relations, the latter continue to propagate delusions about absolute human spontaneity and originality.
Myth:	Myth is one of the three institutions of the SACRED – along with PROHIBITION and

RITUAL. Myth is pre-eminently concerned with *narrating* the sacred. It is characterized by stories that possess a radically incomplete recollection of cultural degeneration and SURROGATE VICTIMAGE. Like rituals, myths represent stereotypically distorted accounts of both the cultural chaos associated with the sacrificial crisis and the cessation of this crisis through collective violence. Myths typically encode such mis-knowing (*méconnaissance*) by representing a primordial chaos – through, for example, 'natural' and cultural calamities that signify the dissolution of difference, such as plagues or the appearance of warring twins or brothers (such as we see, for instance, in the mythical narrative of Romulus and Remus).

Prohibition: Prohibition is one of the three institutions of the SACRED – along with MYTH and RITUAL. For Girard, the main function of prohibition is to control mimetic contagion and thereby proscribe interpersonal conflict. Religious taboos/prohibitions commonly target mimetic behaviour and the mythical transpositions of that behaviour through representation. For instance, taboos are often focused on things such as behavioural mirroring, 'imitative magic', representational art and the problematic of 'twins'. By targeting these domains, prohibition is best seen as a sacred prophylactic that, although manifesting only dim self-awareness, is preoccupied with the forestalling of rivalry and the dissolution of differences that conflictual reciprocity engenders.

Pseudo-masochism: and pseudo-sadism Pseudo-masochism and pseudo-sadism represent two of the primary poles of psychopathology in Girard's understanding. The prefix 'pseudo' in both cases indicates what deconstructionists would call terms 'under erasure' – terms that are considered necessary but problematic because of their traditional constructions. Here, Girard wants to distance himself from the Freudian conceptions under which the notions of masochism and sadism have been developed while wanting to retain something of their ambience or semantic field. From one perspective, pseudo-masochism can be seen as a kind of METAPHYSICAL DESIRE in extremis. In MIMETIC DESIRE, the prestige of the model is sometimes boosted by his or her seeming indifference towards others. The pseudo-masochist concludes that their rejection by the mediator confirms the mediator's supremacy and the absolute desirability of what the mediator desires. The pseudo-masochist looks for objects whose value is conferred and confirmed by the resistance encountered in attempts to attain them. Where a model serves initially as an obstacle to the consummation of a desire, the pseudo-masochist eventually will seek the obstacle itself – the model is valued because of the obstruction that he or she can provide.

Pseudo-sadism involves what Girard calls a 'dialectical reversal' of pseudo-masochism: where the masochist will seek a mediator who will oppose him or her, the pseudo-sadist seeks masochists for the same end, of turning him or her into a demigod. The sadist seeks to be a mediator for imitators for whom he or she will provide violent opposition and, in so doing, hopes to turn this role of human divinity into a reality. For Freud, such social pathologies are externalizations of internal disquiet; for Girard, these psychopathologies represent the internalization of external social dynamics.

Religion: See the SACRED.

Ritual: Ritual is one of the three institutions of the SACRED – along with PROHIBITION and MYTH. Ritual, along with prohibition, functions to control mimetic behaviour. Both freeze into institutional form an imperfect comprehension of SURROGATE VICTIMAGE; they are distorted recollections of both the cultural chaos associated with a sacrificial crisis and its abatement through SCAPEGOATING. The primary form of ritual is sacrifice, which usually begins with carnivalesque features (masks, intoxication, the theatrical erasure or suspension of normal cultural codes and so on) and concludes with the killing of an animal (or, in the past, a human or group of humans). Ritual is the institution of the sacred that is pre-eminently constituted by a performative restaging of a cultural crisis and its resolution through surrogate victimage, usually by means of a sacrifice.

(The) Sacred: Girard continually emphasizes the connections between religion, social structure and culture, which he sees as holding firm in so-called primitive (or pre-state) cultures, in ancient cultures and even in 'modern' (so-called) secular cultures – although the way these features interconnect and function in each case is importantly different. There are two senses of the sacred (*le sacré*) in Girard's work. The first, evinced in early works such as *Violence and the Sacred*, is that the sacred is the anthropological correlate of the social; further, that violence lies at the basis of the sacred and that the institutions of the sacred – MYTH, RITUAL and PROHIBITION – give institutional form and religious underwriting to the culture-forming power and ambit of human violence.

However, beginning with *Things Hidden since the Foundation of the World*, Girard develops a new conception of the sacred that does not so much overturn as supplement his earlier view. He develops this view by posing the question of how it is that we came to know about the (violent) sacred and its effects. His answer is that this knowledge is the product of the radically desacralizing effect of the Judeo-Christian scriptures, beginning with the psalms, the Joseph story, Job and the Servant Songs of Isaiah and culminating in the Gospel narratives of Jesus's passion.

Girard posits a fundamental distinction between myth and biblical narrative; where the former narrates events structured by SURROGATE VICTIMAGE in a way that legitimizes violence, the latter takes the point of view of the victims of that violence – *thematizes* violence – in a way that undermines its legitimacy. In this sense at least, Girard acknowledges the breakthrough insight of nineteenth-century German philosopher Friedrich Nietzsche (1844–1900), whose antithesis between 'Dionysus' and 'the Crucified' anticipates Girard's thesis in many respects – anthropologically, if not ethically, since Nietzsche repudiates Christian regard for victims in favour of Dionysian excess.

Scapegoating: Girard's use of the term 'scapegoating' (scapegoat; *bouc émissaire*) is consistent in many ways with the common-sense uses of that term: the violent and arbitrary convergence around a victim or group of victims who are seen as uniquely responsible for a particular group's misfortunes. Although scapegoats need not be innocent in any strong sense of that word – that is, utterly blameless – they bear the blame for the social disorder surrounding them out of all proportion to their responsibility. In the *Scapegoat*, Girard argues that scapegoats are (mis)represented in remarkably similar ways – with what Girard calls 'victimary signs' – and so we can see scapegoating in certain texts, even when authors do not see this themselves. Scapegoating is a central feature of SURROGATE VICTIMAGE.

Surrogate victimage: In Girard's thought, 'surrogate victimage' (*mécanisme de la victim é missaire/le mécanisme* *victimaire*) names the principal mechanism by which cultures constitute themselves sacrificially. Where MIMETIC DESIRE denotes those dimensions of imitative behaviour oriented by reference to acts of *appropriation*, surrogate victimage has its basis in an increasingly envious and rivalrous MIMESIS of *accusation*. Surrogate victimage is best encapsulated by reference to a hypothetical scenario where a contagion of rivalrous mimesis has swept through a proto-human milieu and levelled the identities of individuals so that mutual suspicion and enmity become pandemic. In such a situation of pervasive DOUBLING, Girard proposes that what invariably occurs is that an individual or group will emerge that is seen to be different enough by the crowd to polarize it in an escalating mimesis of accusation. In other words, the SCAPEGOAT functions in a socio-psychological sense by reintroducing difference when all other differences or markers of identity are collapsing. The mob polarizes around the scapegoat, who is lynched or banished. (Of course, the persecuting community does not see their victim as a *scapegoat*. Rather they see *themselves* as scapegoats of those they are accusing.) The esprit de corps produced by the lynching or banishment then ends up justifying or legitimating the lynching to the mob, post hoc. This accounts for the origin of the SACRED, according to Girard, as the victim – formerly thought to be the malign source of violent contagion threatening the community – is experienced post mortem as the bringer of a seemingly miraculous order and stability by virtue of his or her murder, which spontaneously quenched the mob's mimetic violence.

Thus, religions begin with the deification of victims. Surrogate victimage is the mechanism that lies behind the primitive religio-cultural nexus, giving rise to MYTH, RITUAL and PROHIBITION – the three institutions of the sacred. Girard thus proposes that conflict rooted in rivalry better explains human violence and conflict than either 'aggression' (the biological/zoological explanation) or 'scarcity' (the economistic explanation).

Notes

Introduction

1 Michele Turner, *Telling East Timor: Personal Testimonies, 1942–1992* (Kensington: New South Wales University Press, 1992).
2 Bernard Collaery, *Oil under Troubled Water: Australia's Timor Sea Intrigue* (Melbourne: Melbourne University Press, 2020).
3 The present Democratic Republic of Timor-Leste was known as 'Portuguese Timor' until Portugal's withdrawal in 1974 and 'East Timor' until 2002. These terms will be used during the relevant periods of time discussed in this book.
4 Charles Taylor, *Modern Social Imaginaries* (Durham: Duke University Press, 2004), 23.
5 René Girard, *I See Satan Fall Like Lightning*, trans. J. G. Williams (Maryknoll, NY: Orbis, 2001), xv.
6 René Girard, *The Scapegoat*, trans. Yvonne Freccero (Baltimore: The Johns Hopkins University Press, 1986), 14–23.
7 Don Greenlees and Robert Garran, *Deliverance: The Inside Story of East Timor's Fight for Freedom* (Crows Nest, NSW: Allen & Unwin, 2002), 111; David Scott, *Last Flight Out of Dili: Memoirs of an Accidental Activist in the Triumph of East Timor* (North Melbourne: Pluto, 2005), 347.
8 René Girard, *Violence and the Sacred*, trans. Patrick Gregory (London: Continuum, 1988), 14.
9 The Timor-Leste Commission for Reception, Truth and Reconciliation (CAVR), *Chega! The Final Report of the Timor-Leste Commission for Reception, Truth and Reconciliation (CAVR)*, 2013, part 6:488, para. 8, http://chegareport.org/Chega%20All%20Volumes.pdf (accessed 26 September 2021).
10 Geoffrey Robinson, *If You Leave Us Here, We Will Die: How Genocide Was Stopped in East Timor* (Princeton, NJ: Princeton University Press, 2010), 230.
11 Jill Jolliffe, *Balibó* (Melbourne: Scribe, 2009); D. Pinch, 'Inquest into the Death of Brian Raymond Peters: Coroner's Report', http://www.etan.org/etanpdf/2007/Peterssinquest1.pdf (accessed 10 May 2020).
12 United Nations, UN General Assembly Votes on East Timor (General Assembly Resolutions 1975–82), http://etan.org/etun/UNvotes.htm (accessed 11 May 2020).
13 Joseph Nevins, *A Not-So-Distant Horror: Mass Violence in East Timor* (Ithaca, NY: Cornell University Press, 2005), 62–4.

14 Ibid., 13; Geoffrey C. Gunn, *Complicity in Genocide: Report to the East Timor 'Truth Commission' on International Actors* (Geoffrey C. Gunn, 2006), 118–26.
15 Girard, *The Scapegoat*, 24–44.
16 René Girard, *Things Hidden since the Foundation of the World* (Stanford, CA: Stanford University Press, 1987), 219.

1 A new way of seeing: Mimetic theory

1 René Girard, *I See Satan Fall Like Lightning*, trans. J. G. Williams (Maryknoll, NY: Orbis, 2001), 10.
2 Gabriel Andrade, 'René Girard', *Internet Encyclopedia of Philosophy*, http://www.iep.utm.edu/girard/#H6 (accessed 10 May 2020).
3 Jeramy Townsley, *René Girard's Theory of Violence, Religion and the Scapegoat* (December 2003), http://www.jeramyt.org/papers/girard.html (accessed 1 October 2017).
4 For example, in psychology (Jean-Michel Oughourlian), business (Peter Thiel), theology (James Alison) and literature (J. M. Coetzee). See Cynthia L. Haven, *Evolution of Desire: A Life of René Girard* (East Lansing: Michigan State University Press, 2018); Scott Cowdell, 'Hard Evidence for Girardian Mimetic Theory? Intersubjectivity and Mirror Neurons', in *Violence, Desire, and the Sacred: Girard's Mimetic Theory across the Disciplines*, ed. Scott Cowdell, Chris Fleming and Joel Hodge (London: Bloomsbury Academic, 2012), 223.
5 Duncan Morrow, 'Terrorism and the Escalation of Violence', in *The Palgrave Handbook of Mimetic Theory and Religion*, ed. James Alison, Wolfgang Palaver et al. (New York: Palgrave Macmillan, 2017), 498.
6 For example, the *Colloquium on Violence and Religion (COV&R)*, the journal *Contagion* and the *Australian Girard Seminar* and its publications.
7 Wolfgang Palaver, *René Girard's Mimetic Theory*, trans. Gabriel Borrud (East Lansing: Michigan State University Press, 2013), 275, 295.
8 Scott M. Thomas, 'Culture, Religion and Violence: René Girard's Mimetic Theory', *Millennium: Journal of International Studies* 43(1) (2014): 326; Nathan Jun, *Toward a Girardian Politics* (Wichita Falls, TX: Midwestern State University, 2007), https://www.researchgate.net/publication/252934438_Toward_a_Girardian_Politics (accessed 20 February 2021); Gil Bailie, *Violence Unveiled: Humanity at the Crossroads* (New York: Crossroad, 1997).
9 René Girard, *Battling to the End: Conversations with Benoît Chantre*, trans. Mary Baker (East Lansing: Michigan State University Press, 2010), 109.

10 Paul Dumouchel, 'A Theory of Everything? A Methodological Tale', in Alison et al., *The Palgrave Handbook of Mimetic Theory and Religion*, 465–6.
11 René Girard, *The Girard Reader*, ed. James G. Williams (New York: Crossroad, 1996), 12.
12 Michael Kirwan, *Discovering Girard* (London: Darton, Longman & Todd, 2004), 48–9; Girard, *The Girard Reader*, 104–6, 107–17.
13 Girard, *I See Satan*, xii; *The Girard Reader*, 216.
14 René Girard, *Violence and the Sacred*, trans. Patrick Gregory (London: Continuum, 1988), 14.
15 Girard, *I See Satan*, 72.
16 Girard, *Battling to the End*, xi.
17 Wolfgang Palaver, 'The Ambiguous Cachet of Victimhood: Elias Canetti's "Religions of Lament" and Abrahamic Monotheism', 5 and 12, https://www.scribd.com/document/110863884/Elias-Canetti-s-Religions-of-Lament (accessed 22 February 2021).
18 René Girard, *The Scapegoat*, trans. Yvonne Freccero (Baltimore: The Johns Hopkins University Press, 1986), 24–44.
19 Ibid., 117, 103; *The Girard Reader*, 262.
20 Canadian Broadcasting Corporation, 'The Scapegoat: René Girard's Anthropology of Violence and Religion', *CBC Ideas Transcripts*, 5–9 March 2001, 21, http://www.radio.cbc.ca/programs/ideas/girard/index.html (accessed 31 January 2020).
21 René Girard, *Things Hidden since the Foundation of the World*, trans. S. Bann and M. Metteer (Stanford, CA: Stanford University Press, 1987), 127.
22 Philip Dorling, 'Attorney-General George Brandis Tries to Keep East Timor War Crimes Secret', *Sydney Morning Herald*, 28 January 2014, http://www.smh.com.au/federal-politics/political-news/attorneygeneral-george-brandis-tries-to-keep-east-timor-war-crimes-secret-20140127-31iyb.html (accessed 12 May 2020); Bernard Collaery, *Oil under Troubled Water: Australia's Timor Sea Intrigue* (Melbourne: Melbourne University Press, 2020), xi. Other examples include the often-thwarted efforts of Clinton Fernandes and Kim McGrath to obtain material, for example, https://timorarchives.wordpress.com/2014/04/16/keeping-oz-archives-secret/ (accessed 10 January 2021).
23 René Girard, *Deceit, Desire and the Novel*, trans. Yvonne Freccero (Baltimore: The Johns Hopkins University Press, 1976), 14–17, 290–314.
24 Allan Gyngell and Michael Wesley, *Making Australian Foreign Policy*, 2nd ed. (Melbourne: Cambridge University Press, 2007), 197.
25 Robert J. Schreiter, *The Ministry of Reconciliation: Spirituality and Strategies* (Maryknoll, NY: Orbis, 2005), 5–6, 15, 19.

2 Australian identity and relationships

1. Benedict R. Anderson, *Imagined Communities: Reflections on the Origin and Spread of Nationalism*, rev. ed. (London: Verso, 2006), 7; Charles Taylor, *Modern Social Imaginaries* (Durham, NC: Duke University Press, 2004), 2.
2. Taylor, *Modern Social Imaginaries*, 23.
3. Ibid.
4. Anderson, *Imagined Communities*, 145.
5. Ibid.
6. Taylor, *Modern Social Imaginaries*, 183.
7. Miriam Dixson, *The Imaginary Australian: Anglo-Celts and Identity, 1788 to the Present* (Sydney: University of New South Wales Press, 1999), 30.
8. Ibid., 13; Gregory Melleuish, *The Packaging of Australia: Politics and Culture Wars* (Sydney: University of New South Wales Press, 1998), 14.
9. Hank Nelson, 'Gallipoli, Kokoda and the Making of National Identity', in *The Australian Legend and Its Discontents*, ed. Richard Nile (St Lucia: University of Queensland Press, 2000), 216.
10. John Thornhill, *Making Australia: Exploring Our National Conversation* (Newtown, NSW: Millennium, 1992), 5.
11. James Walter, 'Defining Australia', in *Images of Australia: An Introductory Reader in Australian Studies*, ed. Gillian Whitlock and David Carter (St Lucia: University of Queensland Press, 1992), 10.
12. Ibid., 15.
13. Richard White, *Inventing Australia: Images and Identity, 1688–1980* (Crows Nest, NSW: Allen & Unwin, 1981), 168.
14. James Dunn, *East Timor: A Rough Passage to Independence*, 3rd ed. (Double Bay, NSW: Longueville, 2003), ii.
15. Winton Higgins, *Journey into Darkness* (Blackheath, NSW: Brandl & Schlesinger, 2003), 50.
16. Ibid.
17. Ibid., 51.
18. Ibid., 18.
19. Ghassan Hage, *White Nation: Fantasies of White Supremacy in a Multicultural Society* (Annandale, NSW: Pluto, 1998), 139.
20. Higgins, *Journey into Darkness*, 21–2.
21. Ibid., 256.
22. Ibid., 20.
23. Manning Clark, *The Quest for an Australian Identity* (St Lucia: University of Queensland Press, 1980), 4.
24. Thornhill, *Making Australia*, 106.

25 Louise Metcalfe, 'The Impact of "White Australia" on the Development of Australian National Identity in the Period between 1880 and 1914', *History Initiates* (March 2013): 3, mq.edu.au/pubstatic/public/download.jsp?id=99535 (accessed 12 May 2020).
26 W. E. H. Stanner, *The Dreaming and Other Essays* (Melbourne: Black Inc. Agenda, 2009), 289–308.
27 Bain Attwood, 'The Past as Future: Aborigines, Australia and the (Dis)course of History', *Australian Humanities Review*, no. 1 (April 1996), http://australianhumanitiesreview.org/1996/04/01/the-past-as-future-aborigines-australia-and-the-discourse-of-history/ (accessed 10 May 2020).
28 Martin Thomas, *The Artificial Horizon: Imagining the Blue Mountains* (Carlton, Vic: Melbourne University Press, 2003), 66.
29 Stuart Macintyre, *A Concise History of Australia*, 2nd. ed. (Cambridge: Cambridge University Press, 2004), 31.
30 Stanner, *The Dreaming*, 301.
31 Keith Windschuttle, *The Fabrication of Aboriginal History* (Sydney: Macleay, 2002), 3.
32 Ibid., 2, 3.
33 Ibid., 3.
34 Ibid., back cover; Miranda Devine, 'Truce, and Truth, in History Wars', *Sydney Morning Herald*, 20 April 2006, 2, https://www.smh.com.au/national/truce-and-truth-in-history-wars-20060420-gdne64.html (accessed 12 May 2020).
35 James Boyce, 'Fantasy Island', in *Whitewash: On Keith Windschuttle's Fabrication of Aboriginal History*, ed. Robert Manne (Melbourne: Black Inc. Agenda, 2003), 20–1, 25, 68.
36 Bain Attwood, 'Contesting Frontiers: History, Memory and Narrative in a National Museum', *reCollections* 1(2) (September 2006), https://recollections.nma.gov.au/issues/vol_1_no_2/papers/contesting_frontiers (accessed 10 May 2020).
37 Geoffrey Blainey, 'Native Fiction: A Review of *The Fabrication of Aboriginal History*, by Keith Windschuttle', *New Criterion*, April 2003, http://www.newcriterion.com/articles.cfm/nativefiction-1774 (accessed 10 May 2020).
38 David Walker, 'Cultural Change and the Response to Asia: 1945 to the Present', in *Australia and Asia*, ed. Mark McGillivray and Gary Smith (Melbourne, Vic: Oxford University Press, 1997), 23.
39 Geoffrey Blainey, *A Shorter History of Australia* (North Sydney: Vintage, 1994), 170.
40 White, *Inventing Australia*, 66.
41 Blainey, *A Shorter History*, 174.
42 Michael Klapdor, Moira Coombs and Catherine Bohm, *Australian Citizenship: A Chronology of Major Developments in Policy and Law* (Canberra: Parliament of Australia, 2009), http://www.aph.gov.au/binaries/library/pubs/bn/sp/austcitizenship.pdf (accessed 10 May 2020).

43 National Archives of Australia, *Citizenship in Australia: A Guide to Commonwealth Government Records*, http://guides.naa.gov.au/citizenship/chapter1/citizenship-australia.aspx#chap1note28 (accessed 27 April 2020).
44 Stuart Ward, *Australia and the British Embrace: The Demise of the Imperial Idea* (Carlton, Vic: Melbourne University Press, 2001), 11.
45 Anne Curthoys, 'Mythologies', in Nile, *The Australian Legend and Its Discontents*, 14, 35–6.
46 Melleuish, *The Packaging of Australia*, 22.
47 Ibid.
48 Commonwealth of Australia, 'Security Treaty between Australia, New Zealand and the United States of America [ANZUS]', *Australian Treaty Series 1952 No. 2* (Canberra: Australian Government Publishing Service, 1997), http://www.austlii.edu.au/au/other/dfat/treaties/1952/2.html (accessed 10 May 2020).
49 Alan Renouf, *The Frightened Country* (South Melbourne: Macmillan Company of Australia, 1979), 114–16.
50 Malcolm Fraser (with Cain Roberts), *Dangerous Allies* (Melbourne: Melbourne University Press, 2014), 9.
51 Ibid., 433.
52 Gary Smith, 'Australia's Political Relationships with Asia', in McGillivray and Smith, *Australia and Asia*, 102.
53 Gideon Haigh, 'Packed It In: The Demise of *The Bulletin*', *Monthly*, March 2008, https://www.themonthly.com.au/issue/2008/march/1268869044/gideon-haigh/packed-it (accessed 2 September 2017).
54 Smith, 'Australia's Political Relationships', 104–5.
55 Renouf, *The Frightened Country*, 161.
56 Smith, 'Australia's Political Relationships', 115.
57 Ibid.
58 Patrick Walters, 'Australia and Indonesia', in McGillivray and Smith, *Australia and Asia*, 157.
59 Aaron L. Connelly, 'Keeping Expectations for the Australia-Indonesia Relationship in Check', *Lowy Institute: The Interpreter*, 4 November 2016, https://www.lowyinstitute.org/the-interpreter/keeping-expectations-australia-indonesia-relationship-check (accessed 10 May 2020).
60 The World Bank, 'The World Bank in Indonesia – Overview', http://www.worldbank.org/en/country/indonesia/overview (accessed 10 May 2020).
61 Ross Tapsell, 'Same Old Stereotypes of Indonesia – and Our Politicians Aren't Helping', *Conversation*, http://theconversation.com/same-old-stereotypes-of-indonesia-and-our-politicians-arent-helping-17159 (accessed 10 May 2020).
62 Department of Foreign Affairs and Trade, *Agreement between Australia and the Republic of Indonesia on the Framework for Security Cooperation*, 13 November 2006, http://www.austlii.edu.au/au/other/dfat/nia/2006/43.html (accessed 10 May 2020).

63 'SAS Training with Kopassus Despite Rights Concerns', *ABC News*, 28 September 2010, http://www.abc.net.au/news/2010-09-28/sas-training-with-kopassus-despite-rights-concerns/2276586 (accessed 12 May 2020).
64 Bernard Collaery, *Oil under Troubled Water* (Melbourne: Melbourne University Press, 2020).
65 United Nations Development Programme, *International Human Development Indicators*, 2020, http://hdr.undp.org/en/countries (accessed 27 April 2020).
66 Taylor, *Modern Social Imaginaries*, 36.
67 Ibid., 156.
68 Ibid., 1.

3 World War II

1 These Companies formed part of 'Sparrow Force', a detachment drawn from the 2/40th Australian Infantry Battalion.
2 Paul Cleary, *The Men Who Came Out of the Ground: A Gripping Account of Australia's First Commando Campaign – Timor 1942* (Sydney: Hachette Australia, 2010), 31–2.
3 James Dunn, *East Timor: A Rough Passage to Independence*, 3rd ed. (Double Bay, NSW: Longueville, 2003), 102.
4 Cleary, *The Men Who Came Out of the Ground*, xviii.
5 For example, B. S. Callinan, *Independent Company: The 2/2 and 2/4 Australian Independent Companies in Portuguese Timor, 1941–43* (Melbourne: Heinemann, 1953); Christopher C. H. Wray, *Timor 1942: Australian Commandos at War with the Japanese* (Port Melbourne: Mandarin, 1990).
6 Dunn, *East Timor*, 22. Gerald Kenneally established *ATLAS* in memory of his father John 'Paddy' Kenneally (https://www.atlaseasttimor.com.au/). The 2/2 Commando Association based in Western Australia has supported the Timorese people for many years.
7 Alan Renouf, *The Frightened Country* (South Melbourne: Macmillan Company of Australia, 1979), 1.
8 David Horner, 'Australia in 1942: A Pivotal Year', in *Australia 1942: In the Shadow of War*, ed. Peter J. Dean (Cambridge: Cambridge University Press, 2010), 12.
9 Renouf, *The Frightened Country*, 519 and 528.
10 Peter Stanley, *Invading Australia: Japan and the Battle for Australia, 1942* (Camberwell, Vic: Penguin, 2008), 25.
11 David Walker, *Anxious Nation: Australia and the Rise of Asia, 1850–1939* (St Lucia: University of Queensland Press, 1999), 98–112.
12 Catriona Ross, 'Paranoid Projections: Australian Novels of Asian Invasion', *Antipodes* 23(1) (2009): Article 4, https://digitalcommons.wayne.edu/antipodes/vol23/iss1/4 (accessed 10 May 2020).

13 Stanley, *Invading Australia*, 38.
14 H. V. C. Thorby, *Cabinet Submission: Proposed Air Service Darwin to Dilli (Portuguese Timor)* (Canberra: Australian Government, Department of Foreign Affairs and Trade, 1939), http://dfat.gov.au/about-us/publications/historical-documents/Pages/volume-02/38-cabinet-submission-by-mr-hvc-thorby-minister-for-civil-aviation.aspx (accessed 10 May 2020).
15 Ibid.
16 Ibid.
17 Bob Wurth, *1942: Australia's Greatest Peril*, 2nd ed. (Sydney: Pan Macmillan Australia, 2010), xi.
18 Stanley, *Invading Australia*, 1.
19 Ibid., xi.
20 National Archives of Australia, 'Australia's Prime Ministers: John Curtin', http://primeministers.naa.gov.au/primeministers/curtin/in-office.aspx (accessed 10 May 2020).
21 John Costello, *The Pacific War, 1941–1945* (New York: Harper Perennial, 1981), 472; Steven Bullard, 'Japanese Strategy and Intentions towards Australia', in *Australia 1942: In the Shadow of War*, ed. Peter J. Dean (Cambridge: Cambridge University Press, 2010), 124–39.
22 Ian McPhedran, 'Historians Professor David Horner and Ashley Ekins Question World War II Kokoda Campaign's Iconic Status', News.com.au, 6 September 2012, http://www.news.com.au/national/historians-professor-david-horner-and-ashley-ekins-question-world-war-ii-kokoda-campaigns-iconic-status/news-story/f24aa6bc525df9760fb9070f57e8ad31 (accessed 10 May 2020); Frank Jacobs, 'Is This Map Australia's Clumsy Attempt at Fabricating a Japanese Invasion during WWII?', *Big Think*, http://bigthink.com/strange-maps/australias-invasion-paranoia (accessed 10 May 2020).
23 Peter Stanley, 'Dramatic Myth and Dull Truth: Invasion by Japan in 1942', in *Zombie Myths of Australian Military History: The Ten Myths That Will Not Die*, ed. Craig Stockings (Sydney: University of New South Wales Press, 2010), 140–60.
24 David Ellery, 'WWII Battle for Aust Questioned', Canberra Times.com.au, 6 September 2012, http://www.canberratimes.com.au/act-news/wwii-battle-for-aust-questioned-20120905-25eoy.html (accessed 12 May 2020).
25 Horner, 'Australia in 1942', 18–21.
26 Gary Brown and David Anderson, *Invasion 1942? Australia and the Japanese Threat*, Background Paper Number 6 (Canberra: Parliamentary Research Service, 1992), 4–10.
27 G. Hermon Gill, 'Royal Australian Navy, 1939–1942', 1st ed., Series 2, Volume I, Navy, Chapter 17: 'Prelude to Victory' (Australian War Memorial, Second World War Official Histories Australia in the War of 1939–45, 1957), 643, https://s3-ap-southeast-2.amazonaws.com/awm-media/collection/RCDIG1070351/document/5519639.PDF (accessed 10 May 2020).
28 Bullard, 'Japanese Strategy and Intentions towards Australia', 126–7.

29 Horner, 'Australia in 1942', 19.
30 Ibid.
31 Stanley, *Invading Australia*, 155.
32 Ibid., 154.
33 Horner, 'Australia in 1942', 19.
34 Stanley, *Invading Australia*, 155.
35 Gill, 'Prelude to Victory', 643.
36 Wurth, *1942*, 136.
37 National Archives of Australia, 'The Bombing of Darwin', https://gallery.records.nsw.gov.au/index.php/galleries/war-and-australia/war-and-australia-world-war-ii/war-and-australia-world-war-ii-1942-the-bombing-of-darwin/ (accessed 10 May 2020).
38 Stanley, *Invading Australia*, 108.
39 Horner, 'Australia in 1942', 20.
40 Henry P. Frei, *Japan's Southward Advance and Australia: From the Sixteenth Century to World War II* (Melbourne: Melbourne University Press, 1991), 172.
41 Stanley, *Invading Australia*, 186.
42 Ibid., 1.
43 Ibid., 188, 191.
44 Horner, 'Australia in 1942', 20.
45 Stanley, *Invading Australia*, 158 and 196.
46 Ibid., 186.
47 David Black, 'Menzies and Curtin in World War Two', in *John Curtin Prime Ministerial Library*, http://john.curtin.edu.au/ww2leaders/war.html (accessed 20 July 2017).
48 Stanley, *Invading Australia*, 227.
49 Wurth, *1942*, 136.
50 Cyril Ayris, *All the Bull's Men* (Hamilton Hill, WA: 2/2 Commando Association, 2006), 68.
51 Wray, *Timor 1942*, 42.
52 Department of Foreign Affairs and Trade, *Documents on Australian Foreign Policy, (DAFP) Historical Documents 1941, July–1942, June*, Vol. 5, Document 195, Commonwealth to Lord Cranbourne, 16 December 1941, https://www.dfat.gov.au/about-us/publications/historical-documents/Pages/volume-05/1941-july-1942-june-volume-5 (accessed 9–12 September 2015). (Except where noted, all historical documents that have been made available on this government website are found at this link. Hereafter, only the document number, writer, recipient and date are listed, and all were accessed between 9 and 12 September 2015.)
53 Wray, *Timor 1942*, 23–4.

54 *DAFP*, Document 258, Mr John Curtin, Prime Minister, to Lord Cranbourne, UK Secretary of State for Dominion Affairs, 6 January 1942.
55 Ibid.
56 *DAFP*, Document 153, Commonwealth Government to Lord Cranbourne, UK Secretary of State for Dominion Affairs, 2 December 1941.
57 *DAFP*, Document 234, Lord Cranbourne, UK Secretary of State for Dominion affairs to Mr John Curtin, Prime Minister, 28 December 1941.
58 *DAFP*, Document 62, Mr A. W. Fadden, Prime Minister, to Lord Cranbourne, UK Secretary of State for Dominion Affairs, 8 September 1941.
59 *DAFP*, Document 19, Lord Cranbourne, UK Secretary of State for Dominion Affairs to Commonwealth Government, 26 July 1941.
60 Thomas Keneally, *Australians: A Short History* (Sydney: Allen & Unwin, 2016), 723.
61 Henry P. Frei, 'Japan's Reluctant Decision to Occupy Portuguese Timor 1 January 1942–20 February 1942', *Australian Historical Studies* 27(107) (1996): 286, http://dx.doi.org/10.1080/10314619608596014 (accessed 5 September 2017).
62 Dunn, *East Timor*, 19.
63 *DAFP*, Document 201, Commonwealth Government to Mr David Ross, UK Consul in Dili, 18 December 1941.
64 Ibid.
65 René Girard, *Battling to the End: Conversations with Benoît Chantre*, trans. Mary Baker (East Lansing: Michigan State University Press, 2010), 18.
66 *DAFP*, Document 200, Mr M. de A. Ferreira de Carvalho, Governor of Portuguese Timor, to Lt Col W. W. Leggatt and Lt Col W. Detiger, Commanders of Australian and Netherlands Forces in Portuguese Timor, 17 December 1941.
67 *DAFP*, Document 300, Mr David Ross, UK Consul in Dili, to Department of External Affairs, 25 January 1942.
68 *DAFP*, Document 233, Lord Cranbourne, UK Secretary of State for Dominion Affairs, to Mr John Curtin, Prime Minister, 27 December 1941.
69 Lionel Wigmore, 'Chapter 21, Resistance in Timor', in *Volume IV: The Japanese Thrust*, 1st ed. (Canberra: Australian War Memorial, 1957), 470, https://s3-ap-southeast-2.amazonaws.com/awm-media/collection/RCDIG1070113/document/5519442.PDF (accessed 10 May 2020).
70 Ken'ichi Goto, *Tensions of Empire: Japan and Southeast Asia in the Colonial and Postcolonial World* (Athens: Ohio University Press, 2003), 33.
71 Cleary, *The Men Who Came Out of the Ground*, 19.
72 *DAFP*, Document 233, Lord Cranbourne, UK Secretary of State for Dominion Affairs, to Mr John Curtin, Prime Minister, 27 December 1941.
73 Frei, 'Japan's Reluctant Decision', 281.
74 Dunn, *East Timor*, 19.
75 Frei, 'Japan's Reluctant Decision', 289.

76 Ibid.
77 Clinton Fernandes, 'Two Tales of Timor', in *Zombie Myths of Australian Military History*, 222.
78 Girard, *Battling to the End*, 18.
79 Ibid., 16.
80 Jeremiah L. Alberg, *Beneath the Veil of the Strange Verses: Reading Scandalous Texts* (East Lansing: Michigan State University Press, 2013), xvi.
81 René Girard, *I See Satan Fall Like Lightning*, trans. J. G. Williams (Maryknoll, NY: Orbis, 2001), xi.
82 Ibid.
83 Dunn, *East Timor*, 19.
84 Wray, *Timor 1942*, 98.
85 Cleary, *The Men Who Came Out of the Ground*, 323.
86 Costello, *The Pacific War*, 310.
87 Wray, *Timor 1942*, 134, 138.
88 Cleary, *The Men Who Came Out of the Ground*, 246.
89 Ibid., xi, 368.
90 Ibid., xi.
91 Ibid., 34.
92 Ibid., 277, 353.
93 Ibid., xi.
94 Archie Campbell, *Double Reds of Timor* (Swanbourne, WA: John Burridge Military Antiques, 1995), 82.
95 Michele Turner, *Telling: East Timor, Personal Testimonies, 1942–1992* (Kensington: New South Wales University Press, 1992), 11–12.
96 Ibid., 21–2.
97 Dunn, *East Timor*, 322.
98 Top Foreign Stocks.com, *Chart: World War II Casualties as a Percentage of Each Country's Population*, http://topforeignstocks.com/2016/04/19/chart-world-war-ii-casualties-as-a-percentage-of-each-countrys-population/ (accessed 10 May 2020).
99 Australian Bureau of Statistics, *100 Years of Australian Lives, Second World War 1939–1945*, http://www.abs.gov.au/ausstats/abs@.nsf/Lookup/2071.0main+featu res952012-2013 (accessed 10 May 2020).
100 Brij V. Lal and Kate Fortune, eds, *The Pacific Islands: An Encyclopedia* (Hawaii: University of Hawaii Press, 2000), 244.
101 Hiromitsu Iwamoto, 'Patrol reports: sources for assessing war damage in Papua New Guinea,' Australian National University symposium (October 2000), Canberra: Australian War Memorial, http://ajrp.awm.gov.au/ajrp/remember.nsf/pages/NT000020EE accessed 7 September 2021.

102 Turner, *Telling*, 61.
103 René Girard, *The Girard Reader*, ed. James G. Williams (New York: Crossroad, 1996), 124.
104 David Stevens, '"Australia's Thermopylae?" The Kokoda Trail', in *Zombie Myths of Australian Military History*, 161–2.
105 James Bowen, *Battle for Australia*, http://www.battleforaustralia.org/battaust/JapdebAustinvade.html (accessed 10 May 2020).
106 For example, Peter FitzSimons, *Kokoda* (Sydney: Hodder Australia, 2004).
107 Department of Veterans' Affairs, 'Australia's War 1939–1945', https://anzacportal.dva.gov.au/wars-and-missions/world-war-ii-1939-1945/events/coral-sea-kokoda-and-milne-bay-may-september-1942 (accessed 10 May 2020).
108 'Battle for Australia Association', http://www.battleforaustralia.org.au/index.php (accessed 10 May 2020).
109 Refugee Council of Australia, Australia's Detention Policies, https://www.refugeecouncil.org.au/detention-policies/ (accessed 5 September 2021).
110 Specialist collections on Timor refer to the 1942 events, and some books deal with the Timor campaign in detail. For example, James Dunn's book *East Timor: A Rough Passage to Independence*; Paul Cleary's *The Men Who Came Out of the Ground*; Sir (Lt Col.) Bernard Callinan's *Independent Company*; C. H. Wray's book *Timor 1942* and the memoirs, letters and interviews of John 'Paddy' Kenneally (private collections).
111 Alison Bashford and Stuart Macintyre, eds, *The Cambridge History of Australia* (Port Melbourne, Vic: Cambridge University Press, 2015); Mark Peel and Christina Twomey, *A History of Australia* (Basingstoke, Hampshire: Palgrave Macmillan, 2011), 265; David Day, *Claiming a Continent: A New History of Australia* (Pymble, NSW: HarperCollins, 2001), 437; Geoffrey Bolton, *The Oxford History of Australia: Volume 5, 1942–1995: The Middle Way, 1942–1995*, 2nd ed. (Melbourne: Oxford University Press, 1996); Frank Welsh, *Great Southern Land: A New History of Australia* (London: Allen Lane, 2004); C. D. Coulthard-Clark, *Where Australians Fought: The Encyclopaedia of Australia's Battles* (St Leonards, NSW: Allen & Unwin, 1998), 207–8; A. K. Macdougall, *Australians at War: A Pictorial History*, 2nd rev. ed. (Rowville, Vic: Five Mile, 2007), 245–6, 352.
112 For example, Government of Western Australia, *Western Australian Museum – Debt of Honour Exhibition*, http://museum.wa.gov.au/whats-on/debt-honour; and Timor Awakening, https://www.timorawakening.com/ (both accessed 10 May 2020).
113 'Australian Curriculum', in *Australian Curriculum, Assessment and Reporting Authority*, https://www.australiancurriculum.edu.au/Search/?q=Timor (accessed 10 May 2020).

114 Australian War Memorial, *Far Eastern Liaison Office (FELO) Leaflet Collection*, 'PG 9: Your friends do not forget you', https://www.awm.gov.au/collection/accessing-records-at-the-memorial/findingaids/special/cards/felo#s34 (accessed 10 May 2020).
115 I heard the author Paul Cleary detail this point during an interview in 2010.
116 Denis Kevans, 'Never Forget You', https://www.youtube.com/watch?v=nGhw7ouBGPw (accessed 10 May 2020).
117 ABC Radio National, 'Did the Walls Have Ears?', *Background Briefing*, 23 February 2014, https://www.abc.net.au/radionational/programs/backgroundbriefing/5267456 (accessed 13 February 2020).
118 Wigmore, 'Chapter 21, Resistance in Timor', 470.

4 The Indonesian invasion of East Timor

1 Wendy Way, ed., 'Australia and the Indonesian Incorporation of Portuguese Timor 1974–1976', *Documents on Australian Foreign Policy*, vol. 20 (Carlton South: Melbourne University Press, 2000), https://www.dfat.gov.au/sites/default/files/australia-and-the-indonesian-incorporation-of-portuguese-timor-1974-1976.pdf (accessed 10 May 2020). (The documents also appear on the government website at https://www.dfat.gov.au/about-us/publications/historical-documents/Pages/volume-20/volume-20-australia-and-the-indonesian-incorporation-of-portuguese-timor-1974-1976. Documents on pages 21–45 are not numbered and appear on the site below the numbered list. All documents are noted here by page number.)
2 James Dunn, *East Timor: A Rough Passage to Independence*, 3rd ed. (Double Bay, NSW: Longueville, 2003), 115, 306.
3 Ibid., 161–2, 187.
4 Ibid., 139.
5 Michael Kirwan, *Discovering Girard* (London: Darton, Longman & Todd, 2004), 38.
6 For uniformity, the name of the town 'Balibó' is spelled 'Balibó' in this book.
7 Way, 'Australia and the Indonesian Incorporation', Introduction, 19.
8 Ibid., *Cablegram to Canberra for Barwick from Beale*, 21 January 1963, 24–5.
9 Bernard K. Gordon, 'The Potential for Indonesian Expansionism', *Pacific Affairs* 36(4) (1963): 378–93, Pacific Affairs, University of British Columbia, doi:10.2307/2754684 (accessed 12 May 2020).
10 Ibid., 385.
11 UDT (*União Democrática Timorense* or Timorese Democratic Union) was formed on 11 May 1974. FRETILIN (*Frente Revolucionária de Timor-Leste Independente* or Revolutionary Front for an Independent East Timor) began as ASDT (Timorese

Social Democratic Association) on 20 May 1974 and changed its name on 11 September 1974.
12 James Dunn, 'Communist Influence in FRETILIN Prior to the 1975 Invasion', East Timor Action Network (ETAN), 29 July 1998, https://etan.org/et/1998/july/july29-31/29communi.htm (accessed 10 May 2020).
13 Helen Hill, *Stirrings of Nationalism in East Timor* (Sydney: Contemporary Otford, 2002), 70, 109.
14 Dunn, *East Timor*, 93.
15 Richard Walsh and George Munster, *Secrets of State: A Detailed Assessment of the Book They Banned* (Sydney: Angus & Robertson, 1982), 78–9.
16 Dunn, *East Timor*, 53.
17 Ibid., viii, 141–2.
18 United Nations, *UN General Assembly Votes on East Timor* (General Assembly Resolutions 1975–82), https://etan.org/etun/genasRes.htm (accessed 10 May 2020).
19 Dorelle Pinch, *Inquest into the death of Brian Raymond Peters: Coroner's Report 2007*, 129, Executive Summary, http://www.etan.org/etanpdf/2007/Peterssinquest1.pdf (accessed 11 May 2020).
20 Ben Saul, 'Prosecuting War Crimes at Balibó under Australian Law: The Killing of Five Journalists in East Timor by Indonesia', *Sydney Law Review* 31(1) (2009): 83–120, http://classic.austlii.edu.au/au/journals/SydLawRw/2009/3.html (accessed 11 May 2020).
21 Pinch, *Inquest*, 18.
22 'Australian Federal Police Drop Investigation into the Murders of the "Balibó Five"', News.com.au, 21 October 2014, http://www.news.com.au/world/asia/australian-federal-police-drop-investigation-into-the-murders-of-the-Balibó-five/news-story/a9af0adb251342c3f7e93070c084985f (accessed 11 May 2020).
23 Way, 'Australia and the Indonesian Incorporation', v.
24 Ibid., 1.
25 Ibid., 2.
26 Ibid., 10, 11.
27 Ibid., 20.
28 Ibid., 1.
29 René Girard, *Deceit, Desire and the Novel*, trans. Yvonne Freccero (Baltimore: The Johns Hopkins University Press, 1965), 17.
30 Ibid., 20.
31 Way, 'Australia and the Indonesian Incorporation', 19.
32 Ibid.
33 Ibid., *Submission to Barwick*, Canberra, 16 January 1962, 22–3.
34 Ibid., *Rowland to Waller*, Canberra, 14 January 1963, 23.
35 Ibid., *For Barwick from Beale*, Washington, 21 January 1963, 25.

36 Ibid., Canberra, 28 January 1963, 26.
37 Ibid., *Salazar to Menzies*, Lisbon, 1 March 1963, 29.
38 Ibid., *Menzies to Salazar*, Canberra, 15 October 1963, 36.
39 Ibid.
40 Ibid., *Report*, Canberra, 4 April 1963, 30.
41 Gordon, 'The Potential', 378 and 381.
42 Way, 'Australia and the Indonesian Incorporation', *Cablegram to Washington*, Canberra, 24 November 1964, 39.
43 Ibid., 20.
44 Ibid., Document 3, *Policy Planning Paper*, 3 May 1974, 51.
45 Ibid., Document 11, *Memorandum to Canberra*, Jakarta, 28 June 1974, 61.
46 Ibid., Document 12, *Furlonger to Feakes*, Jakarta, 3 July 1974, 62.
47 Ibid., Document 17, *Furlonger to Feakes*, Jakarta, 30 July 1974, 73.
48 Ibid., Document 18, *Report by Fisher*, Jakarta, July 1974, 76.
49 Dunn, *East Timor*, 151.
50 The Timor-Leste Commission for Reception, Truth and Reconciliation (CAVR), *Chega! The Final Report of the Timor-Leste Commission for Reception, Truth and Reconciliation (CAVR)* (2013), part 3: 176–7, para. 119–21, http://chegareport.org/Chega%20All%20Volumes.pdf (accessed 13 May 2020).
51 Ibid., 3: 176, para. 117–18.
52 Ibid., 3: 175, para. 114.
53 Ibid., para. 116.
54 Dunn, *East Timor*, 196.
55 Way, 'Australia and the Indonesian Incorporation', Document 37, *Woolcott to Renouf*, Canberra, 24 September 1974, 111.
56 Ibid., Document 357, *Woolcott to Feakes*, Jakarta, 3 December 1975, 597.
57 Ibid., Document 147, *Statement by Willesee*, Tokyo, 17 June 1975, 279.
58 Ibid., 13.
59 Ibid., Documents 26 and 27, *Records of Meetings between Whitlam and Suharto*, Yogyakarta (10.00 am), 6 September 1974, 95–8; and Wonosobo (8.00 pm), 99–100.
60 Ibid., Document 123, *Record of Conversation between Whitlam and Suharto*, Townsville (1.00 pm), 4 April 1975, 244–8.
61 Ibid., Document 26, *Record of Meeting between Whitlam and Suharto*, Yogyakarta, 6 September 1974, 96.
62 Ibid., 97.
63 Ibid., 95.
64 Ibid.
65 Ibid., Document 250, *Cablegram to Canberra*, Jakarta, 2 October 1975, 444–6.
66 Ibid., Document 255, *Cablegram to Canberra*, Jakarta, 9 October 1975, 456; Document 365, *Cablegram to Canberra*, Jakarta, 9 December 1975, 613.

67 Ibid., Document 28, *Background Paper*, 11 September 1974, 101.
68 Ibid., Document 127, *Woolcott to Willesee*, Jakarta, 17 April 1975, 253.
69 Ibid., Document 123, *Record of Conversation between Whitlam and Suharto, 2nd Discussion*, Townsville, 4 April 1975, 245.
70 Ibid., Document 137, *Dispatch to Willesee*, Jakarta, 2 June 1975, 268.
71 Ibid., Document 123, *Record of Conversation between Whitlam and Suharto, 2nd Discussion*, Townsville, 4 April 1975, 245.
72 Ibid., Document 37, *Woolcott to Renouf*, Canberra, 24 September 1974, 111.
73 Ibid., Document 360, *DFAT News Release*, Canberra, 7 December 1975, 604.
74 Ibid., 4–5.
75 Ibid., Document 67, *Submission to Willesee*, Canberra, 13 December 1974, 148.
76 Ibid., Document 83, *Record of Conversation between Willesee, Feakes and Joseph*, Canberra, 13 February 1975, 181–3; Document 85, *Joseph to Feakes*, Canberra, 14 February 1975, 184–6.
77 Ibid., Document 66, *Record of Policy Discussion*, Canberra, 11 December 1974, 147.
78 Ibid., Document 81, *Barnard to Willesee*, Canberra, 11 February 1975, 176–80.
79 Ibid., Document 241, *Woolcott to Juddery*, Jakarta, 24 September 1975, 433.
80 Ibid., Document 170, *Woolcott to Canberra*, Jakarta, 17 August 1975, 315.
81 Ibid., Document 219, *Woolcott to Canberra*, Jakarta, 7 September 1975, 394–6.
82 Ibid., Document 229, *Woolcott to Canberra*, Jakarta, 13 September 1975, 410–12.
83 Ibid., Document 243, *Woolcott to Canberra*, Jakarta, 27 September 1975, 435–7.
84 Ibid., Document 275, *Woolcott to Canberra*, Jakarta, 19 October 1975, 488–91.
85 Ibid., Document 306, *Submission to Willesee*, Canberra, 29 October 1975, 526–8.
86 Ibid., Document 12, *Furlonger to Feakes*, 63.
87 Desmond Ball and Hamish McDonald, *Death in Balibó Lies in Canberra* (St Leonards, NSW: Allen & Unwin, 2000), 65–71.
88 Brian Toohey and Marian Wilkinson, 'The Timor Papers 1987', in *Tell Me No Lies: Investigative Journalism and Its Triumphs*, ed. John Pilger (London: Jonathan Cape, 2004), 175.
89 Ibid., 178.
90 Ibid., 181.
91 Ibid., 180–1.
92 Ibid., 175–6.
93 Way, 'Australia and the Indonesian Incorporation', Document 262, *Cablegram to Canberra*, Jakarta, 15 October 1975, 468.
94 Ibid., Document 257, *Canberra to Jakarta*, Canberra, 13 October 1975, 460.
95 Ibid., Document 262, *Cablegram to Canberra*, Jakarta, 15 October 1975, 468.
96 Ibid., 469.
97 Pinch, *Inquest*, 105.

98 Way, 'Australia and the Indonesian Incorporation', Document 169, *Woolcott to Canberra*, 17 August 1975, 314.
99 The Timor-Leste Commission, 3: 178, para. 126.
100 Girard, *Deceit, Desire and the Novel*, 14.
101 The Timor-Leste Commission, 3: 179, para. 128.
102 Ibid.
103 Way, 'Australia and the Indonesian Incorporation', Document 45, *Cooper to Canberra*, Lisbon, 14 October 1974, 119.
104 René Girard, *Battling to the End: Conversations with Benoît Chantre*, trans. Mary Baker (East Lansing: Michigan State University Press, 2010), 57.
105 Girard, *Deceit, Desire and the Novel*, 4.
106 Saul, 'Prosecuting War Crimes at Balibó', 84, n. 4.
107 The Timor-Leste Commission, 7.2: 806, para. 105.
108 Saul, 'Prosecuting War Crimes at Balibó', 85.
109 Pinch, *Inquest*, 129.
110 Ibid.
111 David Jenkins, 'Charismatic, Sinister Suharto Man', *Sydney Morning Herald*, 10 September 2004, http://www.smh.com.au/articles/2004/09/09/1094530768057.html (accessed 11 May 2020).
112 The Timor-Leste Commission, 8, annexe 4, 2413.
113 Australian Federal Police (AFP), *Balibo Five Disclosure Log*, FOI – CRM No. 2015/198: 83–4; 284, https://www.afp.gov.au/sites/default/files/PDF/Disclosure-Log/20/2015 (accessed 10 May 2020). (A search on 29 May 2020 revealed that this document must now be obtained through Freedom of Information, foi@afp.gov.au.)
114 Sara Everingham, 'Balibó Five: Investigation into Deaths of Five Journalists Dropped by Australian Federal Police', *ABC News*, 21 October 2014, http://www.abc.net.au/news/2014-10-21/Balibó-five-investigation-dropped-by-afp/5828814 (accessed 11 May 2020).
115 AFP *Disclosure Log*, FOI – CRM No. 2015/198: 284.
116 George Munster and Richard Walsh, *Documents on Australian Defence and Foreign Policy 1968–1975* (Sydney: J.R. Walsh and G.J. Munster, 1980).
117 Walsh and Munster, *Secrets of State*, vii, viii.
118 Ibid., viii.
119 Ibid.
120 Ibid., ix.
121 Ibid.
122 René Girard, *The Scapegoat*, trans. Yvonne Freccero (Baltimore: The Johns Hopkins University Press, 1986), 37.

123 Way, 'Australia and the Indonesian Incorporation', Document 371, *Cablegram to Canberra*, Lisbon, 10 December 1975, 621–2.
124 Ibid., *Cablegram to Canberra, Jakarta, Washington and New York*, Lisbon, 23 May 1977, 836.
125 Ibid., 'Introduction', 1.
126 Girard, *The Scapegoat*, 37.
127 Girard, *Deceit, Desire and the Novel*, 17.

5 The occupation of East Timor

1 The Timor-Leste Commission for Reception, Truth and Reconciliation (CAVR), *Chega! The Final Report of the Timor-Leste Commission for Reception, Truth and Reconciliation (CAVR)* (2013), part 4: 343, para. 1, http://chegareport.org/Chega%20All%20Volumes.pdf (accessed 13 May 2020).
2 Falintil – *Forças Armadas de Libertação de Timor-Leste* – was the military wing of FRETILIN, established on 20 August 1975 as part of the political conflict with the Timorese Democratic Union (UDT).
3 Max Stahl, 'Massacre among the Graves', *Tapol Bulletin*, no. 108 (December 1991): 6, 8, http://vuir.vu.edu.au/26096/ (accessed 11 May 2020).
4 The Timor-Leste Commission, 4: 344–5, para. 4–7.
5 This even-handed approach strengthens the report's claim to impartiality and negates accusations that investigations into Timor's suffering are anti-Indonesian. The findings are presented in measured tones, focusing on the facts as far as they could be established systematically and scientifically.
6 Ibid., 6: 488, para. 8.
7 Sarah Staveteig, 'How Many Persons in East Timor Went "Missing" during the Indonesian Occupation? Results from Indirect Estimates' (2007), 23, https://www.unsw.adfa.edu.au/school-of-humanities-and-social-sciences/sites/default/files/documents/Staveteig%20death%20toll.pdf (accessed 11 May 2020).
8 The Timor-Leste Commission, 6: 488, para. 10.
9 Joseph Nevins, *A Not-So-Distant Horror: Mass Violence in East Timor* (Ithaca, NY: Cornell University Press, 2005), 30; Geoffrey Robinson, *If You Leave Us Here, We Will Die: How Genocide Was Stopped in East Timor* (Princeton, NJ: Princeton University Press, 2010), 57; James Dunn, *East Timor: A Rough Passage to Independence*, 3rd ed. (Double Bay, NSW: Longueville, 2003), 333–4.
10 The Timor-Leste Commission, 6: 490, para. 19.
11 Ibid., 77.
12 Ibid., 44.

13 John G. Taylor, *Indonesia's Forgotten War: The Hidden History of East Timor* (Leichhardt: Pluto, 1991), 204.
14 Ibid., 117–19.
15 The Timor-Leste Commission, 4: 11, para. 24.
16 Department of Foreign Affairs and Trade (DFAT), *East Timor in Transition 1998–2000: An Australian Policy Challenge* (2001), 13.
17 Phillip Hudson, 'Why Fraser Gave Up on East Timor', *Sydney Morning Herald*, 1 January 2009, https://www.smh.com.au/national/why-fraser-gave-up-on-east-timor-20090101-gdt8a9.html (accessed 6 September 2021).
18 John Waddingham, 'Australia's New Labor Government, March 1983', *Timor Archives: Clearing House for Archival Records on Timor*, https://timorarchives.wordpress.com/2013/03/05/hawke-labor-march-1983/ (accessed 11 May 2020).
19 Peter Hartcher, 'Jakarta Leaves Keating at the Altar', *Sydney Morning Herald*, 24 April 1992, 15.
20 Tony Wright, 'Jakarta Joy as PM Backs Off Human Rights', *Sydney Morning Herald*, 27 October 1993, 3.
21 Michael Millett and Louise Williams, 'PM Defends Soft Line on Indonesia', *Sydney Morning Herald*, 18 September 1996, 1.
22 Gordon Fenney, 'Soeharto a 20th Century Great', *Sydney Morning Herald*, 15 May 1996, 9.
23 Clinton Fernandes, *The Independence of East Timor* (Eastbourne: Sussex Academic, 2011), 183–8.
24 DFAT, *East Timor in Transition*, 181.
25 Ibid., 182.
26 René Girard, *The Scapegoat*, trans. Yvonne Freccero (Baltimore: The Johns Hopkins University Press, 1986), 119.
27 Ibid., 26.
28 Ibid., 18.
29 Michael Kirwan, *Discovering Girard* (London: Darton, Longman & Todd, 2004), 39.
30 DFAT, *East Timor in Transition*, 1.
31 Ibid., vi.
32 Ibid., v.
33 Clinton Fernandes, *Reluctant Saviour: Australia, Indonesia and the Independence of East Timor* (Carlton North, Vic: Scribe, 2004), 2.
34 DFAT, *East Timor in Transition*, v, vi.
35 Ibid., v.
36 The Timor-Leste Commission, 3: 267, para. 483.
37 Ibid., 7.2: 1010–11, para. 610–12.
38 Arnold S. Kohen, *From the Place of the Dead: The Epic Struggles of Bishop Belo of East Timor* (New York: St Martin's, 1999), 171.

39 Bodies continue to be found, for example, Lindsay Murdoch, 'Remains of Dili Massacre Victims Identified', *Sydney Morning Herald*, 19 August 2009, https://www.smh.com.au/world/remains-of-dili-massacre-victims-identified-20090818-ep5f.html (accessed 11 May 2020).
40 DFAT, *East Timor in Transition*, 7. The pro-integration youth's name was Afonso Hendrique, not Gomes. See *Tapol Bulletin*, no. 108 (December 1991): 14, http://vuir.vu.edu.au/26096/ (accessed 11 May 2020).
41 The Timor-Leste Commission, 7.2: 1006, para. 600.
42 Ibid.
43 International Commission of Jurists (ICJ), *Blaming the Victims: The 12 November 1991 Massacre in Dili, East Timor, and the Response of the Indonesian Government* (Geneva, Switzerland: ICJ, February 1992), 5. https://www.icj.org/wp-content/uploads/1992/02/East-Timor-blaming-the-victims-fact-finding-mission-report-1992-eng.pdf (accessed 6 September 2021).
44 DFAT, *East Timor in Transition*, 7.
45 'Report by the Special Rapporteur Bacre Waly Ndiaye, on His Mission to Indonesia and East Timor from 3 to 13 July 1994', in Geoffrey C. Gunn, *East Timor and the United Nations: The Case for Intervention* (Laurenceville, NJ: Red Sea, 1997), 139–71. (The Ndiaye report is referred to in *East Timor in Transition* on page 7 but is omitted from the index, pages 304–12.)
46 Ibid., 145, 147.
47 Ibid., 150.
48 Ibid., 151.
49 Ibid., 143, 151, 152.
50 Ibid., 152.
51 DFAT, *East Timor in Transition*, 7, 8.
52 Ibid., v.
53 Ibid., 8.
54 Ibid.
55 Kohen, *From the Place of the Dead*, 171.
56 DFAT, *East Timor in Transition*, 8.
57 Ibid., 9, 10.
58 Ibid., 9.
59 Ibid.
60 Ibid.
61 Ibid.
62 Ibid.
63 Dunn, *East Timor: A Rough Passage*, 347.
64 Ibid., 354.
65 DFAT, *East Timor in Transition*, 1.
66 The Timor-Leste Commission, 3: 300, para. 626.

67 DFAT, *East Timor in Transition*, 61.
68 The Timor-Leste Commission, 3:305, para. 649.
69 Ibid., 3:279, para. 537.
70 Nevins, *A Not-So-Distant Horror*, 120.
71 Brian Toohey and M. Wilkinson, 'The Timor Papers 1987', in *Tell Me No Lies: investigative journalism and its triumphs*, ed. John Pilger (London: Jonathan Cape, 2004), 174–90; Lance Collins and W. Reed, *Plunging Point: Intelligence Failures, Cover-Ups and Consequences* (Pymble, NSW: HarperCollins, 2005), 324–46.
72 Fernandes, *Reluctant Saviour*, 47–50.
73 Nevins, *A Not-So-Distant Horror*, 145.
74 DFAT, *East Timor in Transition*, 24, 26, 61, 62.
75 Rodney Tiffen, *Diplomatic Deceits: Government, Media and East Timor* (Sydney: University of NSW Press, 2001), 61.
76 Nevins, *A Not-So-Distant Horror*, 247, n.39.
77 Don Greenlees and Robert Garran, *Deliverance: The Inside Story of East Timor's Fight for Freedom* (Crows Nest, NSW: Allen & Unwin, 2002), 111.
78 David Scott, *Last Flight Out of Dili: Memoirs of an accidental activist in the triumph of East Timor* (North Melbourne: Pluto Press, 2005), 347.
79 Dunn, *East Timor*, vii.
80 DFAT, *East Timor in Transition*, 11.
81 Between 1976 and 1981, 2447 Timorese came to Australia by air, some under humanitarian schemes. See Amanda Wise, *Exile and Return among the Timorese* (Philadelphia: University of Pennsylvania Press, 2006), 44–5.
82 DFAT, *East Timor in Transition*, 12.
83 Ibid.
84 Ibid.
85 Ibid.
86 Ibid., 13.
87 Ibid., 12.
88 United Nations, *UN General Assembly Votes on East Timor* (General Assembly Resolutions 1975–82), accessed May 11, 2020, http://etan.org/etun/UNvotes.htm
89 DFAT, *East Timor in Transition*, 3, 4.
90 Australian Information Service, *Transcript of Whitlam/Hastings press conference*, Jakarta, 5 March 1982, accessed May 8, 2020, https://timorarchives.wordpress.com/2012/03/01/whitlam-hastings-1982/
91 UN Press Release, Department of Public Information Press Section, GA/D/2334, November 9, 1982, quoted in The Timor-Leste Commission, 7.1: 695, para 380.
92 The Timor-Leste Commission, 7.1: 631, para. 126.
93 Geoffrey C. Gunn, *Complicity in Genocide: Report to the East Timor 'Truth Commission' on international actors* (Geoffrey C. Gunn, 2006), 125 n.2.

94 Gunn, *Complicity in Genocide,* 125; Taylor, *Indonesia's Forgotten War,* 214, 217.
95 Gunn, *Complicity in Genocide,* 118.
96 Ibid., 121.
97 Ibid., 124.
98 DFAT, *East Timor in Transition,* 12.
99 Ibid., 13.
100 Ibid., 181.
101 Wendy Way, ed., 'Australia and the Indonesian Incorporation of Portuguese Timor, 1974–1976', in *Documents on Australian Foreign Policy,* vol. 20 (Carlton South: Melbourne University Press, 2000), Document 358, *Cablegram to Canberra,* 599, https://www.dfat.gov.au/sites/default/files/australia-and-the-indonesian-incorporation-of-portuguese-timor-1974-1976.pdf (accessed 10 May 2020). (The documents also appear on the *DFAT* website at https://www.dfat.gov.au/about-us/publications/historical-documents/Pages/volume-20/volume-20-australia-and-the-indonesian-incorporation-of-portuguese-timor-1974-1976.)
102 Nevins, *A Not-So-Distant Horror,* 63.
103 The Timor-Leste Commission, 7.1: 632, para. 130.
104 Way, 'Australia and the Indonesian Incorporation', vol. 20, Document 9, *McCready to Feakes,* 59.
105 Ibid., Document 3, *Policy Planning Paper,* Canberra, 50.
106 Ibid., Document 169, *Canberra from Jakarta,* 314.
107 DFAT, *East Timor in Transition,* 12.
108 Roger S. Clark, 'Timor Gap', in *East Timor at the Crossroads: The Forging of a Nation,* ed. Peter Carey and G. Carter Bentley (London: Cassell, 1995), 73–94, 75.
109 Simone King, 'The Fate of Occupied Territory: Recognition, Non-recognition, Self-Determination and Prolonged Occupation' (2005), 29–30, https://www.wsrw.org/files/dated/2008-10-22/simone_king_thesis_2005.pdf (accessed 12 May 2020).
110 DFAT, *East Timor in Transition,* 12.
111 Bernard Collaery, *Oil under Troubled Water* (Melbourne: Melbourne University Press, 2020).
112 Another instance of Australian dependence on Indonesian favour is shown in the case of approximately 1,500 Timorese people who sought asylum in Australia after the Santa Cruz massacre. All were subjected to a protracted legal stalemate. Initially, the Australian government argued that as they were Portuguese citizens, they could apply to Portugal for protection. However, Australia had already argued that Portugal could not act on behalf of East Timor regarding the matter of the Timor Sea, and had argued from 1985 that the Timorese were Indonesian citizens. The Full Bench of the Federal Court ruled against the government in May 1997. After the referendum of 1999 the Australian government then argued that the Timorese could safely return to their homeland. This was again successfully

challenged but for most asylum seekers it was a full twelve years after their application for asylum before residency in Australia was granted.
113 Girard, *I See Satan Fall Like Lightning* (Baltimore: The Johns Hopkins University Press, 1986), xvi, 72.
114 Joel Hodge, *Resisting Violence and Victimisation: Christian Faith and Solidarity in East Timor* (Burlington, VT: Ashgate, 2012), 19, 93–101.
115 Rowena Lennox, *Fighting Spirit of East Timor: The Life of Martinho da Costa Lopes* (Annandale, NSW: Pluto, 2000), vii.
116 Ibid., 130.
117 The Timor-Leste Commission, 3: 247, para. 401.
118 Ibid., 7.3: 1178, para. 20.
119 Ibid., 7.3: 1210, para. 114.
120 Ibid., 7.3: 1178, para. 20.
121 Ibid., 7.3: 1247, para. 203.
122 Ibid., 7.3: 1249, para. 209.
123 Ibid., 7.3: 1254, para. 231.
124 Ibid., 7.3: 1255, para. 236.
125 Ibid., 7.3: 1256, para. 238.
126 Peter Rodgers, 'East Timor: A Continuing Game of Face-Saving?', *Sydney Morning Herald*, 7 November 1979, 7.
127 The Timor-Leste Commission, 7.3: 1347, para. 509.
128 Ibid., 7.3: 1339, para. 502.
129 J. J. Gerry, Letter to Monsignor da Costa Lopes, 11 November 1981, https://timorarchives.files.wordpress.com/2012/02/tis_box13-02_10.pdf (accessed 23 May 2020).
130 Monsignor da Costa Lopes, *Monsignor Lopes Reply to Bishop Gerry*, 19 November 1981, https://timorarchives.files.wordpress.com/2012/02/tis_box13-02_10b.pdf (accessed 23 May 2020).
131 'Backing for Timor Plea', *Northern Territory News*, 11 January 1982, https://timorarchives.files.wordpress.com/2012/03/eto-attic3-02.pdf (accessed 11 May 2020).
132 Australian Information Service, *Transcript*, 12.
133 Timor Information Service, *Interview with Gough Whitlam, ABC Radio 'Frontline'*, 26 March 1982 (unofficial transcript), 3, https://timorarchives.files.wordpress.com/2012/02/eto_w-h_09.pdf (accessed 8 April 2020).
134 Pat Walsh, 'Timor Report: Whitlam and Hastings Observed', *Arena*, no. 60 (1982): 136, https://timorarchives.files.wordpress.com/2012/02/eto_w-h_69.pdf (accessed 12 May 2020).
135 Ibid., 141.
136 Australian Information Service, *Transcript*, 11.

137 Ibid., 2.
138 Timor Information Service, *Transcript*, 2.
139 Ibid.
140 Ibid.
141 Gough Whitlam, 'The Truth about Timor', *Bulletin*, 30 March 1982, 79–81, https://nla.gov.au/nla.obj-1400927193/view?partId=nla.obj-1400978147#page/n59/mode/1up (accessed 10 May 2020).
142 Girard, *The Scapegoat*, 35–6.
143 Timor Information Service, *Transcript*, 3.
144 Nevins, *A Not-So-Distant Horror*, 30.
145 Girard, *The Scapegoat*, 35–6.
146 'Timor Trench', *Sydney Morning Herald*, 12 January 1982, 6.
147 Ibid.
148 Ibid.
149 Geoffrey C. Gunn, *A Critical View of Western Journalism and Scholarship on East Timor* (Manila: Journal of Contemporary Asia, 1994), 218–19.
150 Girard, *The Scapegoat*, 18.
151 Australian Information Service, *Transcript*, 4.
152 Whitlam, 'The Truth about Timor', 79–80.
153 R. K. R. Alston, Chairman, Australian Council for Overseas Aid, 'Timor Bishop Defended', *Sydney Morning Herald Letters*, 5 April 1982, 6.
154 'East Timor Beset by Famine', *Sydney Morning Herald*, 6 January 1984, 4.
155 The Timor-Leste Commission, 3: 252, para. 415; Lennox, *Fighting Spirit of East Timor*, 195.
156 Girard, *I See Satan Fall Like Lightning*, 145–6.
157 Ibid.

6 Collapse and resurgence

1 Bob Breen, *Mission Accomplished: East Timor* (Crows Nest, NSW: Allen & Unwin, n.d.), 18–19. The InterFET assessment of damage ranges from minimal (Lolotoe) to 50 per cent (Remixio) with most places upwards of 60 per cent: Los Palos (east) at 70 per cent and Suai (south) and Balibó (west) both at 95 per cent. The destruction of the capital Dili was assessed at 100 per cent.
2 James Dunn, *East Timor: A Rough Passage to Independence*, 3rd ed. (Double Bay, NSW: Longueville Books, 2003), 362. (The company's name at the time of publishing was 'Longueville Books'. It is now 'Longueville Media'.)
3 John Howard, *Lazarus Rising: A Personal and Political Autobiography* (Sydney: HarperCollins, 2011), 340–1.

4 Hugh White, 'The Road to InterFET: Reflections on Australian Strategic Decisions concerning East Timor, December 1998–September 1999', *Institute for Regional Security* 4(1) (Autumn 2008): 74, https://www.jstor.org/stable/26458869 (accessed 11 May 2020).
5 Ibid.
6 Department of Foreign Affairs and Trade (DFAT), *East Timor in Transition 1998–2000: An Australian Policy Challenge* (2001), 181.
7 Ibid., 182.
8 Grayson J. Lloyd, 'The Diplomacy on East Timor', in *Out of the Ashes: Deconstruction and Reconstruction of East Timor*, ed. James J. Fox and Dionisio Babo Soares (Adelaide: Crawford House, 2000), 88.
9 Don Greenlees and Robert Garran, *Deliverance: The Inside Story of East Timor's Fight for Freedom* (Crows Nest, NSW: Allen & Unwin, 2002), 103.
10 Joseph Nevins, *A Not-So-Distant Horror: Mass Violence in East Timor* (Ithaca, NY: Cornell University Press, 2005), 121.
11 The phrase 'pebble in the shoe' was used by Ali Alatas, Indonesia's foreign minister (1988–99), who subsequently wrote the book *The Pebble in the Shoe: The Diplomatic Struggle for East Timor* (Jakarta: Aksara Karunia, 2006). The phrase has also been associated with Gareth Evans, Australian foreign minister (1988–96), regarding his comments about the Santa Cruz massacre and his role in the Timor Gap agreement. See https://newmatilda.com/2010/02/02/pebble-gareths-shoe/.
12 Clinton Fernandes, *The Independence of East Timor* (Eastbourne: Sussex Academic, 2011), 174.
13 White, 'The Road to InterFET', 73.
14 Paul Kelly, *The March of Patriots: The Struggle for Modern Australia* (Carlton, Vic: Melbourne University Press, 2011), 514.
15 Ricardo Roque, 'Mimetic Governmentality and the Administration of Colonial Justice in East Timor, ca. 1860–1910', *Comparative Studies in Society and History* 57(1) (2015): 92, http://www.jstor.org/stable/43908334 (accessed 5 September 2021).
16 Ibid., 85.
17 Ibid., 73.
18 Ibid., 92.
19 Ibid.
20 The Timor-Leste Commission for Reception, Truth and Reconciliation (CAVR), *Chega! The Final Report of the Timor-Leste Commission for Reception, Truth and Reconciliation (CAVR)* (2013), part 7.1: 709, para. 432, http://chegareport.org/Chega%20All%20Volumes.pdf (accessed 13 May 2020).
21 Arnold S. Kohen, *From the Place of the Dead: The Epic Struggles of Bishop Belo of East Timor* (New York: St Martin's, 1999), 189.

22 Erica Chenoweth and Maria J. Stephan, *Why Civil Resistance Works: The Strategic Logic of Nonviolent Conflict* (New York: Columbia University Press, 2013), 4.
23 Ibid., 3.
24 The Timor-Leste Commission, 3: 263, para. 465.
25 Ibid., 7.1: 723, para. 475.
26 I was present at the Corpus Christi procession in Dili in June 1999 where thousands of people lined the streets as hundreds of religious and priests walked with the Blessed Sacrament, with armed military all along the route. The laity did not walk in procession, such an action being considered too dangerous. The procession ended at the park in Lecidere, where Bishop Belo spoke of human dignity in the context of the self-giving of Christ in the Eucharist. The people then left for their homes in relative silence.
27 Chenoweth and Stephan, *Why Civil Resistance Works*, 7.
28 Ibid., 10.
29 Ibid., 78, 79.
30 Richard Tanter, Mark Selden and Stephen R. Shalom, eds, *Bitter Flowers, Sweet Flowers: East Timor, Indonesia and the World Community* (Annandale, NSW: Pluto, 2001), 123.
31 José Ramos-Horta, 'Former East Timor President José Ramos-Horta's Advice for Syrian Rebels', *Daily Beast*, 18 July 2012, http://www.thedailybeast.com/former-east-timor-president-jose-ramos-hortas-advice-for-syrian-rebels (accessed 11 May 2020).
32 John G. Taylor, *Indonesia's Forgotten War: The Hidden History of East Timor* (Leichhardt: Pluto, 1991), 124, 159.
33 The numerical growth of the church was huge during the occupation, increasing from about 30 per cent to 95 per cent. See Hilton Deakin (with Jim and Therese D'Orsa), *Bonded through Tragedy, United in Hope: The Catholic Church and East Timor's Struggle for Independence – a Memoir* (Mulgrave, Vic: Garratt, 2017), 13, 114.
34 Joel Hodge, *Resisting Violence and Victimisation: Christian Faith and Solidarity in East Timor* (Burlington, VT: Ashgate, 2012), 59.
35 Arnold S. Kohen, *From the Place of the Dead: The Epic Struggles of Bishop Belo of East Timor* (New York: St Martin's, 1999), 120.
36 William T. Cavanaugh, *Torture and Eucharist: Theology, Politics and the Body of Christ* (Malden, MA: Blackwell, 1998), 120.
37 Hodge, *Resisting Violence and Victimisation*, 57.
38 Timor-Leste has not pressured Indonesia for redress against perpetrators, but neither has any other nation or any international body. Cf. the Timor-Leste Commission, 9: 2460–1, para. 102, incl. table 3: Result of Community Reconciliation Program with part 8: 2274, table 1: Perpetrator Responsibility; Clinton Fernandes, 'Indonesia and East Timor: Against Impunity, for Justice',

APSNet Policy Forum, 24 April 2008, http://nautilus.org/apsnet/indonesia-and-east-timor-against-impunity-for-justice/ (accessed 11 May 2020).
39 Raymund Schwager, *Must There Be Scapegoats? Violence and Redemption in the Bible*, 2nd ed. (Herefordshire: Gracewing, 2000), 173. Cf. Mt. 5.39, Rom. 12.17, 1 Thess. 5.15, 1 Pet. 3.9.
40 Schwager, *Must There Be Scapegoats?*, 172.
41 René Girard, *Battling to the End: Conversations with Benoît Chantre*, trans. Mary Baker (East Lansing: Michigan State University Press, 2010), 109.
42 Joel Hodge, *Violence in the Name of God: The Militant Jihadist Response to Modernity* (London: Bloomsbury, 2020), 32–3.
43 Girard, *Battling to the End*, xiv.
44 René Girard, *Violence and the Sacred*, trans. Patrick Gregory (London: Continuum, 1988), 94–7, 317.
45 James Alison, *The Joy of Being Wrong: Original Sin through Easter Eyes* (New York: Crossroad, 1998), 121.
46 Andrew T. Lincoln, *A Commentary on the Gospel according to St John* (London: Continuum, 2005), 469.
47 Ibid.
48 Ibid., 468.
49 Ibid.
50 Girard, *Battling to the End*, xiv.
51 Melissa Browning, *Epistemological Privilege and Collaborative Research: A Reflection on Researching as an Outsider* (Chicago: Loyola University, 2013), http://practicalmattersjournal.org/2013/03/01/epistemological-privilege/ (accessed 11 May 2020).
52 Girard, *Violence and the Sacred*, 14.
53 James Alison, *Raising Abel: The Recovery of the Eschatological Imagination*, 2nd ed. (London: Society for Promoting Christian Knowledge, 2010), 141–2.
54 It could be argued that there were mixed motives behind such forgiveness, for example, evasion of responsibility for the unaddressed violence of the civil war prior to the invasion and the serious crimes committed by Timorese in 1999. Nevertheless, the complicity of its neighbours over decades caused far greater destruction of Timorese life and property than any Timorese internal problems and divisions.
55 Felix Neto, Maria da Conceição Pinto and Etienne Mullet, *Forgiveness and Reconciliation in an Inter-group Context: East Timor's Perspectives* (Hauppauge: Nova Science, 2011), ProQuest Ebook Central, viii (accessed 20 October 2017).
56 John Braithwaite, Hilary Charlesworth and Adérito Soares, 'Networked Governance of Freedom and Tyranny: Peace in Timor-Leste', Canberra: ANU Press, 2012): 193–4, https://www.jstor.org/stable/j.ctt24h2jz.17 (accessed 11 May 2020).

57 Kay Rala Gusmão, *Challenges for Peace and Stability*, Chancellor's Human Rights Lecture (Melbourne: University of Melbourne, 2003), www.unimelb.edu.au/__data/assets/pdf_file/0004/1727572/20030407-gusmao.pdf (accessed 11 May 2020).
58 Robert J. Schreiter, *The Ministry of Reconciliation: Spirituality and Strategies* (Maryknoll, NY: Orbis, 2005), 55–6.
59 Ibid., 55.
60 Ibid., 58.
61 Ibid.
62 Lux Lucis, *A Hero's Journey* (Singapore: Madmax Films, 2006), DVD, http://www.luxlucis.sg/WhereTheSunRises.htm (accessed 11 May 2020).
63 Xanana Gusmão, 'His Excellency Xanana Gusmão accepts Honorary Doctorate and Acknowledges Balibó House Trust', Balibó House Trust (2015), http://balibohouse.com/excellency-xanana-gusmao-accepts-honorary-doctorate-acknowledges-balibo-house-trust/ (accessed 11 May 2020).
64 Sara Everingham, 'Horta Says No to War Crimes Tribunal', ABC Radio National, World Today, 28 August 2009, http://www.abc.net.au/worldtoday/content/2009/s2669794.htm (accessed 12 May 2020).
65 Madalena Pampalk, 'Accountability for Serious Crimes and National Reconciliation in Timor-Leste: Progress or Wishful Thinking?', *Australian Journal for South-East Asian Studies* 3(1) (2001): 19, https://nbn-resolving.org/urn:nbn:de:0168-ssoar-362381 (accessed 11 May 2020).
66 Ibid., 25 and 23.
67 Suzannah Linton, 'Putting Things in Perspective: The Realities of Accountability in East Timor, Indonesia and Cambodia', *Maryland Series in Contemporary Asian Studies* 3(182) (2005): 65, http://digitalcommons.law.umaryland.edu/mscas/vol2005/iss3/1/ (accessed 11 May 2020).
68 The Timor-Leste Commission, 9: 2427, para. 2 and 6: 2429, para. 11; 2461: table 2, http://chegareport.org/Chega%20All%20Volumes.pdf (accessed 9 May 2020).
69 Hodge, *Resisting Violence and Victimisation*, 190.
70 Gusmão, *Challenges for Peace and Stability*.
71 I was present in the cathedral when Fr Doherty made this comment, and I have spoken with him about it since.
72 Annika Kovar and Andrew Harrington, 'Breaking the Cycle of Domestic Violence in Timor-Leste: Access to Justice Options, Barriers, and Decision-Making Processes in the Context of Legal Pluralism', *Justice System Program, UNDP Timor-Leste* (October 2013), http://www.undp.org/content/dam/timorleste/docs/reports/DG/Domesticpercent20Violencepercent20Reportpercent20_withpercent20coverpercent20FINAL.pdf (accessed 11 May 2020).
73 René Girard, *The Scapegoat*, trans. Yvonne Freccero (Baltimore: The Johns Hopkins University Press, 1986), 212.
74 Girard, *Battling to the End*, xiv.

75 Ibid., 13.
76 Robert J. Schreiter, *Reconciliation: Mission and Ministry in a Changing Social Order* (Maryknoll, NY: Orbis, 2000), 45–6.
77 Ibid., 21–3.
78 Ibid., 19.
79 Ibid., 25.
80 Ibid., 45.
81 Ibid.
82 Ibid., 60.
83 Lux Lucis, *A Hero's Journey*.

7 Solidarity and conversion

1 René Girard, *The Girard Reader*, ed. James G. Williams (New York: Crossroad, 1996), 284.
2 René Girard, *Deceit, Desire and the Novel*, trans. Yvonne Freccero (Baltimore: The Johns Hopkins University Press, 1976), 3.
3 Carmen Budiardjo, 'The International Solidarity Movement for East Timor: A Weapon More Powerful than Guns', *Tapol*, 17 May 2002, https://www.tapol.org/news/international-solidarity-movement-east-timor-weapon-more-powerful-guns (accessed 11 May 2020); Clinton Fernandes, *The Independence of East Timor: Multi-dimensional Perspectives – Occupation, Resistance, and International Political Activism* (Eastbourne: Sussex Academic, 2011), 91–7.
4 Kumi Naidoo and Sylvia Borren, 'Civil Society', in *International Development: Ideas, Experience, and Prospects*, ed. Bruce Currie-Alder, Ravi Kanbur, David M. Malone and Rohinton Medhora (Oxford: Oxford University Press, Oxford Scholarship Online, 2014), https://idl-bnc-idrc.dspacedirect.org/bitstream/handle/10625/51588/IDL-51588.pdf?sequence=1&isAllowed=y (accessed 12 May 2020).
5 Monica Ciobanu, 'Civil Society', in *Encyclopedia of Activism and Social Justice*, ed. Gary L. Anderson and Kathryn G. Herr (Thousand Oaks, CA: SAGE, 2007), 2, doi: http://dx.doi.org/10.4135/9781412956215.n185 (accessed 29 September 2016).
6 The Timor-Leste Commission for Reception, Truth and Reconciliation (CAVR), *Chega! The Final Report of the Timor-Leste Commission for Reception, Truth and Reconciliation (CAVR)* (2013), part 7.1: 708, para. 430; 740, para. 526, http://chegareport.org/Chega%20All%20Volumes.pdf (accessed 13 May 2020).
7 Ibid., 7.1: 728, para. 487.
8 See http//:www.etan.org.
9 The Timor-Leste Commission, 7.1: 727, para. 485.
10 Ibid.

11 J. De Groot and Louise Crowe, 'Just Reading No. 2, the Church and East Timor: A Collection of Documents by National and International Catholic Church Agencies', in *Catholic Commission for Justice, Development and Peace* (Melbourne: Catholic Archdiocese, 1993); East Timor Human Rights Centre, *Human Rights Deteriorate in East Timor: Bi-annual Report of Human Rights Violations in East Timor January to July 1997* (Fitzroy: Human Rights Centre, 1997).
12 Arnold S. Kohen, *From the Place of the Dead: The Epic Struggles of Bishop Belo of East Timor* (New York: St Martin's, 1999), 290.
13 Don Greenlees and Robert Garran, *Deliverance: The Inside Story of East Timor's Fight for Freedom* (Crows Nest, NSW: Allen & Unwin, 2002), 22.
14 Rodney Tiffen, *Diplomatic Deceits: Government, Media and East Timor* (Sydney: University of New South Wales Press, 2001), 45.
15 René Girard, *Things Hidden since the Foundation of the World*, trans. S. Bann and M. Metteer (Stanford, CA: Stanford University Press, 1987), 138; René Girard, *The Scapegoat*, trans. Yvonne Freccero (Baltimore: The Johns Hopkins University Press, 1986), 27.
16 Angie Zelter, 'Civil Society and Global Responsibility: The Arms Trade and East Timor', 31 October 1997, http://ad9.org/pegasus/peace/zelter.htm (accessed 11 May 2020).
17 The Timor-Leste Commission, 7.1: 709, para. 430.
18 Ibid., 7.1: 732, para. 499.
19 René Girard, *I See Satan Fall Like Lightning*, trans. J. G. Williams (Maryknoll, NY: Orbis, 2001), 161.
20 Ibid., 165.
21 Ibid., 168.
22 Amanda Wise, *Exile and Return among the Timorese* (Philadelphia: University of Pennsylvania Press, 2006), 45–7.
23 The Timor-Leste Commission, 7.1: 710, para. 437.
24 Charles Taylor, *Modern Social Imaginaries* (Durham, NC: Duke University Press, 2004), 183.
25 *Australian Groups specifically founded for East Timor before 1999 included:*
2/2 Commando Association; Action in Solidarity with Indonesia and East Timor; Australian Coalition for East Timor; Australia-East Timor Association; Australians for a Free East Timor; Australia East Timor Friendship Association; Brisbane East Timor Office; Campaign for an Independent East Timor; East Timor Action Coalition; East Timor Campaign; East Timor Foundation; East Timor Human Rights Centre; East Timor International Support Centre; East Timor Justice Lobby; East Timor Relief Association; Friends of East Timor; Hobart East Timor Committee; Christians in Solidarity With East Timor; Christian Sanctuary Network Australia; Mary MacKillop Institute of East Timorese Studies; Parliamentarians

for East Timor; Timor Aid; Timor Aid for Children; Timor Information Service; University Students for East Timor.

Australian groups adopting a focus on East Timor included:
APHEDA – Union Aid Abroad; Action for World Development; Amnesty International; Australian Campaign against the Arms Trade; Australian Catholic Relief (later Caritas); Australian Council for Overseas Aid; Australian Council of Churches; Australian Forum of Human Rights Organisations; Australian People for Health, Democratic Socialist Perspective; Education and Development Abroad; Campaign against Militarism; Catholic Commission for Justice and Peace (replaced by Australian Catholic Social Justice Council); Churches (numerous); Community Aid Abroad; International Commission of Jurists – Australian Section; Minority Rights Group International; National Council of Major Religious Superiors of Australia; Pax Christi; Service for the Treatment and Rehabilitation of Torture and Trauma Survivors; Trade Unions (numerous); Australian Education Union; Young Christian Workers; Young Christian Students.

26 The Timor-Leste Commission, 7.1: 711, para. 439.
27 Patrick A. Smythe, *The Heaviest Blow: The Catholic Church and the East Timor Issue* (Münster: Lit Verlag, 2004), 102, 115 and 133; The Timor-Leste Commission, 7.1: 728, para. 487; David Scott, *Last Flight Out of Dili: Memoirs of an Accidental Activist in the Triumph of East Timor* (North Melbourne: Pluto, 2005), 63–70.
28 The Timor-Leste Commission, 7.1: 715, para. 450.
29 D. O'Connor, A. C. Thompson, G. C. Hart and A. D. Stevenson, 'Australia's Debt to the Timorese', Letters, *Sydney Morning Herald*, 18 August 1975.
30 Robert Domm interviewed Xanana Gusmão; see Mark Aarons and Robert Domm, *East Timor: A Western Made Tragedy* (Sydney: Left Book Club, 1992), 55–60.
31 For example, Rob Wesley-Smith. See John Izzard, 'Crumbs of Compassion', *Quadrant*, 1 March 2010, http://quadrant.org.au/magazine/2010/03/crumbs-of-compassion/ (accessed 11 May 2020).
32 Shirley Shackleton, *The Circle of Silence: A Personal Testimony before, during and after Balibó* (Millers Point, NSW: Murdoch Books Australia, 2010).
33 Scott, *Last Flight Out of Dili*, 19.
34 J. DeGroot and Louise Crowe, 'Just Reading No. 2', v.
35 Rob Wesley-Smith, 'Radio Maubere and Links to East Timor', in *Free East Timor: Australia's Culpability in East Timor's Genocide*, ed. Jim Aubrey (Milsons Point: Random House, 1998), 84.
36 Ibid., 92–3.
37 'Maubere' was a derogatory term used by the Portuguese to describe the poorer sections of the Timorese people, and it was subsequently used by the Timorese with pride.

38 Wesley-Smith, 'Radio Maubere', 84.
39 Ibid., 83–96; Mark Aarons, 'Truth, Death & Diplomacy in East Timor', *Monthly*, Essays (April 2006), https://www.themonthly.com.au/monthly-essays-mark-aarons-truth-death-diplomacy-east-timor-commission-s-report-confirms-australian (accessed 6 September 2021).
40 Joseph Nevins, *A Not-So-Distant Horror: Mass Violence in East Timor* (Ithaca, NY: Cornell University Press, 2005), 120 and 240 n. 25; Geoffrey C. Gunn, *Complicity in Genocide: Report to the East Timor 'Truth Commission' on International Actors* (Geoffrey C. Gunn, 2006), 118–22.
41 Scott, *Last Flight Out of Dili*, 59.
42 Ibid.
43 'Time to Get Tough with Indonesia', *Australian*, 7 September 1999.
44 'Act to Stop the Slaughter', *Sydney Morning Herald*, 7 September 1999.
45 Kerry Myers, Letters Editor, 'Postscript', *Sydney Morning Herald*, 13 September 1999.
46 'Australia's Anger', *Australian*, 9 September 1999, 2.
47 An account of this action by Gareth Smith and others appears at 'Shame Australia Shame – Appeal for Donations', in www.etan.org, http://www.etan.org/et2001a/january/01-06/01shame.htm (accessed 11 May 2020).
48 'The Tide of Protest Swells', *Weekend Australian*, 11–12 September 1999, 5.
49 Joel Hodge, *Resisting Violence and Victimisation: Christian Faith and Solidarity in East Timor* (Burlington, VT: Ashgate, 2012), 87.
50 Smythe, *The Heaviest Blow*, 1.
51 J. Xie, S. Sreenivasan, G. Korniss, W. Zhang, C. Lim and B. K. Szymanski, 'Social Consensus through the Influence of Committed Minorities', *Physical Review* E 84(1) 011130 (July 2011), https://www.cs.rpi.edu/~szymansk/papers/pre.11.pdf (accessed 11 May 2020); 'Minority Rules: Scientists Discover Tipping Point for the Spread of Ideas', 25 July 2011, http://phys.org/news/2011-07-minority-scientists-ideas.html. (accessed 11 May 2020),
52 Xie et al., 'Social Consensus through the Influence of Committed Minorities'.
53 Erica Chenoweth and Maria J. Stephan, *Why Civil Resistance Works: The Strategic Logic of Nonviolent Conflict* (New York: Columbia University Press, 2013), 36.
54 Paul Kelly, *The March of Patriots: The Struggle for Modern Australia* (Carlton, Vic: Melbourne University Press, 2011), 488.
55 Department of Foreign Affairs and Trade (DFAT), *East Timor in Transition 1998–2000: An Australian Policy Challenge* (2001), v.
56 Clinton Fernandes, *Reluctant Saviour: Australia, Indonesia and the Independence of East Timor* (Carlton North, Vic: Scribe, 2004), 113.
57 Sam Pietsch, 'Australian Imperialism and East Timor', *Marxist Interventions* 2 (May 2010): 7, http://sa.org.au/mi/2/mi2.pdf (accessed 11 May 2020).
58 Ibid., 17.

59 Geoffrey Robinson, *If You Leave Us Here, We Will Die: How Genocide Was Stopped in East Timor* (Princeton, NJ: Princeton University Press, 2010), 19.
60 Ibid., 19, 186.
61 Ibid., 19.
62 Ibid., 95.
63 Ibid., 94.
64 Ibid., 19.
65 Pietsch, 'Australian Imperialism and East Timor', 9.
66 'Agony at Our Doorstep', *Sydney Morning Herald*, 1 November 1979, 1.
67 James Alison, *The Joy of Being Wrong: Original Sin through Easter Eyes* (New York: Crossroad, 1998), 62.
68 Hamish McDonald, 'Failure of the Inevitable', *Sydney Morning Herald*, 29 August 1998.
69 Alan Ramsey, 'Timor: A Debt Dishonoured', *Sydney Morning Herald*, 25 September 1999.
70 Paul Kelly, 'Shattered Myths', *Weekend Australian*, 11–12 September 1999, 25.
71 Hank Nelson, 'Gallipoli, Kokoda and the Making of National Identity', in *The Australian Legend and Its Discontents*, ed. Richard Nile (St Lucia: University of Queensland Press, 2000), 216.
72 Alison, *The Joy of Being Wrong*, 124.
73 The Timor-Leste Commission, 9: 2427. This part of the CAVR concerning community reconciliation remains an ongoing challenge.
74 Jeremiah L. Alberg, *Beneath the Veil of the Strange Verses: Reading Scandalous Texts* (East Lansing: Michigan State University Press, 2013), 120.
75 Ibid., 90.
76 Geoffrey Robertson QC, *Crimes against Humanity: The Struggle for Global Justice*, 3rd ed. (Camberwell: Penguin, 2006), 503.
77 Another related investigation occurred when Portugal took Australia to the world court in 1995 claiming that Australia and Indonesia's Timor Gap Treaty refused to recognize East Timor's right to self-determination. The International Court of Justice, via a minor legal point, declined to state the fact that Indonesia was an illegal occupier. See ibid., 495.
78 Madalena Pampalk, 'Accountability for Serious Crimes and National Reconciliation in Timor-Leste: Progress or Wishful Thinking?', *Australian Journal for South-East Asian Studies* 3(1) (2010): 13, https://nbn-resolving.org/urn:nbn:de:0168-ssoar-362381 (accessed 11 May 2020).
79 Uniya Jesuit Social Justice Centre, *Justice and Reconciliation in East Timor: Australia and the CAVR* (Kings Cross, NSW: Uniya, 2006), 12.
80 Girard, *The Girard Reader*, 82.
81 Ibid., 85.

82 James Alison, *Knowing Jesus* (London: Society for Promoting Christian Knowledge, 1993), 44; Girard, *Things Hidden*, 426.
83 Girard, *Things Hidden*, 426.
84 Girard, *I See Satan Fall Like Lightning*, 158.
85 René Girard, *Battling to the End: Conversations with Benoît Chantre*, trans. Mary Baker (East Lansing: Michigan State University Press, 2010), 205.
86 Ibid., 117.
87 Ibid., xiv, 21.
88 Terry Veling, *For You Alone: Emmanuel Levinas and the Answerable Life* (Eugene, OR: Cascade, 2014), 151.
89 Ibid., 70.
90 Ibid., 76.
91 Ada María Isasi-Díaz, quoted in Melissa Browning, *Epistemological Privilege and Collaborative Research: A Reflection on Researching as an Outsider* (Chicago: Loyola University, 2013), 13, http://practicalmattersjournal.org/2013/03/01/epistemological-privilege/ (accessed 11 May 2020).
92 Veling, *For You Alone*, 70.
93 Ann Astell, 'Violence, Mysticism and René Girard', *Theological Studies* 78(2) (2017): 391, http://journals.sagepub.com/doi/abs/10.1177/0040563917698560?journalCode=tsja (accessed 5 September 2017).
94 Ibid., 40.
95 Girard, *The Girard Reader*, 284.
96 Hodge, *Resisting Violence and Victimisation*, 46.
97 Girard, *The Girard Reader*, 62–5.
98 Girard, *Battling to the End*, 109.
99 Ibid.
100 Girard, *Things Hidden*, 217.
101 Ibid.

Afterword

1 Hank Nelson, 'Gallipoli, Kokoda and the Making of National Identity', in *The Australian Legend and Its Discontents*, ed. Richard Nile (St Lucia: University of Queensland Press, 2000), 216.

Bibliography

Aarons, Mark, and Robert Domm. *East Timor: A Western Made Tragedy*. Sydney: Left Book Club, 1992.

ABC Radio National. 'Did the Walls Have Ears?' *Background Briefing*, 23 February 2014. https://www.abc.net.au/radionational/programs/backgroundbriefing/5267456 (accessed 13 February 2020).

'Act to Stop the Slaughter'. *Sydney Morning Herald*, 7 September 1999.

'Agony at Our Doorstep: Indonesia Didn't Want You to See These Pictures'. *Sydney Morning Herald*, 1 November 1979, 1.

Alberg, Jeremiah L. *Beneath the Veil of the Strange Verses: Reading Scandalous Texts*. East Lansing: Michigan State University Press, 2013.

Alison, James. *The Joy of Being Wrong: Original Sin through Easter Eyes*. New York: Crossroad, 1998.

Alison, James. *Knowing Jesus*. London: Society for Promoting Christian Knowledge, 1993.

Alison, James. *Raising Abel: The Recovery of the Eschatological Imagination*, 2nd ed. London: Society for Promoting Christian Knowledge, 2010.

Alston, R. K. R. 'Timor Bishop Defended'. *Sydney Morning Herald Letters*, 5 April 1982.

Anderson, Benedict R. *Imagined Communities: Reflections on the Origin and Spread of Nationalism*, rev. ed. London: Verso, 2006.

Andrade, Gabriel. 'René Girard'. *Internet Encyclopedia of Philosophy*. http://www.iep.utm.edu/girard/#H6 (accessed 10 May 2020).

Astell, Ann. 'Violence, Mysticism and René Girard'. *Theological Studies* 78(2) (2017): 391. http://journals.sagepub.com/doi/abs/10.1177/0040563917698560?journalCode=tsja (accessed 5 September 2017).

Attwood, Bain. 'Contesting Frontiers: History, Memory and Narrative in a National Museum'. *reCollections* 1(2) (September 2006). http://recollections.nma.gov.au/issues/vol_1_no_2/papers/contesting_frontiers - nav (accessed 10 May 2020).

Attwood, Bain. 'The Past as Future: Aborigines, Australia and the (Dis)course of History'. *Australian Humanities Review*, no. 1 (April 1996). http://australianhumanitiesreview.org/1996/04/01/the-past-as-future-aborigines-australia-and-the-discourse-of-history/ (accessed 10 May 2020).

Aubrey, Jim. 'Jakarta's Trojan Horse in East Timor'. In *The East Timor Question: The Struggle for Independence from Indonesia*, edited by Paul Hainsworth and Stephen McCloskey, 133–47. London: I.B. Taurus, 2000.

Australian Bureau of Statistics. *100 Years of Australian Lives, Second World War 1939–1945*. http://www.abs.gov.au/ausstats/abs@.nsf/Lookup/2071.0main+features952012-2013 (accessed 10 May 2020).

'Australian Curriculum'. In *Australian Curriculum, Assessment and Reporting Authority*. https://www.australiancurriculum.edu.au/Search/?q=Timor (accessed 10 May 2020).

Australian Federal Police. *Balibo Five Disclosure Log*, Reference 20/2015. AFP Disclosure Log FOI – CRM No. 2015/198. https://www.afp.gov.au/sites/default/files/PDF/Disclosure-Log/20-2015.pdf (accessed 10 May 2020).

'Australian Federal Police Drop Investigation into the Murders of the "Balibo Five"'. News.com.au, 21 October 2014. http://www.news.com.au/world/asia/australian-federal-police-drop-investigation-into-the-murders-of-the-Balibó-five/news-story/a9af0adb251342c3f7e93070c084985f (accessed 10 May 2020).

Australian Information Service. *Transcript of Press Conference by Mr Gough Whitlam*, 5 March 1982, 12. https://timorarchives.files.wordpress.com/2012/02/eto_w-h_12.pdf (accessed 8 May 2020).

Australian War Memorial. *Far Eastern Liaison Office (FELO) Leaflet Collection*. 'PG 9: Your Friends Do Not Forget You'. https://www.awm.gov.au/collection/accessing-records-at-the-memorial/findingaids/special/cards/felo#s34 (accessed 10 May 2020).

'Australia's Anger'. *Australian*, 9 September 1999, 2.

Ayris, Cyril. *All the Bull's Men*. Hamilton Hill, WA: 2/2 Commando Association, 2006.

'Backing for Timor Plea'. *Northern Territory News*, 11 January 1982, 1. https://timorarchives.files.wordpress.com/2012/03/eto-attic3-02.pdf (accessed 11 May 2020).

Bailie, Gil. *Violence Unveiled: Humanity at the Crossroads*. New York: Crossroad, 1997.

Ball, Desmond, and Hamish McDonald. *Death in Balibo Lies in Canberra*. St. Leonards, NSW: Allen & Unwin, 2000.

Barker, Anne. 'Declassified Intelligence Documents Shed Light on 1999 Timor Leste Independence'. *Sydney Morning Herald*, 29 August 2019. https://www.abc.net.au/news/2019-08-29/declassified-us-intelligence-documents-sheds-light-timor-leste/11459284 (accessed 25 February 2021).

Bashford, Alison, and Stuart Macintyre, eds. *The Cambridge History of Australia*. Port Melbourne, Vic: Cambridge University Press, 2015.

'Battle for Australia Association'. http://www.battleforaustralia.org.au/index.php (accessed 10 May 2020).

Black, David. 'Menzies and Curtin in World War Two'. *John Curtin Prime Ministerial Library*. http://john.curtin.edu.au/ww2leaders/war.html (accessed 10 May 2020).

Blainey, Geoffrey. 'Native Fiction: A Review of *The Fabrication of Aboriginal History*, by Keith Windschuttle'. *New Criterion* (April 2003). https://www.newcriterion.com/issues/2003/4/native-fiction (accessed 10 May 2020).

Blainey, Geoffrey. *A Shorter History of Australia*. North Sydney: Vintage, 1994.

Bolton, Geoffrey. *The Oxford History of Australia: Volume 5, 1942–1995: The Middle Way, 1942–1995*, 2nd ed. Melbourne: Oxford University Press, 1996.

Bowen, James. 'Battle for Australia'. http://www.battleforaustralia.org/battaust/JapdebAustinvade.html (accessed 10 May 2020).
Boyce, James. 'Fantasy Island'. In *Whitewash: On Keith Windschuttle's Fabrication of Aboriginal History*, edited by Robert Manne, 17–78. Melbourne: Black Inc. Agenda, 2003.
Braithwaite, John, Hilary Charlesworth and Adérito Soares. 'Transitional Justice and Reconciliation'. In *Networked Governance of Freedom and Tyranny: Peace in Timor-Leste*, 175–235. Canberra: ANU Press, 2012. https://www.jstor.org/stable/j.ctt24h2jz.17 (accessed 7 September 2021).
Breen, Bob. *Mission Accomplished: East Timor*. Crows Nest, NSW: Allen & Unwin, n.d.
Brennan, Frank. *Time to Draw the Line: Finding a Just Settlement between Australia and Timor-Leste*. Alexandria: Australian Catholic Social Justice Council, 2013.
Brown, Gary, and David Anderson. *Invasion 1942? Australia and the Japanese Threat*, Background Paper Number 6. Canberra: Parliamentary Research Service, 29 April 1992.
Browning, Melissa. *Epistemological Privilege and Collaborative Research: A Reflection on Researching as an Outsider*. Chicago: Loyola University, 2013. http://practicalmattersjournal.org/2013/03/01/epistemological-privilege/ (accessed 11 May 2020).
Budiardjo, Carmen. 'The International Solidarity Movement for East Timor: A Weapon More Powerful than Guns'. *Tapol*, 17 May 2002. https://www.tapol.org/news/international-solidarity-movement-east-timor-weapon-more-powerful-guns (accessed 11 May 2020).
Bullard, Steven. 'Japanese Strategy and Intentions towards Australia'. In *Australia 1942: In the Shadow of War*, edited by Peter J. Dean, 124–39. Cambridge: Cambridge University Press, 2010.
Callinan, B. S. *Independent Company: The 2/2/ and 2/4 Australian Independent Companies in Portuguese Timor 1941–43*. Heinemann: Melbourne, 1953.
Campbell, Archie. *Double Reds of Timor*. Swanbourne, WA: John Burridge Military Antiques, 1995.
Canadian Broadcasting Corporation. 'The Scapegoat: René Girard's Anthropology of Violence and Religion'. *CBC Ideas Transcripts* 5–9 March 2001. http://www.radio.cbc.ca/programs/ideas/girard/index.html (accessed 31 January 2020).
Catholic Commission for Justice, Development and Peace. *Just Reading No. 2 The Church and East Timor: A Collection of Documents by National and International Catholic Church Agencies*. Melbourne: Catholic Archdiocese, 1993.
Cavanaugh, William T. *Torture and Eucharist: Theology, Politics and the Body of Christ*. Malden, MA: Blackwell, 1998.
'Chart: World War II Casualties as a Percentage of Each Country's Population'. Top Foreign Stocks.com. http://topforeignstocks.com/2016/04/19/chart-world-war-ii-casualties-as-a-percentage-of-each-countrys-population/ (accessed 10 May 2020).

Chenoweth, Erica, and Maria J. Stephan. *Why Civil Resistance Works: The Strategic Logic of Nonviolent Conflict*. New York: Columbia University Press, 2013.

Ciobanu, Monica. 'Civil Society'. In *Encyclopedia of Activism and Social Justice*, edited by Gary L. Anderson and Kathryn G. Herr, 347–50. Thousand Oaks, CA: SAGE, 2007. http://dx.doi.org/10.4135/9781412956215.n185 (accessed 29 September 2016).

Clark, Manning. *The Quest for an Australian Identity*. St Lucia: University of Queensland Press, 1980.

Clark, Roger S. 'Timor Gap'. In *East Timor at the Crossroads: The Forging of a Nation*, edited by Peter Carey and G. Carter Bentley, 73–94. London: Cassell, 1995.

Cleary, Paul. *The Men Who Came Out of the Ground: A Gripping Account of Australia's First Commando Campaign Timor 1942*. Sydney: Hachette Australia, 2010.

Collaery, Bernard. *Oil under Troubled Water: Australia's Timor Sea Intrigue*. Melbourne: Melbourne University Press, 2020.

Collins, Lance, and Robert Reed. *Plunging Point: Intelligence Failures, Cover-Ups and Consequences*. Pymble, NSW: HarperCollins, 2005.

Commonwealth of Australia. 'Security Treaty between Australia, New Zealand and the United States of America [ANZUS]'. *Australian Treaty Series 1952 No. 2*. Canberra: Australian Government Publishing Service, 1997. http://www.austlii.edu.au/au/other/dfat/treaties/1952/2.html (accessed 10 May 2020).

Connelly, Aaron L. 'Keeping Expectations for the Australia-Indonesia Relationship in Check'. *Interpreter* 4 (November 2016). https://www.lowyinstitute.org/the-interpreter/keeping-expectations-australia-indonesia-relationship-check (accessed 10 May 2020).

Costello, John. *The Pacific War 1941–1945*. New York: Harper Perennial, 1981.

Coulthard-Clark, C. D. *Where Australians Fought: The Encyclopaedia of Australia's Battles*. St Leonards, NSW: Allen & Unwin, 1998.

Cowdell, Scott. 'Hard Evidence for Girardian Mimetic Theory? Intersubjectivity and Mirror Neurons'. In *Violence, Desire, and the Sacred: Girard's Mimetic Theory across the Disciplines*, edited by Scott Cowdell, Chris Fleming and Joel Hodge, 219–26. London: Bloomsbury Academic, 2012.

Curthoys, Anne. 'Mythologies'. In *The Australian Legend and Its Discontents*, edited by Richard Nile. St Lucia: University of Queensland Press, 2000.

Day, David. *Claiming a Continent: A New History of Australia*. Pymble, NSW: HarperCollins, 2001.

De Groot, J., and Louise Crowe. 'Just Reading No. 2, The Church and East Timor: A Collection of Documents by National and International Catholic Church Agencies'. In *Catholic Commission for Justice, Development and Peace*. Melbourne: Catholic Archdiocese, 1993.

Deakin, Hilton (with Jim and Therese D'Orsa). *Bonded through Tragedy, United in Hope: The Catholic Church and East Timor's Struggle for Independence – a Memoir*. Mulgrave, Vic: Garratt, 2017.

Department of Foreign Affairs and Trade. *Agreement between Australia and the Republic of Indonesia on the Framework for Security Cooperation*. Mataram, Lombok, 13 November 2006. http://www.austlii.edu.au/au/other/dfat/nia/2006/43.html (accessed 10 May 2020).

Department of Foreign Affairs and Trade. *Documents on Australian Foreign Policy (DAFP) Historical Documents 1941, July–1942, June*, vol. 5. https://www.dfat.gov.au/about-us/publications/historical-documents/Pages/volume-05/1941-july-1942-june-volume-5 (accessed 10 May 2020).

Department of Foreign Affairs and Trade. *East Timor in Transition 1998–2000: An Australian Policy Challenge*. Canberra: DFAT, 2001.

Department of Foreign Affairs and Trade. *Timor-Leste: Political, Economic and Trade Information*. https://www.dfat.gov.au/geo/timor-leste/timor-leste (accessed 22 February 2021).

Department of Veterans' Affairs. *Australia's War 1939–1945*. https://anzacportal.dva.gov.au/wars-and-missions/world-war-ii-1939-1945/events/coral-sea-kokoda-and-milne-bay-may-september-1942 (accessed 10 May 2020).

Devine, Miranda. 'Truce, and Truth, in History Wars'. *Sydney Morning Herald*, 20 April 2006. http://www.smh.com.au/news/opinion/truce-and-truth-in-history-wars/2006/04/19/1145344151509.html (accessed 12 May 2020).

Dixson, Miriam. *The Imaginary Australian: Anglo-Celts and Identity, 1788 to the Present*. Sydney: University of New South Wales Press, 1999.

Dorling, Philip. 'Attorney-General George Brandis Tries to Keep East Timor War Crimes Secret'. *Sydney Morning Herald*, 28 January 2014. http://www.smh.com.au/federal-politics/political-news/attorneygeneral-george-brandis-tries-to-keep-east-timor-war-crimes-secret-20140127-31iyb.html (accessed 12 May 2020).

Dumouchel, Paul. 'A Theory of Everything? A Methodological Tale'. In *The Palgrave Handbook of Mimetic Theory and Religion*, edited by James Alison and Wolfgang Palaver, 463–9. New York: Palgrave Macmillan, 2017.

Dunn, James. 'Communist Influence in Fretilin Prior to the 1975 Invasion'. East Timor Action Network (ETAN), 29 July 1998. https://etan.org/et/1998/july/july29-31/29communi.htm (accessed 10 May 2020).

Dunn, James. *East Timor: A Rough Passage to Independence*, 3rd ed. Double Bay, NSW: Longueville, 2003.

'East Timor Beset by Famine'. *Sydney Morning Herald*, 6 January 1984, 4.

East Timor Human Rights Centre. *Human Rights Deteriorate in East Timor: Bi-annual Report of Human Rights Violations in East Timor, January to July 1997*. Fitzroy: Human Rights Centre, 1997.

Ellery, David. 'WWII Battle for Aust Questioned'. Canberra Times.com.au, 6 September 2012. http://www.canberratimes.com.au/act-news/wwii-battle-for-aust-questioned-20120905-25eoy.html (accessed 12 May 2020).

Everingham, Sara. 'Balibo Five: Investigation into Deaths of Five Journalists Dropped by Australian Federal Police'. *ABC News*, 21 October 2014. http://www.abc.net.au/

news/2014-10-21/Balibó-five-investigation-dropped-by-afp/5828814 (accessed 11 May 2020).

Everingham, Sara. 'Horta Says No to War Crimes Tribunal'. *World Today*, 28 August 2009. http://www.abc.net.au/worldtoday/content/2009/s2669794.htm (accessed 12 May 2020).

Fenney, Gordon. 'Soeharto a 20th Century Great'. *Sydney Morning Herald*, 15 May 1996, 9.

Fernandes, Clinton. *The Independence of East Timor: Multi-dimensional Perspectives – Occupation, Resistance, and International Political Activism*. Eastbourne: Sussex Academic, 2011.

Fernandes, Clinton. 'Indonesia and East Timor: Against Impunity, for Justice'. *Nautilus Institute APSNet Policy Forum*, 24 April 2008. http://nautilus.org/apsnet/indonesia-and-east-timor-against-impunity-for-justice/(accessed 11 May 2020).

Fernandes, Clinton. *Reluctant Saviour: Australia, Indonesia and the Independence of East Timor*. Carlton North, Vic: Scribe, 2004.

Fernandes, Clinton. 'Two Tales of Timor'. In *Zombie Myths of Australian Military History: The Ten Myths That Will Not Die*, edited by Craig A. Stockings, 213–33. Sydney: University of New South Wales Press, 2010.

Firth, Stewart. *Australia in International Politics: An Introduction to Australian Foreign Policy*. St Leonards, NSW: Allen & Unwin, 1999.

FitzSimons, Peter. *Kokoda*. Sydney: Hodder Australia, 2004.

Fraser, Malcolm (with Cain Roberts). *Dangerous Allies*. Melbourne: Melbourne University Press, 2014.

Frei, Henry P. 'Japan's Reluctant Decision to Occupy Portuguese Timor 1 January 1942–20 February 1942'. *Australian Historical Studies* 27(107) (1996): 281–302. http://dx.doi.org/10.1080/10314619608596014 (accessed 5 September 2017).

Frei, Henry P. *Japan's Southward Advance and Australia: From the Sixteenth Century to World War II*. Melbourne: Melbourne University Press, 1991.

Gerry, J. J. *Letter to Mgr da Costa Lopes*, 11 November 1981. https://timorarchives.files.wordpress.com/2012/02/tis_box13-02_10.pdf (accessed 11 May 2020).

Gill, G. Hermon. 'Royal Australian Navy, 1939–1942', 1st ed. Series 2, Volume I, Navy, Chapter 17: 'Prelude to Victory'. Australian War Memorial, Second World War Official Histories Australia in the War of 1939–45 (1957): 625–48. https://s3-ap-southeast-2.amazonaws.com/awm-media/collection/RCDIG1070351/document/5519639.PDF (accessed 10 May 2020).

Girard, René. *Battling to the End: Conversations with Benoît Chantre*. Translated by Mary Baker. East Lansing: Michigan State University Press, 2010.

Girard, René. *Deceit, Desire and the Novel*. Translated by Yvonne Freccero. Baltimore: The Johns Hopkins University Press, 1976.

Girard, René. *The Girard Reader*. Edited by James G. Williams. New York: Crossroad, 1996.

Girard, René. *I See Satan Fall Like Lightning*. Translated by J. G. Williams. Maryknoll, NY: Orbis, 2001.

Girard, René. *The Scapegoat*. Translated by Yvonne Freccero. Baltimore: The Johns Hopkins University Press, 1986.

Girard, René. *Things Hidden since the Foundation of the World*. Translated by S. Bann and M. Metteer. Stanford, CA: Stanford University Press, 1987.

Girard, René. *Violence and the Sacred*. Translated by Patrick Gregory. London: Continuum, 1988.

Gordon, Bernard K. 'The Potential for Indonesian Expansionism'. *Pacific Affairs* 36(4) (1963): 378–93. doi:10.2307/2754684 (accessed 12 May 2020).

Goto, Ken'ichi. *Tensions of Empire: Japan and Southeast Asia in the Colonial and Postcolonial World*. Athens: Ohio University Press, 2003.

Government of Western Australia. *Western Australian Museum – Debt of Honour Exhibition*. http://museum.wa.gov.au/whats-on/debt-honour; *Timor Awakening*, https://www.timorawakening.com/ (accessed 10 May 2020).

Greenlees, Don, and Robert Garran. *Deliverance: The Inside Story of East Timor's Fight for Freedom*. Crows Nest, NSW: Allen & Unwin, 2002.

Gunn, Geoffrey C. *Complicity in Genocide: Report to the East Timor 'Truth Commission' on International Actors*. Geoffrey C. Gunn, 2006.

Gunn, Geoffrey C. *A Critical View of Western Journalism and Scholarship on East Timor*. Manila: Journal of Contemporary Asia, 1994.

Gunn, Geoffrey C. *East Timor and the United Nations: The Case for Intervention*. Laurenceville, NJ: Red Sea, 1997.

Gusmão, Kay Rala (Xanana). *Challenges for Peace and Stability*. Chancellor's Human Rights Lecture, 2003. http://www.unimelb.edu.au/__data/assets/pdf_file/0004/1727572/20030407-gusmao.pdf (accessed 11 May 2020).

Gusmão, Kay Rala (Xanana). *His Excellency Xanana Gusmão Accepts Honorary Doctorate and Acknowledges Balibo House Trust*. Balibo House Trust, 2015. http://balibohouse.com/excellency-xanana-gusmao-accepts-honorary-doctorate-acknowledges-balibo-house-trust/ (accessed 10 May 2020).

Gyngell, Allan, and Michael Wesley. *Making Australian Foreign Policy*, 2nd ed. Melbourne: Cambridge University Press, 2007.

Hage, Ghassan. *White Nation: Fantasies of White Supremacy in a Multicultural Society*. Annandale, NSW: Pluto Press, 1998.

Haigh, Gideon. 'Packed It In: The Demise of the Bulletin'. *Monthly* (March 2008). https://www.themonthly.com.au/issue/2008/march/1268869044/gideon-haigh/packed-it (accessed 2 September 2017).

Hartcher, Peter. 'Jakarta Leaves Keating at the Altar'. *Sydney Morning Herald*, 24 April 1992, 15.

Haven, Cynthia L. *Evolution of Desire: A Life of René Girard*. East Lansing: Michigan State University Press, 2018.

Higgins, Winton. *Journey into Darkness*. Blackheath, NSW: Brandl & Schlesinger, 2003.
Hill, Helen. *Stirrings of Nationalism in East Timor*. Sydney: Contemporary Otford, 2002.
Hodge, Joel. *Resisting Violence and Victimisation: Christian Faith and Solidarity in East Timor*. Burlington, VT: Ashgate, 2012.
Hodge, Joel. *Violence in the Name of God: The Militant Jihadist Response to Modernity*. London: Bloomsbury, 2020.
Horner, David. 'Australia in 1942: A Pivotal Year'. In *Australia 1942: In the Shadow of War*, edited by Peter J. Dean, 11–30. Cambridge: Cambridge University Press, 2010.
Howard, John. *Lazarus Rising: A Personal and Political Autobiography*. Sydney: HarperCollins, 2011.
Hudson, Phillip. 'Why Fraser gave up on East Timor Sydney Morning Herald'. *Sydney Morning Herald*, 1 January 2009. https://www.smh.com.au/national/why-fraser-gave-up-on-east-timor-20090101-gdt8a9.html (accessed 6 September 2021).
International Commission of Jurists (ICJ). Blaming the Victims: The 12 November 1991 Massacre in Dili, East Timor, and the Response of the Indonesian Government. Geneva, Switzerland: ICJ, February 1992. https://www.icj.org/wp-content/uploads/1992/02/East-Timor-blaming-the-victims-fact-finding-mission-report-1992-eng.pdf (accessed 6 September 2021).
'International Human Development Indicators'. United Nations Development Programme, 2016. http://hdr.undp.org/en/countries (accessed 27 April 2020).
Iwamoto, Hiromitsu. 'Patrol Reports: Sources for Assessing War Damage in Papua New Guinea'. Australian National University Symposium (October 2000). Canberra: Australian War Memorial. http://ajrp.awm.gov.au/ajrp/remember.nsf/pages/NT000020EE (accessed 7 September 2021).
Izzard, John. 'Crumbs of Compassion'. *Quadrant*, 1 March 2010. http://quadrant.org.au/magazine/2010/03/crumbs-of-compassion/ (accessed 11 May 2020).
Jacobs, Frank. 'Is This Map Australia's Clumsy Attempt at Fabricating a Japanese Invasion during WWII?' *Big Think*. http://bigthink.com/strange-maps/australias-invasion-paranoia (accessed 10 May 2020).
Jenkins, David. 'Charismatic, Sinister Soeharto Man'. *Sydney Morning Herald*, 10 September 2004. http://www.smh.com.au/articles/2004/09/09/1094530768057.html (accessed 11 May 2020).
Jolliffe, Jill. *Balibo*. Melbourne: Scribe, 2009.
Jun, Nathan. *Toward a Girardian Politics*. Wichita Falls, TX: Midwestern State University, 2007. https://www.researchgate.net/publication/252934438_Toward_a_Girardian_Politics (accessed 20 February 2021).
Kelly, Paul. *The March of Patriots: The Struggle for Modern Australia*. Carlton, Vic: Melbourne University Press, 2011.
Kelly, Paul. 'Shattered Myths'. *Weekend Australian*, 11–12 September 1999, 25.
Keneally, Thomas. *Australians: A Short History*. Sydney: Allen & Unwin, 2016.
Kevans, Denis. 'Never Forget You'. In *Praying for Peace on Anzac Day*. https://www.youtube.com/watch?v=nGhw7ouBGPw (accessed 10 May 2020).

King, Simone. 'The Fate of Occupied Territory: Recognition, Non-recognition, Self-Determination and Prolonged Occupation', 2005. https://www.wsrw.org/files/dated/2008-10-22/simone_king_thesis_2005.pdf (accessed 12 May 2020).

Kirwan, Michael. *Discovering Girard*. London: Darton, Longman & Todd, 2004.

Klapdor, Michael, Moira Coombs and Catherine Bohm. *Australian Citizenship: A Chronology of Major Developments in Policy and Law*. Canberra: Parliament of Australia, 2009. http://www.aph.gov.au/binaries/library/pubs/bn/sp/austcitizenship.pdf (accessed 10 May 2020).

Kohen, Arnold S. *From the Place of the Dead: The Epic Struggles of Bishop Belo of East Timor*. New York: St Martin's, 1999.

Kovar, Annika, and Andrew Harrington. 'Breaking the Cycle of Domestic Violence in Timor-Leste: Access to Justice Options, Barriers, and Decision-Making Processes in the Context of Legal Pluralism', October 2013. http://www.undp.org/content/dam/timorleste/docs/reports/DG/Domesticpercent20Violencepercent20Reportpercent20_withpercent20coverpercent20FINAL.pdf (accessed 11 May 2020).

Lal, Brij V., and Kate Fortune, eds. *The Pacific Islands: An Encyclopedia*, vol. 1: 243–53. Hawaii: University of Hawaii Press, 2000.

Lennox, Rowena. *Fighting Spirit of East Timor: The Life of Martinho da Costa Lopes*. Annandale, NSW: Pluto, 2000.

Lincoln, Andrew T. *A Commentary on the Gospel according to St John*. London: Continuum, 2005.

Linton, Suzannah. 'Putting Things in Perspective: The Realities of Accountability in East Timor, Indonesia and Cambodia'. *Maryland Series in Contemporary Asian Studies* 3(182) (2005): 1–90. http://digitalcommons.law.umaryland.edu/mscas/vol2005/iss3/1/ (accessed 11 May 2020).

Lloyd, Grayson J. 'The Diplomacy on East Timor'. In *Out of the Ashes: Deconstruction and Reconstruction of East Timor*, edited by James J. Fox and Dionisio Babo Soares, 79–105. Adelaide: Crawford House, 2000.

Lopes, Monsignor da Costa. *Reply to Bishop Gerry*, 19 November 1981. https://timorarchives.files.wordpress.com/2012/02/tis_box13-02_10b.pdf (accessed 11 May 2020).

Macdougall, A. K. *Australians at War: A Pictorial History*, 2nd rev. ed. Rowville, Vic: Five Mile, 2007.

Macintyre, Stuart. *A Concise History of Australia*, 2nd ed. Cambridge: Cambridge University Press, 2004.

Manne, Robert. 'Introduction'. In *Whitewash: On Keith Windschuttle's Fabrication of Aboriginal History*, edited by Robert Manne, 1–13. Melbourne: Black Inc. Agenda, 2003.

McDonald, Hamish. 'Failure of the Inevitable'. *Sydney Morning Herald*, 29 August 1998.

McGrath, Kim. *Crossing the Line: Australia's Secret History in the Timor Sea*. Carlton, Vic: Redback Quarterly, 2017.

McPhedran, Ian. 'Historians Professor David Horner and Ashley Ekins Question World War II Kokoda Campaign's Iconic Status'. News.com.au, 6 September 2012. http://www.news.com.au/national/historians-professor-david-horner-and-ashley-ekins-question-world-war-ii-kokoda-campaigns-iconic-status/news-story/f24aa6bc525df9760fb9070f57e8ad31 (accessed 11 May 2020).

Melleuish, Gregory. *The Packaging of Australia: Politics and Culture Wars*. Sydney: University of New South Wales Press, 1998.

Metcalfe, Louise. 'The Impact of "White Australia" on the Development of Australian National Identity in the Period between 1880 and 1914'. *History Initiates* (March 2013): 2–9. mq.edu.au/pubstatic/public/download.jsp?id=99535 (accessed 12 May 2020).

Millett, Michael, and Louise Williams. 'PM Defends Soft Line on Indonesia'. *Sydney Morning Herald*, 18 September 1996.

'Minority Rules: Scientists Discover Tipping Point for the Spread of Ideas'. *Science Daily*, 25 July 2011. http://phys.org/news/2011-07-minority-scientists-ideas.html (accessed 11 May 2020).

Morrow, Duncan. 'Terrorism and the Escalation of Violence'. In *The Palgrave Handbook of Mimetic Theory and Religion*, edited by James Alison and Wolfgang Palaver, 493–9. New York: Palgrave Macmillan, 2017.

Munster, George, and Richard Walsh. *Documents on Australian Defence and Foreign Policy 1968–1975*. Sydney: J.R. Walsh and G.J. Munster, 1980.

Murdoch, Lindsay. 'Remains of Dili Massacre Victims Identified'. *Sydney Morning Herald*, 19 August 2009. https://www.smh.com.au/world (accessed 11 May 2020).

Myers, Kerry. 'Postscript'. *Sydney Morning Herald*, 13 September 1999.

Naidoo, Kumi, and Sylvia Borren. 'Civil Society'. In *International Development: Ideas, Experience, and Prospects*, edited by Bruce Currie-Alder, Ravi Kanbur, David M. Malone and Rohinton Medhora, chapter 46. Oxford Scholarship Online, 2014. https://idl-bnc-idrc.dspacedirect.org/bitstream/handle/10625/51588/IDL-51588.pdf?sequence=1&isAllowed=y (accessed 12 May 2020).

National Archives of Australia. *Australia's Prime Ministers: John Curtin*. http://primeministers.naa.gov.au/primeministers/curtin/in-office.aspx (accessed 10 May 2020).

National Archives of Australia. 'The Bombing of Darwin'. https://gallery.records.nsw.gov.au/index.php/galleries/war-and-australia/war-and-australia-world-war-ii/war-and-australia-world-war-ii-1942-the-bombing-of-darwin/ (accessed 10 May 2020).

National Archives of Australia. *Citizenship in Australia: A Guide to Commonwealth Government Records*. http://guides.naa.gov.au/citizenship/chapter1/citizenship-australia.aspx#chap1note28 (accessed 27 April 2020).

Nelson, Hank. 'Gallipoli, Kokoda and the Making of National Identity'. In *The Australian Legend and Its Discontents*, edited by Richard Nile, 200–17. St Lucia: University of Queensland Press, 2000.

Neto, Félix, Maria da Conceição Pinto and Etienne Mullet. *Forgiveness and Reconciliation in an Inter-group Context: East Timor's Perspectives*. Hauppauge: Nova Science, 2011. ProQuest Ebook Central (accessed 20 October 2017).

Nevins, Joseph. *A Not-So-Distant Horror: Mass Violence in East Timor*. Ithaca, NY: Cornell University Press, 2005.

Nuechterlein, Paul. 'Girardian Anthropology in a Nutshell'. *Girardian Lectionary*. http://girardianlectionary.net/nutshell.htm (accessed 3 February 2020).

O'Connor, D., A. C. Thompson, G. C Hart and A. D. Stevenson. 'Australia's Debt to the Timorese'. *Letters, Sydney Morning Herald*, 18 August 1975.

Palaver, Wolfgang. 'The Ambiguous Cachet of Victimhood: Elias Canetti's "Religions of Lament" and Abrahamic Monotheism'. https://www.scribd.com/document/110863884/Elias-Canetti-s-Religions-of-Lament (accessed 22 February 2021).

Palaver, Wolfgang. 'The Ambiguous Cachet of Victimhood: On Violence and Monotheism'. In *The New Visibility of Religion: Studies in Religion and Cultural Hermeneutics*, edited by G. Ward and M. Hoelzl, 68–87. London: Continuum, 2008. https://www.bloomsburycollections.com/book/the-new-visibility-of-religion-studies-in-religion-and-cultural-hermeneutics/ch5-the-ambiguous-cachet-of-victimhood (accessed 7 September 2021).

Palaver, Wolfgang. *René Girard's Mimetic Theory*. Translated by Gabriel Borrud. East Lansing: Michigan State University Press, 2013.

Pampalk, Madalena. 'Accountability for Serious Crimes and National Reconciliation in Timor-Leste: Progress or Wishful Thinking?' *Australian Journal for South-East Asian Studies* 3(1) (2010): 8–30. https://nbn-resolving.org/urn:nbn:de:0168-ssoar-362381 (accessed 11 May 2020).

Peel, Mark, and Christina Twomey. *A History of Australia*. Basingstoke, Hampshire: Palgrave Macmillan, 2011.

Phan, Grace, dir. *A Hero's Journey*. Singapore: Madmax Films, 2006. Lux Lucis Pvt Ltd. DVD. http://www.luxlucis.sg/A%20HERO%27S%20JOURNEY%20full%20synopsis+director%27s%20bio.pdf (accessed 11 May 2020).

Pietsch, Sam. 'Australian Imperialism and East Timor'. *Marxist Interventions* 2 (May 2010): 7–38. http://sa.org.au/mi/2/mi2.pdf (accessed 11 May 2020).

Pinch, Dorelle. *Inquest into the death of Brian Raymond Peters: Coroner's Report 2007 Executive Summary*. http://www.etan.org/etanpdf/2007/Peterssinquest1.pdf (accessed 10 May 2020).

Ramos-Horta, José. 'Former East Timor President José Ramos-Horta's Advice For Syrian Rebels'. *Daily Beast*, 18 July 2012. http://www.thedailybeast.com/former-east-timor-president-jose-ramos-hortas-advice-for-syrian-rebels (accessed 11 May 2020).

Ramsey, Alan. 'Timor: A Debt Dishonoured'. *Sydney Morning Herald*, 25 September 1999.

Refugee Council of Australia. Australia's Detention Policies. https://www.refugeecouncil.org.au/detention-policies/ (accessed 5 September 2021).

Renouf, Alan. *The Frightened Country*. South Melbourne: Macmillan Company of Australia, 1979.

'Report by the Special Rapporteur Bacre Waly Ndiaye, on His Mission to Indonesia and East Timor from 3 to 13 July 1994'. In Geoffrey C. Gunn, *East Timor and the United Nations: The Case for Intervention*. Laurenceville, NJ: Red Sea, 1997.

Robertson QC, Geoffrey. *Crimes against Humanity: The Struggle for Global Justice*, 3rd ed. Camberwell: Penguin, 2006.

Robinson, Geoffrey. *If You Leave Us Here, We Will Die: How Genocide Was Stopped in East Timor*. Princeton, NJ: Princeton University Press, 2010.

Rodgers, Peter. 'East Timor: A Continuing Game of Face-Saving?' *Sydney Morning Herald*, 7 November 1979, 7.

Ross, Catriona. 'Paranoid Projections: Australian Novels of Asian Invasion'. *Antipodes* 23(1) (2009): article 4, 11–16. https://digitalcommons.wayne.edu/antipodes/vol23/iss1/4 (accessed 10 May 2020).

Roque, Ricardo. 'Mimetic Governmentality and the Administration of Colonial Justice in East Timor, ca. 1860–1910'. *Comparative Studies in Society and History* 57(1) (2015): 67–97. http://www.jstor.org/stable/43908334 (accessed 5 September 2021).

'SAS Training with Kopassus Despite Rights Concerns'. *ABC News*, 28 September 2010. http://www.abc.net.au/news/2010-09-28/sas-training-with-kopassus-despite-rights-concerns/2276586 (accessed 12 May 2020).

Saul, Ben. 'Prosecuting War Crimes at Balibo under Australian Law: The Killing of Five Journalists in East Timor by Indonesia'. *Sydney Law Review* 31 (2009): 83–120. http://classic.austlii.edu.au/au/journals/SydLawRw/2009/3.html (accessed 11 May 2020).

Schreiter, Robert J. *The Ministry of Reconciliation: Spirituality and Strategies*. Maryknoll, NY: Orbis, 2005.

Schreiter, Robert J. *Reconciliation: Mission and Ministry in a Changing Social Order*. Maryknoll, NY: Orbis, 2000.

Schwager, Raymund. *Must There Be Scapegoats? Violence and Redemption in the Bible*, 2nd ed. Herefordshire: Gracewing, 2000.

Scott, David. *Last Flight Out of Dili: Memoirs of an Accidental Activist in the Triumph of East Timor*. North Melbourne: Pluto, 2005.

Shackleton, Shirley. *The Circle of Silence: A Personal Testimony before, during and after Balibo*. Millers Point, NSW: Murdoch Books Australia, 2010.

Smith, Gareth. 'Shame Australia Shame – Appeal for Donations'. East Timor Action Network. http://www.etan.org/et2001a/january/01-06/01shame.htm (accessed 11 May 2020).

Smith, Gary. 'Australia's Political Relationships with Asia'. In *Australia and Asia*, edited by Mark McGillivray and Gary Smith, 100–19. Melbourne, Vic: Oxford University Press, 1997.

Smythe, Patrick A. *The Heaviest Blow: The Catholic Church and the East Timor Issue.* Münster: Lit Verlag, 2004.

Stahl, Max. 'Massacre among the Graves'. *Tapol Bulletin*, no. 108 (December 1991): 6–8. http://vuir.vu.edu.au/26096/ (accessed 11 May 2020).

Stanley, Peter. 'Dramatic Myth and Dull Truth: Invasion by Japan in 1942'. In *Zombie Myths of Australian Military History: The Ten Myths That Will Not Die*, edited by Craig A. Stockings, 140–60. Sydney: University of New South Wales Press, 2010.

Stanley, Peter. *Invading Australia: Japan and the Battle for Australia, 1942.* Camberwell, Vic: Penguin, 2008.

Stanner, W. E. H. *The Dreaming and Other Essays.* Melbourne: Black Inc. Agenda, 2009.

Staveteig, Sarah. 'How Many Persons in East Timor Went "Missing" during the Indonesian Occupation?: Results from Indirect Estimates'. *International Institute for Applied Systems Analysis* Interim Report IR-07–003 (31 January 2007). https://www.unsw.adfa.edu.au/school-of-humanities-and-social-sciences/sites/default/files/documents/Staveteig%20death%20toll.pdf (accessed 11 May 2020).

Stevens, David. '"Australia's Thermopylae?" The Kokoda Trail'. In *Zombie Myths of Australian Military History: The Ten Myths That Will Not Die*, edited by Craig A. Stockings, 161–89. Sydney: University of New South Wales Press, 2010.

Sydney Morning Herald, 'Timor Looking for "Sympathy" over Oil: Downer'. AAP, 25 April 2004. https://www.smh.com.au/world/asia/timor-looking-for-sympathy-over-oil-downer-20040425-gdit0j.html (accessed 25 February 2021).

Tanter, Richard, Mark Selden and Stephen R, Shalom, eds. *Bitter Flowers, Sweet Flowers: East Timor, Indonesia and the World Community.* Annandale, NSW: Pluto, 2001.

Tapol Bulletin, no. 108, December 1991. http://vuir.vu.edu.au/26096/ (accessed 6 April 2016).

Tapsell, Ross. 'Same Old Stereotypes of Indonesia – and Our Politicians Aren't Helping'. *Conversation.* http://theconversation.com/same-old-stereotypes-of-indonesia-and-our-politicians-arent-helping-17159 (accessed 10 May 2020).

Taylor, Charles. *Modern Social Imaginaries.* Durham, NC: Duke University Press, 2004.

Taylor, John G. *East Timor: The Price of Freedom.* London: Zed, 1999.

Taylor, John G. *Indonesia's Forgotten War: The Hidden History of East Timor.* Leichhardt: Pluto, 1991.

'The Tide of Protest Swells'. *Weekend Australian*, 11–12 September 1999, 5.

The Timor-Leste Commission for Reception, Truth and Reconciliation (CAVR). *Chega! The Final Report of the Timor-Leste Commission for Reception, Truth and Reconciliation (CAVR).* 2013. http://chegareport.org/Chega%20All%20Volumes.pdf (accessed 13 May 2020).

The Timor-Leste Commission for Reception, Truth and Reconciliation (CAVR). *Chega! The Report of the Commission for Reception, Truth and Reconciliation in Timor-Leste Executive Summary.* Dili, Timor-Leste: CAVR, 2005.

Thomas, Martin. *The Artificial Horizon: Imagining the Blue Mountains*. Carlton, Vic: Melbourne University Press, 2003.

Thomas, Scott M. 'Culture, Religion and Violence: René Girard's Mimetic Theory'. *Millennium: Journal of International Studies* 43(1) (2014): 308–27.

Thorby, H. V. C. 38 *Cabinet Submission: Proposed Air Service Darwin to Dilli (Portuguese Timor)*. Canberra: Australian Government, Department of Foreign Affairs and Trade, 1939. http://dfat.gov.au/about-us/publications/historical-documents/Pages/volume-02/38-cabinet-submission-by-mr-hvc-thorby-minister-for-civil-aviation.aspx (accessed 10 May 2020).

Thornhill, John. *Making Australia: Exploring Our National Conversation*. Newtown NSW: Millennium, 1992.

Tiffen, Rodney. *Diplomatic Deceits: Government, Media and East Timor*. Sydney: University of New South Wales Press, 2001.

'Time to Get Tough with Indonesia'. *Australian*, 7 September 1999.

Timor Information Service. Interview with Gough Whitlam, ABC Radio 'Frontline', 26 March 1982 (unofficial transcript). https://timorarchives.files.wordpress.com/2012/02/eto_w-h_09.pdf (accessed 8 April 2020).

'Timor Trench'. *Sydney Morning Herald*, 12 January 1982, 6.

Toohey, Brian, and Marian Wilkinson. 'The Timor Papers 1987'. In *Tell Me No Lies: Investigative Journalism and Its Triumphs*, edited by John Pilger, 174–90. London: Jonathan Cape, 2004.

Townsley, Jeramy. *René Girard's Theory of Violence, Religion and the Scapegoat*. December 2003. http://www.jeramyt.org/papers/girard.html (accessed 1 October 2017).

Turner, Michele. *Telling East Timor: Personal Testimonies 1942–1992*. Kensington: New South Wales University Press, 1992.

United Nations. *UN General Assembly Votes on East Timor* (General Assembly Resolutions 1975–82). https://etan.org/etun/genasRes.htm (accessed 10 May 2020).

United Nations Development Programme. *International Human Development Indicators*. 2020. http://hdr.undp.org/en/countries (accessed 12 February 2020).

Uniya Jesuit Social Justice Centre. *Justice and Reconciliation in East Timor: Australia and the CAVR*. Kings Cross: Uniya, Jesuit Social Justice Centre, 2006.

Veling, Terry. *For You Alone: Emmanuel Levinas and the Answerable Life*. Eugene, OR: Cascade, 2014.

Waddingham, John. 'Australia's New Labor Government, March 1983'. *Timor Archives: Clearing House for Archival Records on Timor*. https://timorarchives.wordpress.com/2013/03/05/hawke-labor-march-1983/ (accessed 11 May 2020).

Walker, David. *Anxious Nation: Australia and the Rise of Asia 1950–1939*. St Lucia: University of Queensland Press, 1999.

Walker, David. 'Cultural Change and the Response to Asia: 1945 to the Present'. In *Australia and Asia*, edited by Mark McGillivray and Gary Smith, 11–27. Melbourne, Vic: Oxford University Press, 1997.

Walsh, Pat. 'Timor Report: Whitlam and Hastings Observed'. *Arena*, no. 60 (1982): 136–45. Timor Archives: Clearing House for Archival Records on Timor. https://timorarchives.files.wordpress.com/2012/02/eto_w-h_69.pdf (accessed 12 May 2020).

Walsh, Richard, and George Munster. *Secrets of State: A Detailed Assessment of the Book They Banned*. Sydney: Angus & Robertson, 1982.

Walter, James. 'Defining Australia'. In *Images of Australia: An Introductory Reader in Australian Studies*, edited by Gillian Whitlock and David Carter, 7–22. St Lucia: University of Queensland Press, 1992.

Walters, Patrick. 'Australia and Indonesia'. In *Australia and Asia*, edited by Mark McGillivray and Gary Smith, 156–77. Melbourne, Vic: Oxford University Press, 1997.

Ward, Stuart. *Australia and the British Embrace: The Demise of the Imperial Ideal*. Carlton Vic: Melbourne University Press, 2001.

Way, Wendy, ed. 'Australia and the Indonesian Incorporation of Portuguese Timor, 1974–1976'. Carlton South: Melbourne University Press, 2000. https://www.google.com.au/search?q=Australia+and+the+Indonesian+Incorporation+of+Portuguese+Timor%2C+1974-1976&ie=utf-8&oe=utf-8&client=firefox-b&gfe_rd=cr&dcr=0&ei=uQOuWfLIBIbr8wfRh4GwCQ (accessed 9 August 2014).

Welsh, Frank. *Great Southern Land: A New History of Australia*. London: Allen Lane, 2004.

Wesley-Smith, Rob. 'Radio Maubere and Links to East Timor'. In *Free East Timor: Australia's Culpability in East Timor's Genocide*, edited by Jim Aubrey, 83–102. Milsons Point: Random House, 1998.

White, Hugh. 'The Road to INTERFET: Reflections on Australian Strategic Decisions concerning East Timor, December 1998–September 1999'. *Institute for Regional Security* 4(1) (Autumn 2008): 69–87. https://www.jstor.org/stable/26458869 (accessed 11 May 2020).

White, Richard. *Inventing Australia: Images and Identity 1688–1980*. Crows Nest, NSW: Allen & Unwin, 1981.

Whitlam, Gough. 'The Truth about Timor'. *Bulletin*, 30 March 1982, 79–81. https://nla.gov.au/nla.obj-1400927193/view?partId=nla.obj-1400978147#page/n59/mode/1up (accessed 10 May 2020).

Wigmore, Lionel. 'Chapter 21, Resistance in Timor'. In *Volume IV, the Japanese Thrust*, 1st ed., 466–97. Canberra: Australian War Memorial, 1957. https://s3-ap-southeast-2.amazonaws.com/awm-media/collection/RCDIG1070113/document/5519442.PDF (accessed 10 May 2020).

Windschuttle, Keith. *The Fabrication of Aboriginal History*. Sydney: Macleay, 2002.

Wise, Amanda. *Exile and Return among the Timorese*. Philadelphia: University of Pennsylvania Press, 2006.

The World Bank. 'The World Bank in Indonesia – Overview'. http://www.worldbank.org/en/country/indonesia/overview (accessed 10 May 2020).

Wray, Christopher C. H. *Timor 1942: Australian Commandos at War with the Japanese*. Port Melbourne: Mandarin, 1990.

Wright, Tony. 'Jakarta Joy as PM Backs Off Human Rights'. *Sydney Morning Herald*, 27 October 1993, 3.

Wurth, Bob. *1942: Australia's Greatest Peril*, 2nd ed. Sydney: Pan Macmillan Australia, 2010.

Xie, J., S. Sreenivasan, G. Korniss, W. Zhang, C. Lim and B. K. Szymanski. 'Social Consensus through the Influence of Committed Minorities'. *Physical Review* E 84(1) 011130 (July 2011): 1–9. http://phys.org/news/2011-07-minority-scientists-ideas.html (accessed 11 May 2020).

Zelter, Angie. 'Civil Society and Global Responsibility: The Arms Trade and East Timor'. *International Relations* 18(1) (March 2004): 125–40. http://ad9.org/pegasus/peace/zelter.htm (accessed 11 May 2020).

Index

Note: Folios with "n" indicates endnotes in the text.

2/2 Commando Association 149, 214n.25
2/2nd Independent Company 26, 41, 47, 53, 55–6, 63, 151
2/4th Independent Company 41, 53

ABRI. *(Angkatan Bersenjata Republik Indonesia)* 87, 94–5, 117
advocacy 149–51
  of civil society 144
  for justice 149
  of solidarity movement 18, 144, 149–51, 168
AETA. *See* Australia-East Timor Association (AETA)
aid 50–1
  food 80, 150
  foreign 36
  international 117
  military assistance 112–13
Alatas, Ali 209n.11
Alison, James 135–7, 160
Amnesty International 145, 215n.25
Angkatan Bersenjata Republik Indonesia (ABRI) 87, 94–5, 117
Anglo-Celtic 26, 34
Annan, Kofi 147, 159
Anzac Day 59
ANZUS Treaty 32–3, 35
Armed Forces for the Liberation of East Timor 94. *See* Falintil
Armed Forces Movement in Portugal 67
Armed Forces of the Republic of Indonesia 94. *See* ABRI
Asia 5–6, 31, 33–6, 42, 66, 68, 79, 146
Asia-Pacific Coalition for East Timor (APCET) 146
atrocity(ies) 2, 117, 119–20, 130, 146, 148, 153, 156
Attwood, Bain 29–30

Australia, Indonesia and Portuguese Timor 1945–1974 70
Australia and the Indonesian Incorporation of Portuguese Timor 1974–1976 69, 71–2, 75–6, 78, 84, 89, 91, 102
Australia-East Timor
  history 15
  policy changes 126–31
  relationship 2–3, 8, 11–12, 17, 129
Australia-East Timor Association (AETA) 149–50, 214n.25
Australia-East Timor relationship 2–3, 8, 11–12, 17, 23, 129, 160
Australian
  account of 1999 107–9
  breach of Portuguese neutrality 49–50
  campaign in Timor WWII 52–3, 60–3
  contradictions 22–5, 40, 70, 113, 128
  contradictory policies 10, 76–82
  'conversion' 160–4
  dependence on Indonesia 40, 66, 128, 206n.112
  fear of invasion 42–4, 48–9
  government 6, 69–71, 97–8
  groups (advocacy) 214–15n.25
  identity 10, 21, 23–8
  involvement in Indonesian invasion 75–81
  knowledge of Indonesian desires 71–4
  military assistance to Indonesia 97, 112–13
  mimetic dependence 81–5
  moral insights in documents 90–1
  nationalism (civic and ethnic) 25–8
  policy changes 126–31
  policy during the occupation of East Timor 97–8
  prime ministers 97–8
  public 78–80

recognition of Indonesian
    sovereignty 110–11
self-perceptions 10, 21, 23–5, 27
solidarity with East Timor 147–8, 153–7
values 23–5
voting and argument in UN 111–12
Australian (Murdoch newspaper) 154
Australian Attitude in Event of Indonesian Aggression 72
Australian Council for Overseas Aid (ACFOA) 118, 122, 150
Australian Federal Police (AFP) 88
Australian National University 45
Australianness 24
Australian Official War History 45
Australian relationships 21–40
    with Asia 33–6
    with East Timor 38–9
    with Great Britain 31–2
    with Indigenous peoples 28–31
    with Indonesia 36–8
    with United States 32–3
Australian Security Intelligence Organisation (ASIO) 150
Australian War Cabinet 48
authority
    disrespect for 23
    local 49
    political questions 13
    of victim as judge 135–7
authorship and balance 101–2

Balibó Five 7, 66, 68–70, 82, 85–8, 148, 150, 156 (*See also* atrocity(ies))
Ball, Desmond 80
Battle for Australia Day 59
Battle of Kokoda 46
Beevor, Antony (Sir) 45
bias 4, 17, 77, 102
    pro-Indonesian 108
    Santa Cruz massacre 106–7
Bible 12, 175
bin Laden, Osama 14
Blainey, Geoffrey 30
Blessed Sacrament 210n.26
Bomford, Lance 55
Boyce, James 30
Brereton, Laurie 98
British-Australian relationship 32

Bulletin 34, 120
Burma 44–5

Callinan, Bernard (Lt Col. Sir) 55
Calvert, Ashton 101
campaign effects on Timorese (WWII) 56–8
Campbell, Archie 55
Canada 108, 145
Canberra 67, 72, 78–9, 81, 118, 159
Caritas Australia 150
Catholic Church 9, 115, 121, 133, 156
Catholic Mass 102
Catholics in Coalition for Justice and Peace (CCJP) 150
Cavanaugh, William 133
Centre for Strategic and International Studies (CSIS) 80, 118
challenges
    egalitarianism 40
    faced by Australia 62, 74, 89–91
    to foreign policy 102
    global 175
    to government 34, 86
    political 74, 137
    to reconciliation (with Indigenous peoples) 29
change 158–60
    Labor Party policy 98
    political 9–10, 126–31
    positive 29
Chenoweth, Erica
    Why Civil Resistance Works 132
China 37, 43, 45, 76
Christ 169
    death 16, 135
    passion of 9, 15–16, 133
    resurrection 135
    victimized 19
Christianity 12, 38, 133
Churchill, Winston 44
civic nationalism 25–8
civil society 18, 131, 144–53, 156, 159, 168–9, 171
Cold War 33, 35
Collins, Lance 108
Colombo Plan 26
colonialism 29, 67, 71, 127
colonization 6, 31

British (of Australia) 31–3
Dutch 38, 67
European 38
Portuguese 38, 67, 113, 116, 134
communications 31, 46, 49, 53, 85,
    91, 151–3
Community Reconciliation Program 139
complicity 7–8, 14, 16, 18, 37, 69, 80–1,
    86, 88, 90, 93, 109–10, 115–16,
    163, 165
contradictions 23–5, 40, 70, 76, 78,
    113, 128
contradictory policies 5, 45, 76–8,
    92–3, 142
conversion 3–4, 9, 11
    in Australia 160–4
    mimetic theory 17–19
    solidarity and 143–69
Cooper, Frank (Australian Ambassador to
    Portugal) 83, 90
Corpus Christi 210n.26
criados 53–5
crime 6, 15, 118–21
    against humanity 144, 163
    scapegoat guilty of 14, 115–16
crisis 5–6, 15, 116–18
    Asian financial 126
    Indonesian financial 159
    moral 10
    social 14
    violent 174
Critchley, Thomas 153
criteria for selection of victim 6–7, 121–2
critical mass 144, 157–8
criticism
    of Australian policies 71, 75
    of Girardian theory 12
    of Timorese leaders 137–42
Crucifixion 136
cultural cringe 24
Cunningham, Gary 86
Curtin, John 44, 47–8

da Costa Lopes, Monsignor Martinho
    8–9, 115–23
Darwin 46, 48–9, 151–2, 155
da Silva, Cristoforo 87
death toll, Timorese
    1999 independence 95

Indonesian occupation 95
    Santa Cruz (Dili) massacre 103, 159
    World War II 54, 57
de Carvalho, Manuel Ferreira (Governor
    of Portuguese Timor) 49
decolonization 67, 74, 76–7, 113
de Mello, Sergio Vieira 138
Department of Defense and Security
    (Indonesian) 75
Department of Foreign Affairs and Trade
    (DFAT) 70, 100–1, 155
Department of Veterans Affairs 59
desire 12, 16, 173
    Australian knowledge of
        Indonesian 71–4
    and identity 18
    imitation of Indonesian 81–3
    mimetic 3, 6, 8, 11, 82, 114, 143,
        162, 173
    of others 11, 17
    self-centred 18
    shared 6, 11, 18
Devil's Island 123
Dili massacre 1, 105, 112
Dili Massacre Commemoration Mass, St
    Mary's Cathedral, Sydney 140
Dili Santa Cruz cemetery 95
Diocesan Catholic Commissions for
    Justice and Peace 150
distortion 64, 102, 103–6, 173
diversity 24, 26, 145, 149
*Documents on Australian Defence and
    Foreign Policy 1968–1975* 89
Doherty, Tony Fr. 140
double transference 15
doubling 173
Downer, Alexander (Foreign
    Minister) 69, 101–2, 109, 128,
    158, 162
Dreyfus, Alfred 122–3
Dumouchel, Paul 13
Dunn, James 57
Dutch East Indies 36, 45, 47
Dutch West Timor 39

East, Roger 7, 68
East Timor 38–9, 42, 93–123
    Australian government account of 1999
        events 107–9

Australian policy during occupation of 97–8
Australian voting and argument in UN 111–12
crime 118–21
crisis 116–18
criteria for selection of victim 121–2
Indonesian occupation of (1975–99) 94–7
as scapegoat 5–8, 98–102, 109–10, 115–23
Timor Sea 37, 114–15
victimization of (*see* victimization)
East Timor Action Network (ETAN) 146
East Timor Human Rights Centre 150, 214n.25
East Timor in Transition 1998–2000: An Australian Policy Challenge 100–6, 108–15
East Timor Relief Association (ETRA) 150
egalitarianism 23–5, 28, 40
embellishment 8, 101–2, 106–7
ethnicity 21, 25–6
ethnic nationalism 25–8
Europe 23–6, 32–6, 38–9, 50–1, 67, 112, 130
exoneration 99, 102, 108–9, 121, 165

Fabrication of Aboriginal History, The (Windschuttle) 30
Falintil *(Forças Armadas de Libertação Nacional de Timor-Leste)* 94, 132–3
false imaginary 4, 22, 30, 148, 161–2 (*See also* social imaginary)
fear 1, 4, 7, 16–17
 of Australia of invasion 42–4, 58–60
 of communism 33
 of Japanese invasion of Australia 46
Fernandes, Clinton 101, 108
Fischer, Tim 98
food aid 80, 150
Ford, Gerald (President) 68, 80–1
foreign aid 36
foreign policy 13, 22, 32–3, 35, 42, 44, 69–70, 75, 79, 89, 91, 102, 127, 165
forgiveness 4, 9, 10, 19, 141, 211n.54
 expressions and criticisms 137–40
 mercy and 164

of perpetrator 141
Fraser, Malcolm 33, 97, 151
FRETILIN *(Frente Revolucionária de Timor-Leste Independente)* 67, 80, 106, 151–2
friendship 166–7
Frightened Country, The (Renouf) 42
Furlonger, Robert 80

Germany 50, 57
Girard, René
 and conversion 3, 9–10, 17–19, 143, 160–3, 169, 171–2
 criticisms of 12
 and mimetic dependence 81–5
 and mimetic desire 3, 6, 8, 11, 82, 114, 143, 162, 173
 and mimetic theory 2–3, 5, 10, 11, 40, 49, 58, 88, 165
 and myth 8, 16–18, 82, 174
 and rivalry 3, 11, 13, 50–1, 143, 171, 173–4
 and romantic lie 8, 65, 71–2, 84–6, 90
 Scapegoat, The 140
 and scapegoating 3, 5–8, 13–17, 98–101, 115–23, 165, 173
 and stereotypes of persecution 5–8
  crime 6, 14–15, 115–16, 118, 163
  crisis 5, 15, 43, 116, 128, 179
  criteria for the scapegoat 6–7, 15, 99, 115–16, 121
  divinization 15
  violence 3, 7, 9, 13, 16, 52–3, 105, 135, 139–40, 175
 and texts of persecution 3, 16–17, 58–63, 90
 and victimization of the innocent 18, 135, 156, 169
Gomes, Alfonso 103
Gomes, Costa (Portugal's President) 74
Gomes, Sebastião 102
Goodman, Amy 146
Gospel 16, 18
Great Britain 31–2, 35, 43, 108
Great Southeast Asia Co-prosperity Sphere scheme 44–5
Greece 57
Gusmão, Xanana (Former President of East Timor) 133, 138–40, 142

Guterres, António (Secretary General of
    United Nations) 138
Guterres, Eurico 139

Habibie, B. J. 98, 126–7, 159
Hage, Ghassan 26
Haigh, Bruce 160
Hastings, Peter 118
Hawke, Bob 97
Hero's Journey, A (documentary) 142
Hideki, Tojo 45
Higgins, Winton 25–7
Horner, David 45
Howard, John 98, 126–7

Iberian Peninsula 50
imitating the good 167–8
Indian Ocean 47
Indigenous peoples 25, 27–32, 38, 61
Indonesian
    financial crisis 159
    invasion of East Timor 5, 65–92
        covert operations before 74–5
        entanglement of Australia 69–74
        involvement of Australia 75–81
        military assistance from
            Australia 112–13
        mutual mimetic dependence with
            Australia 81–5
        occupation of East Timor 94–7, 125–6
        relationships with Australia 36–8
        responsibility for Balibó Five
            deaths 85–8
Indonesian National Armed Forces 94.
    See TNI
Indonesian Special Forces
    (Kopassus) 87, 112
international aid 117
International Commission of Jurists 87
International Force for East Timor
    (InterFET) 9, 100, 125, 158,
    161, 208n.1
international support for East
    Timor 145–7
invasion
    Australian fear of 42–4, 58–60
    of East Timor by Indonesia 5, 65–92
    fiction 43
    Indonesian covert operations before 74–5

Japanese plans for Australian 44–7
    of Portuguese Timor by Australia
        47–9, 52–3
    of Portuguese Timor by Japan 47–8,
        50–1

Jakarta 80
Japan 34–5
    breach of neutrality 50–2
    expansionism 5
    intentions 44–7
Japanese High Command 45
Jesus of Nazareth 136
Judeo-Christian 39, 174

Kalbuadi, Dading 87
Keating, Paul 37, 59, 97
Kevans, Denis 62
Kirby, Michael 1
Kissinger, Henry 68
Kokoda Track 46
Korea 43
Kraras massacre 95

Labor Party 98, 128
Lacluta massacre 95
leaflet "Your friends do not forget
    you" 61–2
Levinas, Emmanuel 166
lies and myths 8–9
Lisbon 50
London 32, 44
Lord Cranborne 48

MacArthur, Douglas 53
Malaysia 67
Manchuria 45
Manne, Robert
    Whitewash 30
Mao Zedong 35
Matignon Accords 127
McDonald, Hamish 80, 160
mediation 83, 88, 141, 173
Melleuish, Gregory 32
Menzies, Robert (Prime Minister) 72
metaphysical desire 174
Middle East 44
military assistance to Indonesia
    112–13

mimesis 3, 10, 11, 16, 69, 88, 91–2, 129, 131, 134, 143, 160, 174
mimetic desire 3, 6, 8, 11, 82, 114, 143, 162, 173
mimetic theory 2–3, 5, 10, 11–19, 135
  conversion 17–19
  myth 16–17
  rivalry 3, 13
  scapegoat 13–16
  texts of persecution 16–17
Minority Rights Groups International 150
modern-day myths 17 (*See also* myths)
Moertopo, Ali 83
moral insights in documents 90–1
Morrison, Bill 81
multiculturalism 26
Munster, George 89–90
Murdani, Benny 87
mutual mimetic dependence 83–5
myths 8–9, 16–17, 174

Nairn, Allan 146
National Australian Archives 70
National Crime Authority 87
national security 5, 37, 58, 135, 165, 171–2
Ndiaye, Bacre Waly (UN Special Rapporteur) 104–5
Netherlands 36, 47
Netherlands East Indies 44, 49
New Caledonia 127
New Guinea campaign 46
New Testament 12
New Zealand 108
non-violence 4, 9, 131–4, 145, 156, 168 (*See also* violence)
Northern Territory 46

Official Australian War History 60
Operasi Flamboyan campaign 74–5
Operasi Komodo campaign 74
'other,' the 166–7
Otto, Rudolf 174
Oxfam 150

Pacific 32, 45–6, 59, 112
Palaver, Wolfgang 13
Papua New Guinea (PNG) 45–6, 52, 57
Peacock, Andrew (Foreign Minister) 78, 110

persecution 9
  stereotypes of 5, 7, 116
  texts of 3, 8, 11, 13, 16–17, 58, 99, 109, 120, 163
Peters, Brian 86
Phillip, Arthur 29
Poland 57
politics 13, 36, 133, 135, 153–60, 164, 172
  changes 9–10, 126–31, 157–61
  compliance 75–6
  as part of violence 13
Pontius Pilate 136
Portugal 6, 47–51, 67, 72, 103, 130, 206n.112, 217n.77
Portuguese East Timor 38–9, 41–2, 47–52, 66–9
positive mimesis 167–8
prime ministers, Australian 97–8
prohibition 174
pseudo-masochism 174
pseudo-sadism 174

racism 24
Ramos-Horta, José (Former President of East Timor) 138–9
Rangel, Sebastião Gomes 103
recognition of Indonesian sovereignty 110–11
reconciliation 131, 138–42
Red Cross 117
Reed, Warren 108
relationships. *See* Australian relationships
Remembrance Day 59
remythologization 165–6
Rennie, Malcolm 86
Renouf, Alan 24, 33, 78
  Frightened Country, The 42
revenge, lack of 131, 138, 139–42, 153, 164
Revolutionary Front for an Independent East Timor (FRETILIN) 67, 106, 151
Reynolds, Henry 29
Ribeiro, José (Bishop) 115
ritual 174
romantic lie 8, 18, 51, 65–6, 69–71, 76, 81, 85–6, 89–91, 162, 166
Roque, Ricardo 129–30
Ross, David 49

Royal Australian Air Force (RAAF) 53
Russia 43, 57

sacred 174
Salazar, António (Portuguese Prime Minister) 72
Santa Cruz massacre 102–7, 131, 159, 206n.112, 209n.11
  bias 106–7
  distortion 103–6
  embellishment 106–7
scapegoat 5–8, 109–10, 115–23, 173
  East Timor as 98–102
  and the Gospel 147
  guilt 14
  innocence 9, 14–15, 87, 137, 153
  mimetic theory 13–16
  peace and violence 122–3
  and the text 98–102
Scapegoat, The (Girard) 140
Schreiter, Robert 138, 141
Secrets of State 89
Shackleton, Greg 86
Singapore 32, 44, 71
Sisters of St Joseph of the Sacred Heart 2
Smith, Gary 33
Smythe, Patrick 156
social crisis 5, 14, 118
social imaginary 4, 21–4, 28, 32–3, 39–41, 168
solidarity 143–69
  advocacy 49–50
  Australian 147–8, 153–7
  friendship 166–7
  groups 148–9, 214 n.25
  imitating the good 167–8
  international 145–7
  welfare and aid 150–1
Southeast Asia 6, 35
South East Asian Treaty Organization (SEATO) 35
Soviet Union 76
Sphere of Co-Prosperity (Great Southeast Asia Co-Prosperity Sphere) 44–5, 51
Stanley, Peter 43, 45
Stanner, W. E. H. 28–30
starvation 7, 42, 54, 95, 116–17, 119–21, 123, 159

Stephan, Maria J.
  Why Civil Resistance Works (Chenoweth and Stephan) 132
stereotypes of persecution 5, 7, 116 (*See also* Girard, René)
Stewart, Tony 86
St John's Gospel 136
substitutionary victim 14
Suharto (President) 36–7, 68, 73, 75–7, 83, 95, 98, 100, 107, 118, 126, 159
Sukarno (President) 36, 72
Sumatra 74
support
  Australian of Indonesians 7, 36, 68, 80, 88, 98, 109–10, 128
  Australian of Timorese 113, 128, 133, 148, 150–3
  international of Timorese 145–7, 168
  Timorese of Australians 52–4, 56
surrogate victimage 175
Sydney Morning Herald 120, 122, 150, 154–5

Taylor, Charles 4
  social imaginary 21, 39
Telling East Timor: Personal Testimonies, 1942–1992 (Turner) 1
texts of persecution 3, 8, 11, 13, 16–17, 58, 99, 109, 120, 163 (*See also* persecution)
Timorese Democratic Union (UDT) 67
Timor Gap Treaty 114, 217n.77
Timor-Leste 38–9, 185n.3
Timor-Leste Commission for Reception, Truth and Reconciliation (CAVR) Report 87, 95, 103, 108, 112, 117, 131–2, 145, 147–8
Timor Sea 2, 8, 37, 66, 68, 79, 82, 93, 110, 114–15
TNI *(Tentara Nasional Indonesia)* 94, 106, 108
Toohey, Brian 80, 108
Treaty on Security Cooperation (Lombok) (2006) 37
triangular desire. *See* mimetic desire
Turner, Michele 55
  Telling East Timor: Personal Testimonies, 1942–1992 1

UN Human Development Index (2020) 39
União Democrática Timorense (UDT) 67
United Nations 7, 9, 36, 68, 87, 106, 110–12
United Nations Assistance Mission for East Timor (UNAMET) 107
United Nations General Assembly 112
United Nations Refugee Convention (1951) 26
United Nations Special Committee on Decolonization 112
United Nations Transitional Administration in East Timor (UNTAET) 94
United States 5, 12, 14, 32–3, 108
UN Security Council 108, 164
USSR 35

values 4, 10, 19, 21–5, 27, 31, 52, 79, 140, 145, 172
Veling, Terry 166
victim 14 (*See also* scapegoat)
   authority as judge 135–7
   characteristics 99
   defined 14
   innocent 16–17, 99, 132, 156–7, 159–60
   of invasion 47–52, 66–9
   selection criteria (*see* criteria for selection of victim)
   substitutionary 13–14
   truth of 64–6
   turning towards 9–10
   of violence 52–8, 94–6, 144
victimization 2, 7–8, 14–15, 18, 48, 58, 60, 62–3, 68, 77, 87, 89, 100, 146, 165, 174
Vietnam War 69
violence 2–3, 7–8 (*See also* Girard, René; non-violence)
   'all against all' 13
   'all against one' 13
   global 16

   ignoring or justifying 58
   internal strife and 13
   militia 108
   victims of 52–8, 94–6, 144

Walsh, Richard 89–90
War Damages Commission 57
Weil, Simone 32
welfare 150–1
West New Guinea 66, 71
Whitewash (Manne) 30
Whitlam, Gough (Prime Minister) 8, 69, 73, 75–6, 83–4, 92–3, 97, 118–22
Why Civil Resistance Works (Chenoweth and Stephan) 132
Wilkinson, Marian 80, 108
Willesee, Don (Foreign Minister) 75, 77
Windschuttle, Keith 29
   Fabrication of Aboriginal History, The 30
Woolcott, Richard (Australian Ambassador) 73, 75, 78, 114
World War I 24, 123
World War II 2, 5–7, 10, 16, 23, 25–6, 32–3, 35–6, 41–64, 134, 143, 168
   Australia, protection of 48–9
   Australian breach of neutrality 49–50
   Australian campaign in Timor 60–3
   Australian fear of invasion 42–4, 58–60
   Australians in Timor 52–3
   campaign effects on Timorese 56–8
   invasions of Portuguese Timor 47–8
   Japanese breach of neutrality 50–2
   Japanese intentions 44–7
   support by the Timorese 53–6
   texts of persecution 58–63
   Timorese suffering 52–6

Yosfiah, Yunus 87
Yugoslavia 57

Zedong, Mao 35